The Rise of Writing

Millions of Americans routinely spend half their working day or more with their hands on keyboards and their minds on audiences – writing so much, in fact, that they have less time and appetite for reading. In this highly anticipated sequel to her award-winning *Literacy in American Lives*, Deborah Brandt (2001) moves beyond laments about the decline of reading to focus on the rise of writing.

What happens when writing overtakes reading as the basis of people's daily literate experience? How does a societal shift toward writing affect the ways that people develop their literacy and understand its value? Drawing on recent interviews with people who write every day, Brandt explores this major turn in the development of mass literacy and examines the serious challenges it poses for America's educational mission and civic health.

DEBORAH BRANDT is Professor Emerita of English at the University of Wisconsin-Madison.

The Rise of Writing

Redefining Mass Literacy

Deborah Brandt

CAMBRIDGE
UNIVERSITY PRESS

University Printing House, Cambridge CB2 8BS, United Kingdom

Cambridge University Press is part of the University of Cambridge.

It furthers the University's mission by disseminating knowledge in the pursuit of education, learning, and research at the highest international levels of excellence.

www.cambridge.org
Information on this title: www.cambridge.org/9781107462113

First published 2015
3rd printing 2017

Printed in the United Kingdom by Clays, St Ives plc

A catalogue record for this publication is available from the British Library

Library of Congress Cataloguing in Publication data
Brandt, Deborah, 1951– author.
The rise of writing : redefining mass literacy in America / Deborah Brandt.
　pages　cm
Includes bibliographical references and index.
ISBN 978-1-107-46211-3 (paperback)
1. Authorship – United States.　2. Literacy – United States.　3. Literacy – Social aspects – United States.　I. Title.
P145.B723　2015
808.02 – dc23　　2014034061

ISBN 978-1-107-09031-6 Hardback
ISBN 978-1-107-46211-3 Paperback

For Nadine

Contents

Acknowledgments

The kind of research I do would be impossible if not for the good graces of the people, mostly trusting strangers, who answer the questions I ask them. Their patience and perceptiveness are evident everywhere in this work, even though they will be known only by pseudonym. I also relied on several individuals who kindly put me in touch with potential study participants. I thank: Nancy Cotter, Abigal Swertz, Ann Scoby, Melissa Tedrowe, Ron Wallace, Maria Bibbs, Mary Fiorenza, Manuel Herrero Puertas, Jani Koester, Steve Wajda, Charles Hoslet, Larry Edgerton, Marty Blalock, Chloe Clark, Katie Krueger, Jacqueline DeWalt, Chad Navin, Brian Schmoldt, Kate Vieira, Andrew Stendhal, Antonio Galvan, Bob Hanle, Linda Aronnsavath, Lupita Montoto, Jennifer Green Johnson, Suzanne Gittleman, Cory Foster, Lisa Aarli, Mike Peters, and Angela Woodward for their assistance.

Several friends and colleagues provided timely support and guidance as this project developed. Thanks to Charles Bazerman, Harvey Graff, Andrea Lunsford, Mike Rose, Min-Zhan Lu, Marilyn Moller, Tim Laquintano, John Schilb, Clive Thompson, Carol Mattingly, Ann-Catrine Edlund, Alison Farrell, Annette Vee, Ursula Howard, and David Barton. Colleagues, students, and alumni from the University of Wisconsin-Madison have been a constant catalyst for my thinking. Working around people who set high standards and find joy in their vocation helped me overcome bouts of confusion and ebbs in energy in the course of this long project. I especially thank former students Julie Nelson Christoph and Rebecca Lorimer Leonard for their sweet reminders of the value of our shared enterprise.

This work would not have come to fruition without the inspiring material support of the University of Louisville Watson Professorship (which provided time and a stimulating atmosphere in 2006 to do early thinking about this project), the National Endowment for the Humanities, the Spencer Foundation, and the Guggenheim Foundation. Thanks to Andrew Winnard, Helena Dowson, Chloe Harries and the anonymous reviewers at Cambridge University Press for their careful attention to this project and their advice for trying to make it better. Thanks too to the production team of Nitesh Sharma and Grace Fairley for their kind and expert contributions.

Earlier versions of Chapter 1 appeared as "When people write for pay," *JAC*, 29 (2009): 165–198; and "Who's the President? Ghostwriting and shifting values in literacy," *College English*, 69 (July 2007): 549–571 (copyright 2007 by the National Council of Teachers of English, reprinted with permission). Parts of the conclusion appeared as "Deep writing: new directions in mass literacy," in Ann-Catrine Edlund, Lars-Erik Edlund and Susanne Hauger, eds., *Vernacular Literacies: past, present, and future* (Umea University, 2014).

Finally, to Mike, Carrie, and Nadine, my thanks for your encouragement and winning company. And to Steve, here is yet another inadequate word of thanks for forty years of forbearance.

"Change is structured and structures change."
Peter Burke (2005)

Introduction: the rise of mass writing

In meetings of the First Federal Congress in June 1789, as James Madison experimented with wording that would eventually become the First Amendment, he proposed to include the following:

The people shall not be deprived or abridged of their right to speak, to write, or to publish their sentiments.

Roger Sherman, representative from Connecticut, concurred in a committee report filed in the following month, declaring that among the "natural rights" of the people are "speaking, writing, and publishing their sentiments with decency and freedom."

But by the time that the Bill of Rights was enacted, references to the people's right to write and publish had been subsumed into what we know today as the free-speech clause of the First Amendment, which states simply that: "Congress shall make no law . . . prohibiting the freedom of speech, or of the press."[1]

Why the people's explicit right to write was excised from the language of the Bill of Rights is lost to history. Perhaps it was merely to repair a redundancy, as writing is a form of speech. Perhaps it was to more singularly enshrine the press as "the greatest bulwark of liberty," to borrow language from yet another early version of the amendment. Perhaps it was a concession to the fact that few commoners of that day would have had the literacy skills necessary to render their political sentiments in publishable form – let alone access to material means to publish them. Or perhaps it was a point of deliberate semantic retrenchment, from fear that a popular claim to the full powers of writing might take this experiment in democracy a step too far. While the founders would have been ready to foster and protect a nation of readers, it would have been difficult, for a variety of reasons, to imagine a nation of writers.

But erasing writing from the language of the Bill of Rights may have had ramifications that are especially felt now as digital technologies finally make feasible the idea of the writing/publishing citizen. For in the intervening years the rights of everyday Americans to write and publish became enmeshed in

1

complicated legal and economic encumbrances that had long been associated with writing and publishing: systems of patronage, control, regulation, and surveillance through which written expressions emerge as products of modified ownership, multiple interests, and distributed responsibility and reward. Not a week goes by without a headline that brings attention to some of these complications, whether about the employee fired for the injudicious blog entry or Facebook's latest strategy for exploiting those who publish on its pages.

From the earliest years of the Republic, mass reading – but not mass writing – was considered indispensable to liberty and to the workings of democracy. Citizens needed unfettered access to the widest array of information in order to vote intelligently and be critical watchdogs of their government. The quintessential citizen was the informed citizen, the reading citizen. Where the press and other expressive dimensions of literacy were protected, it was in order to serve this reading citizenry (Brown 1997). Over time, deep-seated connections between literacy and democracy heaped legal protections upon people's reading freedoms; justified the spread and continued maintenance of public libraries; led to massive investments of time and money in reading education; and fed the anxiety that changes in people's reading habits or skills were threats to the health of the democracy.

All the while, mass writing developed through a different cultural heritage. It became connected not to citizenship but to work, vocation, avocation, and practical living. The writing skills of everyday people were captured largely for private enterprise, trade, and artisanship. Writing belonged to the transactional sphere, the employment and production sphere, where high-vaulted values of personal autonomy, critical expression, or civic activism rarely found traction and where, in fact, unauthorized writing could well lead to recrimination, if not incrimination. Rather than being protected in the Bill of Rights, the people's writing came to be regulated by contract, labor law, and copyright, as writing skills were rented out as part of production and profit-making. It is not surprising, given this heritage, that the idea of the quintessential citizen as an informing citizen, as an independent writing citizen, would have a wobblier presence in the national imaginary. If, as the founders reasoned, the people's literacy developed through their reading and the people's democracy developed through their reading, then people's writing and the civic protections around it mattered less from a political or educational perspective. Reading was the dominant literate skill, the skill of consequence, and democratic values tacitly relied on its standing as such. From the founding of the Republic forward, these assumptions about reading as dominant and writing as recessive conditioned the ways that mass literacy was supported, experienced, regulated, and valued. But do these relationships still hold?

The rise of mass writing

When it comes to what is new about literacy these days, digital technology tends to capture the attention, as it is likened to the printing press (only speedier) in its radical impact on communications and social organization (Bolter 2001, Eisenstein 1982). But this attention glosses over what may be a more radical – if quieter – transformation, namely, the turn to writing as a mass daily experience. Largely congruent with the rise of digital communication but not synonymous with it, the rise of mass writing has accompanied the emergence of the so-called knowledge or information economy, first identified by Fritz Machlup in 1962 (Machlup, 1972) and elaborated by Marc Uri Porat in 1977, an economy based not in the manufacturing of things but in the manufacturing of services – knowledge, ideas, data, information, news. In this economy texts serve as a chief means of production and a chief output of production, and writing becomes a dominant form of manufacturing. Millions of Americans now engage in creating, processing, and managing written communications as a major aspect of their work. It is not unusual for many American adults to spend 50 percent or more of the workday with their hands on keyboards and their minds on audiences, spending so much time and energy in acts of writing, in fact, that their appetites for reading often wane. As the nature of work in the United States has changed – toward making and managing information and knowledge in increasingly globalized settings – intense pressure has come to bear on the productive side of literacy, the writing side (Brandt 2004, Drucker 2003). For perhaps the first time in the history of mass literacy, writing seems to be eclipsing reading as the literate experience of consequence. What happens when writing, not reading, becomes the dominant grounds of daily literate experience? How does a societal shift in time and energy toward writing affect the ways that people develop their literacy and understand its worth? How does the ascendancy of a writing-based literacy create tensions in a society whose institutions were organized around a reading-based literacy, around a presumption that readers would be many and writers would be few? Of special concern is the alienation of mass writing from the civic protections afforded mass reading. What happens to the associations between literacy and democracy when writing takes over?

In the fanfare over the digital revolution, the intensifying recruitment of writing literacy into economic productivity on a mass scale has been largely overlooked – as has its inevitable spillover into the leisure lives of young people, who are being invited by commercial interests to invest their scribal skills (as well as money and time) in online writing activities. Writing – paid and unpaid – is keeping the economy, especially the Internet economy, afloat. While until recently it would have been difficult to fathom how people could be writing more than reading, it is indeed happening for many. This shift represents a new, uncharted, and unsettling stage in the history of mass literacy, one with serious social, political, and cultural implications for which we are unprepared.

Mass literacy has almost exclusively been understood and described from the reading perspective. Now we must take writing seriously, in its own right, as a set of practices and dispositions that is shaping the experience of mass literacy and the values associated with it. *The Rise of Writing* weaves together historical perspectives on mass writing and mass reading with an analysis of the experiences of everyday, contemporary literates to understand the dynamic, human consequences of this major cultural transition. In each chapter and from different angles, the focus moves backward into the past to attend to writing as initially a minor strain of mass literacy, one with a distinctively different and even alienated cultural heritage from mass reading. Then, I explore how these legacies come forward into contemporary literate experience, as I study the accounts of ninety people, aged 15 to 80, who use writing regularly in their vocations and avocations. In in-depth interviews that I conducted between 2005 and 2012, people discussed with me the writing they do, how they learned it, how it affects them and their families, and how they experience shifting relationships between reading and writing, whether directly in their own literacy experiences or in the wider world. Through their experiences we will be able to see how a growing rivalry between writing and reading sets up potential contradictions in the meanings and values of literacy upon which our society has long rested.

In educational circles it is not uncommon to think of reading and writing as mutually supportive and interrelated processes, drawing on similar underlying language skills and similar social, pragmatic, and rhetorical knowledge (Tierney and Shanahan 1991). In school especially, reading typically initiates writing assignments and writing is often used to assess reading. Reading is always part of a writing process (if only to read over one's own words) and writing is often part of a reading process. In many literacy practices, the two are thoroughly intertwined. But these conjunctions of reading and writing within contemporary school experience gloss over their different cultural histories or what I would call their sponsorship histories. Initially mass reading spread under the auspices of church and State, institutions that sought to universalize reading in order to integrate initiates into shared belief systems. Reading was for learning how to be good – in worship, citizenship, work, and school. Books had value because their goodness was thought to rub off on readers. This moral valence around reading still holds strong today, as reading to young children is treated as the hallmark of good parenting and reading is almost always treated as a wholesome alternative to rival entertainments. Writing has played a role in this moral system when it has served as part of spiritual practice or a tool for learning or disciplining the mind (Burton 2008; Foucault 1988; Miller 1998). But writing has always been less *for* good than it is *a* good. While reading has productive value for a reader, writing has surplus value that fuels other enterprises. The commercial value of writing, the way it can be transacted and enhance other transactions, the way it can fit into systems of work, wage, and market, all make writing unique among the so-called language arts, giving it a different cultural history from reading. In the colonial period, writing was taught separately from reading, often in private pay settings and as part of practical training for the world of work. It took longer to democratize, and its subversive and deceptive powers marked it for heightened control (Monaghan 2005). Practically speaking, writing has flourished not in the civic sphere but in the realm of patronage, where writers enter into some sort of give-and-take relationship with more powerful others in exchange for access to tools, audiences, or remunerations of various kinds. "To be a writer," David D. Hall (2007) observed of literacy conditions in the seventeenth century "was to enter into a relationship of dependence" (p. 76). This statement remains most true today – the only difference being that many more people are writing now.

For most of the history of mass literacy, the value of writing has resided in the reading of it, not the doing of it. Authorship gained its prestige from its power to morally uplift a civic readership. Reading has been seen as the avenue to intellectual and moral improvement. The capacity for ordinary, functional writing to develop a person's character, or ensure social well-being, or strengthen democratic processes has gotten little consideration in our public discourse about literacy, and paltry protection from our legal institutions. In short, at least until now, the potentials (and pitfalls) of mass writing as a grounds for democracy have been stifled within the ideological arrangements of a reading literacy – not only in the nation's educational mission but more broadly in the culture. Now, as writing gains in economic and social power, attraction, and consequence and as writing takes on a more formative role in literacy development across the lifespan, reading inevitably grows more subordinate and writing's alternate sponsorship history surges into prominence. With it comes potential challenge to bedrock beliefs, values, and practices associated with a healthy mass literacy.

Origins of this study

In 2001 I published *Literacy in American Lives*, a book that sought to characterize the changing conditions for literacy learning as they were felt in the lived experiences of everyday Americans across the twentieth century. The book was based on eighty in-depth interviews conducted in the mid-1990s with a diverse group of people born between 1895 and 1985, individuals who were asked to recount everything they could remember about how they learned to read and write across their lifetimes. Working closely with their accounts led me to develop an analytic concept I called *sponsors of literacy* – constellations of agents and entities who develop, exploit, or suppress people's literacy and gain economic or political advantage by doing so. As the society grew more reliant on literacy, sponsors of literacy proliferated, their competing interests palpable at the recollected scenes of literacy learning. This competition of literacy sponsors lent to conditions of stratification and change in literacy across the twentieth century, raising standards for literacy achievement while shaping the manners in which everyday people pursued their literacy. Sponsors of literacy leave their mark not only on individual learners but also on whole communities, regions, economies, and social eras in ways that linger, for better or worse, for subsequent generations.

Two major discoveries came out of that project (discoveries at least for me!). One was the curious contrast in the ways that most people cast their earliest memories of reading versus their earliest memories of writing, more readily associating reading with leisure, worship, pleasure, intimacy, and social approval and writing more readily with work, adult business, trouble, embarrassment, subterfuge, and trauma. As I came to realize, these modern-day memories carried echoes of the earliest arrangements of mass literacy, especially the divergent sponsorship histories of reading and writing and their different statuses in schooling. The other discovery was the enormous influence of the workplace as a reported site of significant literacy learning and relearning. Over the lifespan, literacy change reached people most directly through their jobs, making once serviceable skills obsolete and new skills compulsory, affecting, in turn, how reading and writing took place at home. On any given day, workplaces may expend more time, effort, and resources in the teaching and learning of literacy than schools do, merely as part of routine word production, putting enormous technological and linguistic know-how into the hands of (at least some) employees while putting enormous pressure on everybody's literacy performance. In retrospect, I knew that I had only scratched the surface of these two phenomena: differences between reading and writing; and the role of the workplace in catalyzing change in literacy. More research was needed. Adding to this imperative was the fact that all of my interviewing for *Literacy in American Lives* had concluded in 1995, the year, according to most observers, that the Internet went into mass circulation, affording stupendous changes in how communication could occur and where and when work was done, as well as inviting new ways of encountering literacy, including new genres for writing and reading.

The Rise of Writing was born, then, out of these gaps. I set to work by studying available cultural histories of mass reading and writing, helped by the publication of the multi-volume *A History of the Book in America* (Hall 2007–2010), a comprehensive project that makes unusual attempts to attend to the social history of writing where it can, even as those efforts reconfirm that we know much more about reading and readers than writing and writers.[2] Paul Starr's *Creation of the Media* (2004) was an influential resource, as it shows how communication systems tend to remain entrenched in the political arrangements through which they are initially developed and regulated. I also found help in Charles Bazerman's *Handbook on Writing Research* (2007), a multidisciplinary and multi-thematic volume that puts writing at the center of attention, as well as Nancy Torrance and David Olson's *Cambridge Handbook of Literacy* (2009), another transdisciplinary collection that takes a broad cultural and historical approach. I also continued reading economic theory and history, particularly work that focused on the formation of the so-called information or knowledge society, as well as cultural and legal studies having to do with literacy and labor. Especially helpful were Alfred Chandler's classic *The Visible Hand* (1977), which showed how symbol-based work grew out of speed-ups in production and communication; JoAnne Yates's *Control Through Communication* (1993), a work rich with incidental evidence of how workplaces manufacture new literacy practices; Catherine Fisk's highly informative, *Working Knowledge* (2009), an account of employers' gradual legal control over employees' skills, including their mental and scribal skills; as well as such work as Alan Burton-Jones's *Knowledge Capitalism* (2001) and the prescient writings of Peter Drucker (2003).

Cumulatively, this background reading provided theoretical and historical perspectives helpful for the design of another interview-based project, preparing me to trace the phenomena that interested me most: how divergent sponsorship histories of reading and writing might continue to manifest and matter in current literacy experiences and how an intensifying use of writing for work might affect how people experience and value their literacy. The aim was to investigate along two main tracks: (1) to explore how writing's differences from reading might be pulling mass literacy in new directions; but also (2) to see, despite differences in circumstances, whether people might consider writing a site for the same kinds of moral and intellectual growth that is habitually attributed to reading. What does day-in-day-out writing do for – and to – the people who carry it out? Reading is associated (some would say overly associated) with just about every positive human quality imaginable, from empathy to critical thinking to civic engagement. How does writing stand in relationship? These two lines of investigation – one focused on differences and one on similarities – were meant to attend to what Harvey Graff (1987) has called contradictions and continuities in the history of mass literacy, as they are being carried forward through the rise of writing over reading.

Framework

The Rise of Writing borrows most directly from the methodological perspective of French sociologist Daniel Bertaux (1981), who uses interviews and other biographical material to understand how sociopolitical developments register in felt experience – how people move through history and how history moves through them. Sometimes called a "realist" approach to narrative inquiry, with antecedents in the work of Oscar Lewis, C. Wright Mills and others in the Chicago School, Bertaux's biographical sociology uses systematic comparisons of biographical materials to uncover the structuring forces behind a given social phenomenon (in his case, intergenerational social mobility). The method is not designed to explicate individual lives or individual intentions or to celebrate individual heroics. It is "to make explicit the traces of social phenomena and processes that are showing – to the informed eye – on the surface of somebody's life, [as] experiences narrated to the interviewer" (Bertaux 2003, p. 40). Like oral history, biographical sociology often explores the lives of the overlooked, everyday people whose voices are usually absent from official representations. The aim is to gather facts about their lives, in the words of Bertaux, to learn: "what people have done, where and when, with whom, in which local contexts, with what results" as well as "what has been done to people *and how they reacted to it*" [author's italics] (Bertaux 2003, p 39). Uncovering systematic patterns across these facts reveals the structuring forces, or what Bertaux calls the social logics, up against which people live their lives (Bertaux and Delacroix 2000).

As in Bertaux's work, *The Rise of Writing* treats research participants not so much as objects of study but as witnesses to socio-historical change. Individuals and their stories are not my focus per se. Rather, what matters is what can be systematically and objectively gleaned from them about how the history of mass literacy – past, present, and future – manifests in particular times, places, and social locations; how particular members of society enter into its force; and with what effects on them and others. While people's accounts provide a finite universe of available facts for study, those facts must be queried and interpreted to yield understanding. The subjective viewpoints of research participants are an essential ingredient – but not where the interpretation begins or where it ends. What matters is how and when people appeal in their accounts to historical and social formations of mass literacy, as resources, constraints, explanations, puzzles, and problems of their existence. The more these appeals turn up across contexts, the closer I come to what I pursue.

This realist perspective has been subject to criticism, above all, for its lack of attention to the interview event itself as a powerful structuring agent – considering, for instance, how a researcher uses questions to structure attention or how both interviewer and interviewee use available discourse to structure their sense of history, meaning, or identity and do so on the spot, as a production of the interaction itself. Another limitation of this perspective, according to critics, is how it takes what people say at face value, without concern about memory failure, unconscious drives, or the influence of power dynamics or anxiety as elements of questions and answers.[3] These criticisms are serious and legitimate. Yet it is a fundamental assumption of this study that the field of literacy studies, in both its research and pedagogical dimensions, could better appreciate – from a sociological perspective – how an accumulating history of mass literacy and its transformations manifest as individual literate experience; how anyone's literacy development is inside that contingent historical development, not in a fated, deterministic way but in a practical way that matters and can be analyzed. The macro-force of literacy is an ongoing cultural production that exceeds any single verbal version of it, making itself present in stories about reading and writing. Understanding this historical contingency is important for understanding aspirations, problems, and practices around literacy, whether they show up as educational policy, in a legal ruling, or at the scene of an individual's learning.

Project design

In 2005 I began to interview people who held positions that required them to write on average for at least 15 percent of the workday. Given constraints of time and resources, I sought participants whom I could meet face-to-face in the general region where I also lived and worked, a Midwestern, mid-sized city that is home to a large public university and state government with an additional economic base principally in health care, insurance, biotechnology, light industry, and retail. Using information from the US Census Community Survey, I identified economic sectors that employed large numbers of people as well as occupations that depended on writing, and I began what amounted to a process of cold calling to recruit participants to the study. I emailed individuals directly when their addresses (and often brief bios) appeared on company or agency websites, or I called business owners or personnel or information officers in business and government for leads. Sometimes colleagues or friends provided contacts after learning about the study, and in a few cases those I interviewed encouraged me to talk with co-workers, which I did. I sought avenues and contact strategies that I hoped would lead to an inclusive pool of participants in terms of gender, age, race, and ethnicity, as well as occupation and size of organization. As the questions of the study clarified themselves, I crafted the participant pool into thirty people working in the private sector and thirty people working in the public sector.

Interviewing continued over a period of seven years, as I could find the time and willing participants. About half the people I contacted declined to participate or declined permission to allow me access to their employees. One CEO explained that her employees did not have time to talk with me. Other people simply did not respond or declined without explanation. As with other projects of this kind, my ideal aim of developing a census-based sample of the workaday writing population gave way to exigency as I began to take any interview I could get, resulting in overrepresentation of some populations and occupations and underrepresentation of many populations and occupations.[4] Missing from this study, by design, are people whose jobs require little or no writing. Heavily represented are people who do a lot of writing and thereby participants who have higher levels of education and higher-paying jobs than the population overall. Characteristics of the sixty participants appear in Appendix 1. Additional information about particular participants appears in individual chapters.

Interviews took place at times and places chosen by the interviewees, sometimes at work, sometimes in public places like restaurants and coffee shops, and occasionally in their homes. Interviews lasted about one hour, sometimes two, and were semi-structured, focusing on straightforward questions about the writing people do at work, how they learned to do it, and how it relates to other aspects of their literacy experiences. Reading–writing relationships also were probed. Of course, many unanticipated topics emerged in the conversation, leading to gradual adjustments in subsequent interviews. The basic interview script appears in Appendix 2. I audiotaped all interviews and transcribed them myself for analysis.[5] Using principles of grounded theory (Charmaz, 2006), I coded each interview for evidence of sponsorship histories, differences between reading and writing, and effects of writing on self and others, coding and recoding over a number of years as patterns evolved into consolidated concepts. Additional information about coding appears in individual chapters.

In 2011 I added a third population to the study: thirty young adults aged 15 to 25 who pursue writing as an avocation. Specifically I sought participants who wrote on a regular basis outside of school for creative or political/civic expression or else as journalists, freelance writers, or entrepreneurs. This sub-study allowed me to examine current elective writing and publishing practices and to include a younger population not present in the larger study.[6] I found participants locally by contacting guidance counselors, teachers, coordinators of pre-college programs, people who worked with community youth, and other personal and professional connections. I also searched websites and campus and community publications to locate writers to contact. In all cases I used recruitment strategies that would favor inclusion in terms of gender, race and ethnicity, and socioeconomic background. Parental permissions were obtained for minor participants. Agreement to participate was higher in this study than the employee study, perhaps because I relied more on intermediaries; five individuals declined requests to be interviewed. Characteristics of participants in this sub-study appear in Appendix 3 and additional information about particular participants appears in Chapter 3. Interviews were held at mutually arranged times and places, during lunch hours or after school at high schools, in community centers, public areas of college campuses, local coffeehouses, public libraries, and occasionally at the interviewee's home. Interviews in this sub-study took a more lifespan perspective on participants' reading and writing experiences and adapted to the different forms of writing they pursued (creative, political, entrepreneurial, etc.). But the main thrust of the questions remained the same as in the other study, with a focus on the kind of writing these young people did, how they learned it, what effect it had on them, and how it related to reading. The basic interview script appears in Appendix 4. I recorded and transcribed all the interviews. Coding took similar directions as in the other study, attending to histories of sponsorship, reading and writing relationships, and effects of writing intensity on self and others. Additional information about coding for this sub-study appears in Chapter 3.

Limits of the study

As will become clear, this book does not focus mainly on digital technologies or social media as catalysts for changes in writing literacy. For that, readers will need to look at the burgeoning research addressed to the so-called digital revolution and multi-modal communication. Here, the focus remains on alphabetic writing and its rise as a second stage of mass literacy in the United States, a quieter and subtler revolution, one of longer duration, into which digital forms of communication have become fruitfully absorbed. This book steadfastly draws attention to the hard daily work of mostly anonymous people who produce the kind of written texts that, at least for now, still have consequence in this society, texts that turn the wheels of finance, law, health care, government, commerce. The book also draws attention to the developmental experiences of youth who elect to write the kind of texts that young people are usually admonished to read, including literature, news, and civic writing. Amid all the excitement (and unease) about new communication technologies, the enduring labor of everyday writers tends to get overlooked and underestimated, even though this labor is what spawned new communication technologies and will always significantly inform the practices associated with them.

Another limitation of this study must be underlined: it is grounded in the facts of the lives of the ninety people I interviewed as they responded to the questions I asked them. My project was to make sense of what these ninety people told me. Consequently, many important forms of experience, writing, work, and change in the wider society are omitted, because they did not arise in the finite universe of data I worked with and beyond which I did not go. These omissions will likely occur to readers in the course of engaging with this book. What I do hope, however, is that the considerable scope of the experiences represented here and the conceptual arguments that I make from them will prove sufficiently generative, even as they might encourage readers to problematize and overtake the limits of this study.

Further, in a work that emphasizes the historicity of literacy, it is important to acknowledge the horizon of time in which this research was conducted, a period in the early twenty-first century when relationships between reading and writing and print and digital technologies were in new, complicated, and often tentative flux. There is nothing about the cultural, social, economic, legal, political, or technological conditions in place at the time of this study (nor the contours of the writing lives represented here) that would be immune to change in the years ahead. But that is why it is important to stress that the perspectives and methods of this study are interpretive and not predictive. Just as the study makes no claim to generalize from the accounts of ninety individuals to other people in the demographic categories or professions to which they belong, neither does it claim that these findings predict an inevitable future for literacy. Rather, the evidence that unfolds in the following chapters is used to build a general conceptual claim. The claim is that earlier sponsorship arrangements of mass writing (including its past relationship to reading) manifest and matter in people's literacy and can be made visible through analysis. Whatever happens in the future, that past – in some form – will still be present, mattering, and available for analysis. But in what way it is present, mattering, and available for analysis will need ongoing research and conceptual development.

Finally, a definitional note. Throughout the book I refer to "workaday" or "everyday" writers. The phrase is deliberately non-technical. It is meant to denote those who write as a routine part of their work, whose pay depends to some degree on their writing literacy, who often write anonymously and ephemerally, and who may not necessarily feel the designation of writer is even appropriate to their situation, given their place in a culture where that term is usually reserved for published professionals associated with a few, highly regarded genres. As I hope will be made abundantly clear, the term is chosen not to diminish the craft or social worth of the writing that workers create. On the contrary, the aim is to shine a light on writing that has become part of everyday life and to expose the ethical, intellectual, and rhetorical efforts that millions of people expend on writing on a daily basis. Indeed, it is through the efforts of workaday writers that the streambed of mass literacy is changing course – even though this change is going largely unrecognized by the institutions that should most be paying attention.

Outline

Chapter 1, The status of writing, draws on the accounts of sixty adult working Americans to explore writing as a form of labor, one that has come to define the experience of a growing number of people as their literacy skills are drawn into the production and management of knowledge and information. As writing takes up more time and mental energy, it changes ratios between reading and writing in people's daily literacy experiences. Increasingly, reading occurs within acts of writing and often as an interaction between one writer and another. Further, when people write for pay, they must grapple as a matter of routine with difficult questions surrounding writing as contractual labor, including matters of ownership, ethical responsibility and accountability, control, and consequence. As the chapter demonstrates, these questions can infiltrate even the most mundane writing tasks, engaging workaday writers in ethical and compositional deliberations of the hardest kinds as they put their minds and language into authoring texts that they do not own but for which they feel responsible.

Tensions between the high status of consequential writing and the low status of the hired writer come to a head in ghostwriting, a labor practice with which, as we will see, a surprising number of individuals in my study were engaged. Ghostwriting, that is, writing something for which someone else will take authorship credit, is on the rise in this society, dramatizing some of the changes in literacy values that accompany writing as a form of labor, including the rising role of writing in economic and communicative competition. As we will see, ghostwriting is breaking down established arrangements between writing and reading, as it simultaneously relies upon and erodes conceptions of authorship that have shaped literacy practices over time. In the middle of this wrenching shift, of course, are workaday ghostwriters themselves, who are buffeted and sometimes bruised by conflicting sets of values as they try to do their job. Above all, Chapter 1 explores writing's alienated cultural heritage, as a form of labor that was never expected to be the primary grounds on which everyday citizens would experience and exercise their literacy. As a result, there has been little interest in what these daily exercises of literacy do for (and to) those who must carry them out.

Chapter 2, Writing for the State, looks at reading–writing tensions in the experiences of a subset of thirty people who write from paid positions inside federal, state, and local governments. The aim is to consider how these citizens bring democratic processes to life through their writing even though they write in settings that are not democratic. Whether as police officers, policy analysts, scientists, political aides, social workers, licensers, or information officers, to name a few, government employees must enact the statutes, policies, procedures, obligations, and powers of government, and they do so largely through writing. As a consequence, government writers engage in ongoing reflections about democratic processes and their duties toward them, developing writing styles, where they can, that satisfy their own standards for what is fair and equitable and civically valuable. While positioned at the gears of a democracy, however, public employees, like private employees, must carry out the official missions they are paid to carry out. They are contractually obliged to advance the interests of the government even if they disagree and must tolerate high levels of government intrusion into their writing. Under these complicated conditions, the expressive civic voices of government writers are muted not only on the job but often off the job as well. The chapter also considers how government's long-standing obligation to provide information and protect the interests and freedoms of a reading public enters into the composing processes of government employees. On the one hand, these obligations can inspire responsiveness, but on the other hand can invite caution and fear, as government writers, as part of the public interest, compose in highly regulated contexts and with the prospect of broad public scrutiny. In sum, Chapter 2 looks closely at the experiences of everyday government personnel to examine how they navigate relationships between democracy and literacy from a perspective rarely considered – from the writing perspective – and with what implications for them and others.

Chapter 3, Occupation: author: writing over reading in the literacy development of contemporary youth, explores writing–reading relationships in the lives of thirty writing-oriented young adults, aged 15 to 25, who pursue avocations as creative writers, journalists, political commentators, and entrepreneurs. Most of these individuals developed an avid interest in writing from an early age and, beyond school or work, write copiously on a daily or near daily basis, composing novels, poetry, songs, screenplays, news, non-fiction, and political commentaries, among other genres. They write on and off the Internet; many publish and perform in public venues. The chapter contrasts their writing-based literacy development outside of school with the kind of reading-based literacy development that is both presumed and promoted by the school, one in which writing ability is treated as a subsidiary or an outgrowth of reading ability. The chapter demonstrates how, rather than reading, it is vocational aspiration – a growing awareness of how writing is associated with occupations and life work – that motivates and supports writing-based literacy development among this group. The commercial world of writing, as well as contact with practicing writers, both peers and older mentors, provide these young people with insights into textual composition as well as material and conceptual props that they leverage in their writing pursuits. Further, in school and other social contexts that construct them as readers, these young adults teach themselves to "write over reading," commandeering, redefining, and, in some cases, refusing reading to maintain and advance their writing development. Above all, the chapter shows, these young people manage to make contact with the recessive heritage of writing that links it to craft, art, apprenticeship, vocation, publicity. This is the very heritage that initially alienated writing from the common school, and it is a heritage that today remains obscured and attenuated in literacy education at all levels, including, sadly enough, most writing instruction.

Chapter 4, When everybody writes, is an exploratory chapter that reunites the accounts of all ninety research participants to look at how the state of mass writing enters into shared social consciousness, how people in this study structure into their sense-making practices the assumption that they live and write among other people who also write. The chapter draws on the concept of *mentalities*, an analytic developed by sociologically oriented French historians who attribute historical change to shifts in what people take for granted about the world around them. Literacy scholars who take this perspective have shown not only how reading has functioned historically to spread new realities but also how the spread of reading itself, including the assumption that other people can and do read, came to affect social structure and social life. In Chapter 4, within the confines of the interview method, I search for evidence of writing mentalities as they surfaced in my conversations with research participants. The analysis reveals how seeing others writing and being seen writing by others play an extraordinarily strong role in the making of writing mentalities. The Internet has been especially influential in this regard as it makes visible the writing activity of so many people. Working or living with others who write invites cognizance about other people's writing processes and the conditions in which they write. The aim of the chapter is to show how those who live in a writing society and experience casual, ongoing contact with other members of that society come to take that world for granted and project it into their practices of living, creating new social realities with which everyone must contend, whether positioned in that writing society or not.

The conclusion, Deep writing, brings together the major findings of the study to contemplate a literacy practiced primarily through writing. Writing as a production imperative can only be expected to spread. More people will dwell for longer periods of time within deeply interactive networks and in immersive mental states that consequential writing demands. The requirement to traffic in written symbols will continue to seep deeply into places that have not traditionally been associated with literacy. The implications of this deep writing for education and for literacy going forward cannot be ignored.

1   The status of writing

Writing has always been used for work, production, output, earning, profit, publicity, practicality, record-keeping, buying, and selling. Increasingly, writing itself is the product that is bought and sold, as it embodies knowledge, information, invention, service, social relations, news – that is, the products of the new economy. At the turn of the twentieth century, knowledge workers represented 10 percent of all employees. By 1959 this proportion had increased to more than 30 percent of the workforce, and by 1970 it was 50 percent. In 2000, knowledge workers were estimated to account for 75 percent of the employed population, with the biggest gains found among highly educated professional and technical workers in government and service-producing industries (Wyatt and Hecker 2006). If, as Thomas Stewart (1998) asserts, "Knowledge has become the primary ingredient in what we make, do, buy, and sell" (p. 12), then writing has become a dominant form of labor as it transforms knowledge and news into useable, shareable form.

"I write the entire day. My whole job is on paper," a mortgage broker told me. An historical society librarian said, *"I write all day. I may work on as many as 50 texts of one sort or another."* An Internet entrepreneur reflected: *"If you think about what I do for a living, I type on my computer. And I'm not writing software. I'm writing words to people. Even when I'm on the phone I'm writing."* *"Seventy percent of my job is writing,"* estimated a corporate manager. *"At least 75 percent writing,"* said a legislative aide. *"Eighty percent,"* reported both a policy analyst and a communications specialist. *"Fifty percent of the day,"* said a clinical social worker. *"Four hours a day,"* said a police officer. *"Conservatively, a fourth to a third of my time,"* estimated an insurance underwriter. *"Twenty percent of my time,"* said a bookkeeper. *"Close to 40 or 50 percent of the time,"* said a farm manager. *"I spend a lot of time writing,"* said a nurse. *"A lot when production must be done in a short period of time,"* explained a sales coordinator. *"It goes in spurts,"* said a scientist. *"How much time? Too much time,"* reflected a social service provider.

The status of writing as a dominant form of labor in the US economy puts an unusual degree of pressure on people's scribal skills, as their writing literacy is pulled deeply into manufacturing, processing, mining, and distributing information and knowledge. Writing is a time-intensive form of labor that tends to follow people home. As one information security officer reported: *"It's hard to get writing done when you are in the office. You're stopping and dealing with the day-to-day, people coming and going, needing answers. So I'll go home and write. After my family is asleep, I'll get out my laptop. It's my most productive writing time."* A revenue specialist said: *"If it's something that's more analytical, I'll take it home. I get too many interruptions during the day."* A public licensing administrator explained: *"If I get behind, I take writing home on the weekend. It's quieter and easier to concentrate and* [the documents] *are ready when I come back on Monday."* An insurance industry lobbyist said: *"I have spent a lot of Sunday afternoons clacking away on my system, just trying to keep up with it because people expected it done."* A lawyer told me: *"I can get a nice extra half hour of writing in after the children are in bed if I'm not too tired."* A police detective said: *"When I go to bed I think about the* [investigative] *interviews I held that day. I find myself starting to write my reports in my head. It saves me time the next morning."* And a public policy analyst explained: *"It depends on what you mean by taking writing home. I think about my writing all the time. I may have the basic idea but it takes me a day to figure out how to express it."*

These brief testimonies illustrate how writing has grown central to, indeed synonymous with production and productivity; how people can spend major parts of a working day in the throes of written communication; how routinely they can dwell in the mindset of the writer throughout their waking hours. (If bedtime used to be for reading, it is now for writing too.) While writing has always been used for work, more and more people are now involved in it and spend more time at it. Writing as a dominant form of labor means that for the first time in the history of mass literacy, writing has become a major form of mass literate experience.[1] So rapacious are the production pressures on writing, in fact, that they are redefining reading, as people increasingly read from the posture of the writer, from inside acts of writing, as they respond to others, research, edit, or review other people's writing or search for styles or approaches to borrow and use in their own writing. Reading is being subordinated to the needs of writing (Brandt 2009, pp. 161–175).[2] Consider this from an IT manager:

When I'm reading I'm always looking for little nuggets of information. It's rare that I enjoy sitting down and reading a novel, it's rare that I have the time for it. Usually I'm reading a magazine or a technical journal trying to figure something out. I'm going through it, scanning it for little bits of stuff I can use in my reports. You are always looking for these nuggets all over the place. Email. Surfing the web. Looking for little pieces of information that will complete the puzzle for you.

Or this from an attorney who considers herself *"more of a writer than a reader"*:

So when I am writing, a lot of times I will stop and look around, trying to find things more on point to make more sense of what I'm writing or things I want to cite. So I'm reading in that sense. But just reading for pleasure, I don't often experience that, I don't get lost in the thing. I spend more time writing than I do reading.

Or this from a stockbroker, who manages a branch office of a national investment firm and has the duty of monitoring all email that goes in or out of his office to make sure it complies with SEC regulations. It is a task that can take a couple of hours a day and, as the following illustrates, has changed the way he reads in private life:

I read for the high points. I just go bing, bing, bing. Even when I read for pleasure, which I don't do enough of, I find myself reading just for the high points. Just the way I read emails. I seldom sit down and just let the book take me.

Or this from an elder care specialist:

I find myself reading more newspapers than I ever thought I would because they're online. I have moved away from fiction. I don't know how much my work has to do with it. I guess it does. I want to know how things are organized. I want to know how things work. I want to know what difference things make in people's lives.

This chapter explores the status of writing as a dominant form of labor that is reshaping relationships between writing and reading, and reshaping the character of mass literacy in the process. But the title of this chapter is also meant to evoke other dimensions of the status of writing that have a bearing on this transformation, including the economic, legal, and cultural power and prestige afforded to writing as a product, a form of property, and a cultural and intellectual resource. So powerful and lucrative is writing in these regards that it has always attracted competing interests and ownership claims around it, making the question of authorship a murky, and increasingly murkier, issue. As we will see, the social, political, economic, and aesthetic powers of writing are not lost on workaday writers; in fact, these powers course through them on a regular basis – sometimes inspirationally and sometimes uncomfortably. At the same time, as texts have become chief vehicles for economic transactions, they have also become potential vehicles for expensive errors, impropriety, and even crime. As a result, regulation and regulatory agencies have a widespread presence in the oversight of everyday writing and its writers, bringing constraint, circumspection, even censorship to individual acts of writing (Brandt 2005; Brandt 2009, pp. 149–153).[3]

In contrast to mass reading, mass writing has grown up under forms of sponsorship and control that do not necessarily honor the integrity and freedom of the individual literate – a concern that may have been incidental to the society when readers were presumed to be many and writers were presumed to be few. But now writers are becoming many. The legacies that came to shape – and control – mass writing in the past are now erupting into view, increasingly defining the ways that more and more people engage with literacy. As a result, the values we have traditionally associated with literacy will change (and already are changing). What that means for society going forward is the major question underlying this chapter, and answers will be sought by listening carefully to the voices of everyday writers. The chapter begins by examining the legal regimes that surround writing at work and then takes an in-depth look at the peculiar, fascinating, and surprisingly ubiquitous practice of ghostwriting, through which the shift from values associated with mass reading to values associated with mass writing can be most provocatively illuminated.

When people write for pay

In his account of the formation of copyright law in early eighteenth-century England, Mark Rose (1995) explores the competing interests that pressed in on writing at the time and shaped the legislative deliberations. Printers and booksellers in England wanted secure returns on their financial investments. Government wanted to be able to track and prosecute sedition. Authors wanted remuneration and control over the publishing circumstances of their texts. People in the provinces wanted broader and cheaper access to the world of books. As each side jockeyed for primacy, they invoked widely various conceptions of writing. Depending on who was talking, writing could be depicted as: a form of sweat-of-the-brow labor; a form of common-law property; progeny in need of tender protection; a commodity to be bought and sold; an inalienable embodiment of personality; a potential enemy of the State; or a communal good. Rose argues that out of this cacophony emerged a flawed yet enduring concept of the author as an individual originator and proprietor of writing – but only because, in the end, it was this concept of authorship that pacified the most number of interests: governments could pin down seditionists; authors could control their reputations and textual products; and English publishers – in the name of authors' rights – could squeeze out their provincial competition. The idea that a text belongs naturally and uniquely to the person who writes it has been much criticized over time for romanticizing writers, masking the collaborative nature of writing, and impoverishing the cultural commons (Ede and Lunsford 1990; Jaszi 1994; Lessig 2005). But that controversy is not the central focus here. Rather, Rose's account serves to underscore that the question of who owns writing is a convoluted and largely irresolvable matter, one that engages interests far beyond the writer's. Embedded as writing usually is in contexts of production, publicity, profit, and control, it takes shape in contentious and dynamic systems of mutual dependency, conflicting interests, and distributed reward. These conditions not only account for the reams of legislation, law-suits, and scholarly debates that continue to flow around questions of writing and ownership. More profoundly – and of most concern here – they can give common acts of writing an ideological complexity (and instability) unrivaled by the other language arts.

Indeed, the idea that a text belongs to the person who writes it is not the only concept of authorship that can be found in current US copyright law. When it comes to writing undertaken within the scope of employment – in other words, the writing done by most people in society – copyright turns inside out: under a provision called "Work Made for Hire," the law is careful to *sever* writers from ownership claims over the texts that they write at work. As will be explored in more depth below, workaday writing is not owned by those who undertake it. Rather, it is owned by those who pay wages and provide the tools for writing. In the eyes of the law, the employer is the author of their texts. As individuals, workplace writers are not allowed to profit individually from the writing they do. Even the knowledge they may produce in their heads as a result of the writing they do at work is technically not theirs to benefit from. Further, workaday writers are not legally entitled to express their own views through their workplace writing. They can be fired for doing it, and they won't get much support from the courts if they appeal. According to the Supreme Court, people do not really write at work as citizens or free beings but rather as willingly enlisted corporate voices. At least in their official capacities, workaday writers don't write as themselves at work, according to the Court. They are not individually responsible for what they are paid to say. Consequently, they don't really mean what they say. In fact, according to the Court, people who write for pay can't really mean what they say. Their speech rights are corrupted and, hence, inoperable. From this perspective, writing starts to look a lot less romantic and a lot more feudal.[4]

My aim here is to inquire into these lesser considered corners of law and custom, not merely because they condition the experiences of so many everyday people but because they invite ways of looking at writing that rarely enter the traditional public discourse about the meaning and value of mass literacy. How do people compose texts that are not theirs in any legal, economic, or moral sense? How do legal and cultural conceptions of writing as labor, property, personality, or social good play out in such workaday writing endeavors? And how might writing for hire complicate public understandings of literacy and its value?

To be clear, my concern is not ultimately to weigh in on who is right or wrong about the ownership of writing, and it is certainly not to try to resolve the question. Rather, my aim is to explore how workaday writers negotiate the competing interests and ideological complexities associated with a history of struggle around the ownership of writing and the regulatory systems it has spawned. Manifestations of this struggle can be quite lively and consequential for the workaday writer, appearing not as philosophy or fine points of law but as practical ethical matters amid the ad hoc work of writing. Intriguing parallels emerge at times between the reflective deliberations of workaday writers and the arguments mounted by litigants, judges, and legal commentators engaged in disputes about the ownership of writing. At the same time, though, gaps can open up between how the law and its regulatory systems treat workaday writers and how those writers treat themselves. Where these gaps occur, they can bring considerable ideological turmoil and psychic wear and tear to people who write for pay.

On the other side of ownership: the work made for hire

From the standpoint of intellectual property law, most workaday writing – what Orbach (2009) refers to as "humdrum" writing – is authorless and beneath the concern of copyright regimes. Ephemeral, functional, typically anonymous, and usually exhausted at the point of use, this writing is considered to have no residual value in need of protecting or redeeming. Although case law does recognize labor as an entitling factor when it comes to ownership claims, copyright is reserved for texts that are considered creative or artistic, or that otherwise promote learning, or have some other enduring social utility (Ginsberg 1990). However, should such copyrightable texts be composed by salaried employees within the scope of their employment, the employer – not the writer – is considered to be the author. Salaried employees were severed legally from ownership of their writing by the Copyright Act of 1909, and again by the Copyright Act of 1976, which states:

In the case of the work made for hire, the employer or other person for whom the work was prepared is considered the author for purposes of this title, and unless the parties have expressly agreed otherwise in a written instrument signed by them, owns all the rights comprised in the copyright.

Interestingly, when disputes have broken out over works made for hire, the usual criteria that courts have used for determining ownership (namely, whose powers of mind created the work) are put aside and a different set of criteria is considered: Who set the manner and means of production? Who owned the tools, provided the space, and shouldered the expense (Clark 1997; Hardy 1987)? In the workplace, authorship is associated not with writing a text but with managing the writer. The work-made-for-hire doctrine has been the object of considerable commentary by legal scholars, most of whom agree that this doctrine does not confer authorship to employers in the regular sense but rather, as Clark (1997) suggests, "it was merely that by deeming employers to be authors, employers would be saved the trouble of obtaining obligatory assignment of rights" (p. 139). Some commentators consider the doctrine an inevitable and long overdue recognition of the corporate and collaborative nature of workplace production. But other critics see the clause as illustrating how deeply courts are mired in the idea of the single, solitary author, such that the role is merely projected onto the employer despite its inappropriateness. Others say this doctrine grows out of an unfortunate conflation in US copyright law between a moral right to one's work (i.e., the right to claim credit and enjoy the reputation of creation) and commercial rights (i.e., the right to reap financial reward from a text). These critics suggest that moral rights – those that come from the real work of creation – can never be transferred to someone else but that fact is clumsily occluded in current US copyright concepts.[5]

Other commentators are much more positive toward the work-made-for-hire doctrine as, in their view, it simply puts creative employees on par with other workers who make things for pay. Some consider it to be in appropriate alignment with the social-good theory of copyright. If copyright exists ultimately to protect and benefit society – to ensure fresh knowledge is produced and shared with the public – then the doctrine merely recognizes that employers have the greater capacity to develop and disseminate socially useful material. Therefore the financial incentive should be theirs. Further, they say, employers are the ones who take the risks and responsibilities, provide the tools, often contribute ideas and direction, and compensate employees in the form of salary – all factors that argue for the legitimacy of treating the employer as author-in-chief.[6]

Finally, some commentators provide a different interpretation. They suggest that the roots of the work-made-for-hire doctrine reach way back into older common law that has to do with what was known as master–servant employment relations, whereby the landowner or master was seen to hold legal property interest in the worker's or apprentice's labor and work products.[7] In a treatment of the early origins of master–servant relations and their manifestation in modern labor law, Tomlins (1993) observes:

> What emerged was a legal discourse of employment increasingly leaving it to employers to exercise detailed control over the employed, a translation of master/servant concepts of the authoritative employer and the subordinate employee into the secular language of "management" – internal and internalized regulation. This was a devolution justified in the name of free contractual assent. (pp. 284–285)

It is worth observing that, prior to 1850, according to Catherine Fisk (2000, 2003), employees were much more likely to be considered the authors and owners of what they created on the job. Fisk suggests that because people who wrote for a living at the time enjoyed higher levels of literacy and education than common laborers, they (along with inventors) tended to receive exemption from master–servant hierarchies. (Interestingly, teachers and academics still enjoy this privileged exemption and, by dint of long-standing tradition, retain rights to their own writing and other intellectual property even when done on an employer's premises.) At any rate, throughout the early nineteenth century in the US, it was not uncommon for court stenographers, for instance, to publish crime fiction based on the real-life trial transcripts they recorded on the job (Cohen 1993). Further, in the absence of government printing capacities at the time, some court reporters published for sale books of judicial decisions, even in some cases gaining copyright to the rulings of the US Supreme Court (Surrency 1981). Should these practices strike us now as most dubious acts of authorship and ownership, it would only go to show how deeply we have internalized the separation of people from their work products – as well as, perhaps, how a rise in literacy has made writing a much more common and less privileged form of labor.

Passage of the 1909 work-for-hire doctrine, then, was partially a response to the needs of government to clarify its control over the written products of its institutions and bureaucracies.[8] But the work-made-for-hire doctrine was also a response to the growing production of collaborative, corporate texts – maps, atlases, databases, reports, and analyses – that in an emerging information economy were becoming a significant source of profit-making for many companies. So the 1909 Act provided some clarity about ownership of corporate texts. Finally, according to Orren (1991), the doctrine was a culmination of a gradual process through the late nineteenth century by which a series of legal rulings sharpened the private sector's jurisdiction over employee rights, rights that came to be seen as separate and distinct from the civil domain (and much more limited). Through such clarifications, mass writing literacy diverged sharply from the civic foundations of mass reading literacy. Although reading clearly can be (and often is) a form of labor, it has never been treated nor regulated as such, and is generally recognized as a private, independent, inalienable experience of the reader.[9]

Constitutional scholar C. Edwin Baker (1989) has written most compellingly of what happens to a citizen's voice once it is put into paid service – when it becomes (someone else's) rented property. Such coerced speech necessarily loses its free-speech protections because it is no longer self-directed: "Once a person is employed to say what she does, the speech usually represents not her own self-expression but, at best, the expression of the employer" (p. 54). Baker elaborates:

The First Amendment protects a person's use of speech to order and create the world in a desired way and as a tool for understanding and communicating about the world in ways he or she finds important. These uses are fundamental aspects of individual liberty and choice. However, in our present historical setting, commercial speech reflects market forces that require enterprises to be profit-oriented. This forced profit orientation is not a manifestation of individual freedom or choice. Unlike the broad categories of protected speech, commercial speech does not represent an attempt to create or affect the world in a way that has any logical or intrinsic connection to anyone's substantive values or personal wishes. (p. 196)

In this excerpt, Baker addresses private sector conditions. However, similar constraints pertain to government employees and for many of the same reasons. In the Supreme Court case *Garcetti* v. *Ceballas*, in which a Justice Department attorney was disciplined for disagreeing (in writing) with his superiors in a way that wound up damaging a prosecution, the justices ruled against the employee, reaffirming that speech made pursuant to official duties receives no First Amendment protection. Like private employers, government may control its employees' speech in order to protect and promulgate its own interests.[10]

As we can see from this review of legal doctrine around writing, workaday writers are legally severed – economically, ethically, and politically – from the words they write on the job. They compose in environments that are shot through with competing interests, rival owners, and contentious ideas about the value and status of their writing. Most strikingly, they write in contexts where normative notions of authorship in US society, including a long tradition of respecting the personality and expressive rights of individual writers, do not pertain. In the words of Baker, they write without the prerogative to "create the world in a desired way" or to use language "as a tool for understanding and communication about the world" as they know it to be. These at least are the official conditions. But, as we will see further below, these conditions are routinely exceeded and contradicted in the ad hoc worlds of workaday writers.

The discussion to follow has been aided by a number of important previous studies that bring attention to the ideological texture of workplace writing, especially its corporate, collaborative, and hierarchical nature, including those by Ede and Lunsford (1990), Doheny-Farina (1986), Henry (2000), and Slack *et al.* (2006). Katz (1998) has explored stances that workplace writers take toward their writing. Others, including Anson and Forsberg (1990), Beaufort (1999), and Schryer (1994), have considered the effects of competing notions of authorship on workplace writers. Still others, like McCarthy (1991) and Pare (2002) have examined the ways that writers can feel pushed around by authoritative genres and practices at work. Spinuzzi (2003) has explored the ad hoc innovations made by workplace writers in the course of carrying out their work. I have been especially helped by the work of Anthony Pare (1993), who examines the effects of legal constraints on the writing of social workers; and Dorothy Winsor, who attends to the personal investments and power struggles that swirl around the writing of corporate texts. Winsor (1993) looks at experiences of ownership and non-ownership in the writing of press releases in a large manufacturing company. In echoing Baker, she considers "the way texts can be seen to represent honest knowledge ... without reflecting what any individual thinks of the products" (p. 181), even as, behind the scenes, individual employees struggle with each other over wording, assign fabricated quotes to others, and worry about the ethics of their work, all while being guided by traditional notions of authorship. It is this strange, often contradictory environment for composing that also interests me here.

At one level, the people I interviewed could easily articulate and embrace the legal conditions that surround writing for pay – particularly the need to advance the interests of the employer – even as the location of these interests was sometimes hard to discern, or would intermingle back and forth with the interests or experiences of the writer. The following observations show the typical range of responses to the basic interview questions, "Whose voice do you use in your writing?" or "What interests do you voice in your writing?"

Here a speechwriter for a high profile public figure speaks of the classic sublimation and self-monitoring that is most associated with writing for pay, particularly the need to separate subjectivity from word production:

When I go into these assignments I need to make sure that I'm not asking myself how I feel about what I am writing about, that I'm not thinking about advancing my personal agenda. We are all creatures of our own influence, so there may be times when I'm affected by how I'm feeling. But I try to make certain that I'm not saying it.

For most of the writers I talked with, however, such separation was hard to maintain. Here a court administrator expresses a view typical of those I interviewed, showing leakages between words and self:

I represent the institution, so I try to be a reasonable voice of the institution. I can't go outside it in my role. I have to respect the constraints of the institution. That has to come first. Now, as an individual I can make choices about how I represent that institution. And I try to do it in as helpful a manner as I can, always with an eye to the restraints that I have to obey according to the institution.

Here is how a housing specialist described the situation:

I have to convey the [agency's] *policy. It's not me. It's not my policy. It's not my position. It's the* [agency's] *position. I might have a different opinion. This is about the position of the organization that you should be conveying, whether you agree or not. It's not my role to give my personal opinion. I have to convey the policy of the city. But if someone may say to me, "Here's a problem, what have you done about it?" then I can say "I have done this or this or this."*

Or this from an adoption lawyer:

I'm hired by a client and, on the face of it you think, well, you represent your client. And especially if I'm doing persuasive writing, I'm trying to persuade a fact finder to see things the way my client wants them seen. However, we're hired by adults and not the children so before I take that client, our office, our rule of how we sleep at night is that I will not take a case unless if I were to win it, it would be in the best interest of the child. I'm not going to advocate for a position I don't think is in the kid's best interest.

Or this from an army recruitment officer:

I have been deployed to the Middle East myself, back in '90 during the Gulf War and then in 2003 at the beginning of Operation Iraqi Freedom. So [in correspondence with recruits] *I like to give my personal experiences of what it was like for me to be deployed. But when it comes to opinion-based* [experience] *then I'm held between certain guidelines. I really can't share my certain opinions on certain things because it gets misconstrued as the Department of the Army is saying this. Or it's coming from the army, whereas it might be my own personal views on something. So I have to stick between certain guidelines because I am an army representative. But I believe I am in there. With some people* [in his unit] *I can tell they are writing based on the army and the nature and the discipline of the army. Then in my case I want to put that personal aspect upon it so others can understand it's not just the army.*

Or from an insurance company policy analyst:

Obviously it can't be "I think." It's always "it would appear" or "this seems to be the best solution." I dare say when I was a rookie I would plagiarize on somebody who had this writing. You got a drift of the tone, the tack you should take. So, yep, the company's interest. As long as you're not doing something illegal. You had to stay within the law. And actually you want to give the policy-holders as many benefits as you can because if you don't they'll go someplace else. So it impacts the sales too. So it's kind of a fine line. I'd have to be careful. I'd want to express but I wasn't going to do something that was going to make me look bad and then have my employer on me. I mean you had to kind of stay with the company line pretty much, which wasn't that hard because contrary to what some people think [the company] *doesn't operate illegally or anything. And they are very concerned. A lot of our mission statement is that we'll provide a valuable policy, peace of mind protection for people. I like to think that I have a lot of integrity and feel* [the company] *does too.*

Under law, those who employ people to write for them take full responsibility and full credit for the work produced. But for those tasked with word pro-duction, neither credit nor responsibility seems able to be completely lent nor relinquished. The sense of walking "a fine line", or being "held between certain guidelines", or negotiating a "how we sleep at night" rule permeated reports of workaday writers about their writing for hire. Some of this can, of course, be attributed to the multiple sets of interests that often bear on professional writing. Lawyers, for instance, must hold to a professional code of ethics even as they sell their services to others. Health care insurance is a social good that operates in a fiercely competitive commercial environment. So even uphold-ing official policy can itself be a conflicted endeavor. But it would be fair to say that most of the people I interviewed "believe [they are] in there" when it comes to their authorless writing. And, depending on the context, they are able to ascertain that "I have done this or this" even as what they are writing is "not me." The inevitable intermingling of self and corporate interest could often amplify individual writers' sense of impact in the world. For example, the insurance agent's personal integrity found satisfaction, even manifestation in his company's philosophy. The adoption lawyer could advocate for children while organizing facts the way an adult client "wants them seen." At other times, though, this intermingling registers as a problem, as a human diminishment; the recruitment officer, for instance, must enhance pure army-speak with some sort of "personal aspect" in order to communicate that his writing is "not just the army." As this continuing analysis will make clear, adding, borrowing, and lending [of power, knowledge, integrity, experience, selfhood, and efficacy] are major elements of workaday writing.

As was mentioned above, copyright law classifies writing according to its perceived social worth. It reserves for copyright protection only literary writing strongly associated with the personality of the writer, or other writing that has some sort of instructive or lasting social value. In this way, copyright converts moral value into commercial value – the more copious the moral value, the more it deserves to win profit. In this scheme, workaday writing has negligible worth in itself, not only because its creators are considered interchangeable (their personalities being irrelevant to the creation) but also because its value is used up in the course of a particular communication. Once a piece of writing does its immediate job (conveys a message, wins a case, implements a policy, seals a deal, etc.) it has no residual value to worry about or protect. It is considered utterly instrumental. Workaday writing also draws no interest or protection under First Amendment law, largely for the same reasons. It is not considered a source of genuine political or aesthetic expression and legally it is considered bereft of any authorial quality that would connect back to the personality or personhood of the composer. Further, writers are not technically allowed to profit in any way – including intellectually – from what they write. They must often, for instance, sign trade secret agreements or contracts agreeing not to take what they know to a competitor company (Fisk 2009). In knowledge industries particularly, employee skill and knowledge – their cultural capital – is often counted among company assets, much as buildings or equipment might count as assets of traditional companies (Burk 2004). So these are the official rules and practices, but they obviously neither originate in nor address the existential work of writing.

In their interviews with me, workaday writers routinely reported having aesthetic, intellectual, ethical, and political experiences during acts of workaday writing. They also often reported carrying away changes in themselves as a result of having written. I want to call all of this experience the residue of authorship, a value that can be neither separated from their person nor accounted for in any legal or economic sense. Sometimes this residue is additive and sometimes it is subtractive. None of it finds recognition – let alone protection – under law.

First, and not surprisingly, several people described the satisfaction of authorship, even when they remained anonymous and credit-less. These sentiments typically came in response to the basic interview question: What do you find most satisfying about the writing that you do at work?

Here is a policy analyst for state government:

Having the feeling that it did have an impact somewhere along the line. There is the little bit of ego that gets into it even when you're watching the news on television and they say, according to a report released by the governor today and you're thinking, hey, that was my number, hey that's from a table I did.

Or the adoption lawyer:

Sometimes thinking of a succinct way to put something and then seeing it picked up. Years ago we were trying to think of a way of saying something in a brochure to describe what people then were calling non-traditional families, and that term sort of didn't seem right because from a child's point of view, what child wants to live in a non-traditional family? Non-traditional suggests there is a traditional family. So we were sitting around throwing out words and I said, you know, it's a family in fact, 'cause there is a contract of law and a contract of fact. They're not families in law because there was no legal recognition of that family. But to the children, they were families in fact. Now, I see [that phrase] in flyers all over the country. I don't claim it, I don't want to. I just want it to be out there.

It was common for the people I interviewed to report aesthetic experience that would come from writing. Some individuals explicitly likened themselves to creative writers, if only at times to exempt themselves from that category.

Here, a police officer describes how he writes incident or arrest reports:

I write my reports as if I were writing a movie. I want you to be able to read my report and visualize everything that happened. I want to envelope the whole human element while I'm writing about the facts. I get enjoyment in finding the right word. That's the way I interject myself into any particular story, through the words that I use, the way that I structure the sentences that I write.

Or this from a housing administrator about the satisfactions of writing:

I don't think of myself as a writer or a poet who writes. But I do like making the case, having done the creative process to make an argument.

These residues also could register as a permanent change in a person. If writing has material effects in the world, it also leaves material effects upon the people who write. Consider this description by a writer who held a string of jobs with mostly technical and industrial clients, preparing brochures, websites, and other authorless texts. This response comes in answer to a basic interview question: How does your work writing affect you?

I feel like I've grown intellectually and maybe even emotionally. If I'm writing about anything that has any value to me personally, it can be really gratifying to sink your teeth into a set of ideas, make them your own, and then say them in your own words. I have had a couple of projects for people who are doing really interesting, cool things and just the process of getting to learn what they do well enough to become comfortable enough to speak about it, I grow and I change as a result of that process. I can meet people at a certain level of knowledge or maybe challenge somebody or have a new set of opinions about something as a result, as an intellectual by-product of what I get paid to do.

Or this from an employment lawyer:

Here is one thing that writing does. It crystallizes you. It crystallizes your thought. All these loose pieces come together and present a picture and that picture, once you've written it down, not only helps you see things but may in fact affect your views. My views on a number of things have changed over time because I had to address them. I'm not a creative person but if I haven't written in a while I feel I have lost the ability to see relevant things.

Work writing is frequently described as politically fraught or politically formative for many people. Consider this reflection by an intake clinician at a drug rehabilitation clinic:

The clients are complex. A lot of them are homeless, jobless, returning from Iraq and so they are complicated. Anything I write can end up as a court document and what I write can influence a jail sentence. So you have to kind of wrestle with the criminal justice system. When I'm writing I can struggle over one stupid word for half an hour and the next day I'll come back and change it. For a half an hour you think about a word.

Or this from a government policy analyst in discussing the effects of work writing:

I'm probably more moderate in some ways than I used to be. You sort of recognize how difficult the [political] process is, how difficult it is to keep going. As a child of the '60s you begin to realize that some of the solutions that people thought up in the '60s were kind of simple minded. Society is a lot more complicated and the sheer number of people in social institutions and all of this stuff. The people I related to in the '60s would scare the hell out of me now.

Or this from a communications specialist:

I think the amount of information I come in contact with daily gives me a fairly good, broad, and, if not a world sense then a national sense of what is going on out there, and I probably have a little bit better understanding of what's going on than the average citizen. Sometimes I'll get into a conversation about politics or about what's going on but I'm learning to sit there quietly and ignore it because I dealt with that for forty hours already this week. I don't need to deal with it for another two.

Roberta Rosenthal Kwall (2001) has argued that authors' accounts of their own creative experiences have largely been submerged and discounted in US copyright law. She writes:

History shows that delineating the exact nature of the author's interest has always been problematic. This difficulty can be attributed to the fact that works of authorship are like other forms of property in that they have the potential for commodification but they differ from more tangible types of property such as real estate because they also entail important personal interests. (p. 16)

This absence of authorial perspective in work-for-hire doctrine – as well as First Amendment case law – is even more complete when it comes to workaday writing, since it is considered to be without authorial perspective at all: below the threshold of creative production and below the standards for protected speech. Workaday writing is most accepted as a form of labor and is thereby conducive to commodification and contract. But what kind of labor it is remains poorly understood, and what it does to and for the people who undertake it remains ill considered in the laws that regulate it. If these interviews are a guide, nearly every way the courts have characterized workplace writing is exceeded or contradicted at the level of writing experience. The very materiality of writing – that which makes it a commodity – appears to bring inalienable, unavoidable effects upon the writer. These effects are amplified through the consequential processes and structures in which the workaday writer works. As a result, both the rewards of writing and its risks seem unable to be shifted wholly to the employer as author. Writing for pay can be both more precious and more costly than any wage can represent. Especially provocative is the last example above, involving the communication specialist, whose testimony suggests what can happen to the expressive civic voice when it is rented and exhausted by the political needs and interests of the employer. (For more on this issue, see Chapter 2.)

As the next section will explore, the relationship of paid writing to the personality or personhood of the writer became especially apparent (but in convoluted ways) during discussions with people who ghostwrite – that is, people who compose words for which some other named individual takes the credit.

While it may be expected that a ghostwriter would take considerable care trying to match their writing to the style of the purported author, this process was described as far from straightforward and involved the same, complicated lending and borrowing that we saw take place among other workaday writers. Further, ghostwriting places writers up against conflicting ideologies of writing that, on the one hand, associate it with the highest cultural values of creativity, independence, and moral right (i.e., authorship) and, on the other hand, regulate it as a form of property and labor. As we will see, these wildly contradictory associations and regulations saturate the tasks and practices of workaday ghostwriters – sometimes with great dissonance and even damage to their personhood.

Ghostwriting and shifting values of literacy

The last time that former Congressman Dennis Kucinich ran for the Democratic nomination for president, he publicly criticized other candidates for hiring collaborators to help them write their campaign books. "If a president has a ghostwriter," he asked, "who's the president?" (quoted in Meadows 2004). With his jabbing question, Kucinich could remind the public that he was the sole author of his own campaign book, implying that he was more genuine, more commanding, harder working, maybe even more literate, and certainly more authoritative than his competitors. Of course, he, along with most of the public, had to know that presidents, like other executives, rely all the time on speechwriters and other assistants to do their writing, just as we know that the book industry increasingly relies on the fame of national politicians and other celebrities to produce ghostwritten books that will boost sales (Hitt 1997). Nevertheless, Kucinich could needle other candidates for misusing the prestige of book publishing to enhance their images while reserving for himself the prestige of real authorship, including a direct and reliable connection between the man and his words.

This incident suggests how ghostwriting (and its critics) can both clarify and complicate values that circulate along with writing and literacy in this culture. For now, we might define ghostwriting as taking on substantial parts of a composing process for which someone else, not you, will be credited – whether by byline, signature, institutional title, or oral delivery, or in some other way. As we will see, ghostwriting especially highlights power exchanges between writing and social structures, and also illuminates assumptions about underlying reading and writing processes that enable such exchanges. In the case of the ghostwritten campaign books, for instance, we see how a "name" – that is, a person with currency, social importance, celebrity, or notoriety – can endow a piece of writing with power. Their status brings status to the writing; they are connected to it by name, and it is this connection that authorizes the writing and warrants the reading of it. From this perspective, the actual working out of the words – the writing – is treated with lesser importance: the writer is a mere instrument in completing the connection, a presence not considered meaningful to the reading. Not only ghostwritten books but also much of the writing we encounter in bureaucratic society participates in this power arrangement, whereby words are made significant not by having been written but by the status of the official issuer.

At the same time, though, writing – particularly literary writing but not exclusively so – enjoys its own prestige. Through the sometimes convoluted history of literacy in this culture and the ideologies it produces, writing is associated with creativity, talent, intellect, sensibility, knowledge – in a word, authority. In general, writing is a desirable skill, a somewhat scarce skill, respected for its difficulty and the achievement it represents, particularly when it results in publication. Writing benefits most of all from the cultural prestige of reading. Because many forms of reading over time have been marked with high cultural value, this value has come to extend to those who can write in those forms. In this climate, then, writing may bequeath its high status to an individual who engages in it. One can "make a name" through writing. Writing is also its own verifiable record of a powerful engagement with literacy and all of its goodness – including the human growth that is presumed to be entailed in an artistic or intellectual experience. This achievement of the writing per se certifies the writer and warrants the reading. Writing, then, can be an independent source of social value and power and, with some exceptions, it enhances the stature of anyone who claims authorship.

These two different valences in writing – person-power and writing-power – are at play in Kucinich's gibe. The other presidential candidates undoubtedly wanted their ghostwritten books to indicate their prominent political status – their arrival as names on the national scene. However, Kucinich accuses them instead of self-aggrandizement: making an unearned claim on the social value of writing in order to puff themselves up. He invokes the social value of writing to insinuate shallowness, dependency, even deception on the part of his rivals (all damaging qualities in a leader). On his part, Kucinich can lay claim to a double status: he is well known enough to publish and authoritative enough to do his own writing. He invites a different kind of reading of his book, one in which the words actually do count and the presence of the writer is meaningful. In this way, he signals his own integrity, authenticity, reliability, and earned entitlement to the attention of his audience (all positive qualities in a leader). In his barb, Kucinich recruits underlying values associated with reading, writing, and literacy to advance a political campaign.

In the following discussion, ghostwriting and criticisms of it are examined for what they can say about how the status of writing operates as a site of power. It dwells first on the experiences of individual ghostwriters in a range of corporate and government settings. Of the 60 workaday writers I interviewed for this project, 22 reported doing at least some occasional ghostwriting as part of their employment, and several ghostwrote as a major aspect of their job. Ghostwriting took the form of memos, letters, speeches, editorials, legal rulings, and, in one case, articles. Ghostwriting was reportedly done by: legislative aides; various publicists, information officers, and communication specialists; a translator; a law clerk; a clerical worker; a member of a small, family-owned business; a social service planner; a bank employee; and several freelance writers. As we will see, most ghostwriters wrote "up," on behalf of supervisors, superiors, or paying clients, although several voluntarily wrote for peers or, in one case, family members who sought or agreed to their help. Most ghostwriters I interviewed wrote in the voice of someone who belonged to a different age cohort (usually, but not always, someone older). Several wrote in the voice of a different gender; two ghostwriters wrote cross-ethnically. I also interviewed one person (the head of a large public institution) who used the services of ghostwriters on his staff.

Ghostwriting depends explicitly on the elaborate borrowing and lending of status, including the status of writing itself, and it is in the handling of these exchanges that both the effectiveness of ghostwriting and its controversies will usually be found. Further, because ghostwriting can both artfully exploit and at times offensively violate normal assumptions about writing and reading, it opens a window on the ways in which social institutions and organizations rely on a normative literacy to run smoothly. Beliefs and values developed as part of mass reading literacy have come to saturate social systems, affecting the sense of how things work, or should work. These tacit assumptions become visible in, and often disturbed by, the practice of ghostwriting. Therefore, it is worth contemplating how the status of writing is recruited to institutional, organizational, and personal interests and how that process registers in the experiences of actual ghostwriters. I will then consider how normative beliefs about the status of writing appear in critiques of ghostwriting. My aim is not to pass judgments on ghostwriting, good or bad, but rather to explore the sometimes ineffable but potent cultural values that have accrued to writing and how those cultural values are themselves turned into rhetorical prerogative and transactional advantage. Just as the centrality of writing is on the rise in economic, social, and political life, ghostwriting is on the rise at the same time. How the prestige of writing is being harnessed in these new, writing-intensive times could transform the meanings, values, and practices of literacy, not to mention institutions and organizations that have come to rely on them. Above all, these transformations affect the literacy and lives of people who undertake the labor of ghostwriting.

Ghostwriters have been the focus of attention in a number of areas, including political science, speech communication, literary studies, and biography. Lois J. Einhorn (1988) provides fascinating profiles of speechwriters in high echelons of government, and Jennie Erdal (2004) supplies a book-length account of her long-term role as a ghostwriter for a quirky public figure and author. Boesky (2013) also recounts her own problematic experiences as a ghostwriter. Lively debates over ghostwriting have been conducted among scholars in speech communication, especially regarding the methodological challenges it poses to those rhetorical critics who are accustomed to drawing on an author's background to account for the style of a text (Bormann 1960, 1961; Buss 2011; Medhurst 1987; Nichols 1963). Others have explored the effects of ghostwriting on writer–reader relationships, particularly the trust that is crucial to certain kinds of written communication. Linda Riley and Stuart C. Brown (1996), for example, surveyed reader perceptions and attitudes, revealing sophisticated public awareness of the phenomenon of ghostwriting. Work by John J. Auer (1984), Donald K. Smith (1961), and Larry Witham (2000) direct attention to the contexts of ghostwriting, particularly the institutional roles of the people who depend on ghosted work, their motivations, the understanding or assumptions of their audiences, their manner of involvement with the writing, and their capacity to take responsibility for it. All of the studies cited above could be usefully mined for what they say about the ethical and interpretive habits that underlie common acts of writing and reading.

The ghostwriter at work

Not surprisingly, recognizing their employers as the controlling agents, pleasing them, or giving them what they want, is essential to ghostwriters' sense of what constitutes responsible or effective ghostwriting (and no doubt job security). But there is more to it than that. They need to recognize the client or employer not just as the controller or material provider but also as the creator, the author in the normative sense. This attribution is essential to their idea of what constitutes ethical ghostwriting. The goodness of their ghostwriting (what makes it worth their wage and makes it honest) depends on locating the status of authorship in the mind or person of the client/employer. To that end, they spend considerable effort trying to elicit and honor everything from the ideas to the prose style of the author-employer. Even further, though, and intriguingly so, in describing their practices, ghostwriters seem at the same time to suggest that part of their art involves bringing an author into being – as one ghostwriter put it, creating "an improved version of her," or as another facetiously put it, "saying what he would say if he knew what he was talking about." At yet another level, however, most ghostwriters also said they experience an authorial stake and intellectual ownership over the words that they write and at times derive pleasure, status, and growth from this writing even as their role remains hidden from the public.

All but one of the ghostwriters I interviewed said it was important to ascertain their client's or employer's *thoughts* or *ways of thinking* to serve as the origination of the writing.[11] "*It took me a long time,*" said a ghostwriter for a CEO of a major institution, "*to understand how his mind operates.*" This need usually entailed meeting with the clients or employers, interviewing them, reading their previous work, or, in some cases, audiotaping conversations. For example, one freelancer who writes personal newsletter columns for banking executives said she always interviews her clients first:

I try the interview technique of picking up themes. If it's important they will typically repeat themselves or if it's a thought they've had it won't be hard to catch because they will emphasize it in some way.

A government speechwriter described a similar process:

For me it was largely a question of paying attention to people like [R.], who was a bright guy and by the time I spent ten or fifteen minutes with him I usually had a pretty good idea of what he wanted to say. Then it was just an iterative process to get things down.

A marketing director for a health maintenance organization communicated regularly with doctors, clinics, and community members under the name of the organization's medical director:

It's odd. Sometimes it's difficult. You almost have to think like they think. Okay, this is a medical director writing this letter. How would a medical director write this letter? It's gotten easier because you just know how. It's the same medical director I've been writing for for a number of years so I just know how he's going to want it to read and what he is not going to want to say.

A legislative aide described how he worked back and forth with his boss when he drafted letters to constituents, calibrating his judgments with her feedback:

I'm writing as if I were her, which makes it important to be quick learning about what a person's moods are and how they feel about certain issues, because if you don't, you're going to be constantly rewriting and struggling with that. I will put a thought forth. Is this true? And sometimes she'll say, "No, I'm not comfortable with that." And sometimes she'll go, "Yeah, that's exactly how it is." Every time the "exactly" happens or the "no" happens, I learn more about it and the "no's" become fewer.

Others reported similar kinds of calibration. A law clerk told me that she read a number of cases decided by the judge who employed her as a way to draft rulings under his name, and studied closely the revisions and edits he would return to her, *"so I could learn from them."* A government speechwriter said he tries to witness the delivery of the speeches he prepares: *"If I'm writing a speech for somebody it's really important to go and hear their speech so I can hear how they use the material,"* he said. *"If they change something, I'll make sure the next time that it's written that way."* Concomitantly, several interviewees said ghostwriting became difficult when they did not get adequate access to a client's thoughts. *"The worst thing is when somebody is not very expressive,"* said one freelance ghostwriter. *"What flips this guy's switch?"* A communications specialist spoke of a generic "leadership style" he would resort to if he did not have access to an executive for whom he needed to write. And then there was this squirmy episode, recounted by a banker about an early stage in his career:

The chairman of a petroleum company had just died, one of our biggest clients. I was working in the petroleum department and the word came down from the president of the bank to write a regret letter to the widow. The head of the department didn't want to do it so it went all the way down to the lowest guy in the room, which was me. I must have written that thing ten or fifteen times. I never knew the guy. I didn't know how well the president knew him. I would keep trotting back to the vice president and he would say, well, I think it should be a little more like this. Back and forth. Finally I had a version he was comfortable with. The secretary put it on the letterhead of the president and put it in a glossy sleeve and I was one who had to take it up to the president in his big old mahogany office and let him have a look. He looked it over, signed it and said thank you very much, and off it went.

In any case, whenever possible, ghostwriters expend a great deal of energy trying to capture the "signature" style of thoughts or values of an author-client. Through the sharing of thoughts or revealing of systems of thought, clients lend their status or position to the ghostwriter. This is the site of authorization that serves both practical and integrity functions for the ghostwriter. At the same time that ghostwriters described the controlling and authoring role played by an employer, they also talked about the powers they as writers lent in the process, which often included bringing an author into being, as part of their creative labor or skill. Here there were references to a "puppet quality", or "a producer–director role", or "script writing." The following is a particularly telling observation in which the writer becomes the controller of the purported author, for his own good. The quote is from a freelancer who writes mostly for the banking industry:

I try to make people smarter. Well, they are probably very intelligent. They are running a financial institution. But I try to use quotes that they probably wouldn't think of. I try to pull things together structurally where they might have these thoughts but they probably didn't think of them in a cogent way. That's my job, to take what's in their head and pull it through a process so the words work and somebody reading it says, yeah, that Bob's a great guy, he's out there for our benefit.

Not surprisingly, having superior knowledge of a topic or superior rhetorical acumen often authorized a writer to take control of the author. As one interviewee observed, *"I'm fascinated to hear my ideas play out through an entirely different voice from my own."* Here we see how the status associated with writing and the writer buys purchase for the ghostwriter, evoking and authorizing authorship. The ghostwriter as the real author was sometimes acknowledged and even joked about within the ghostwriter–employer relationship. The law clerk I interviewed found it "exciting" when another judge cited an opinion that she had written, even though, of course, her name was not on it. *"I kidded around with* [the judge I worked for] *once or twice on that one,"* she said.

Along with expressions of pride of ownership came expressions, interestingly, of both authorial responsibility and abdication of authorial responsibility.

These mixed experiences could occur as part of the same writing event because, as I have been arguing, they emerge from the flow of power from the status of writing into the employee–employer relationship. Consider this account of a speechwriter for a high-profile CEO. The ghostwriter called this elaborate borrowing and lending of authorship "oddly powerful." Here he describes sitting anonymously in an audience as his boss delivered a speech he had written:

First, he is saying what you wrote and that has a weird puppet feel to it. But then you're also in an audience surrounded by people who are reacting for the first time to what you have written and nobody knows that you wrote it. And it's humbling too because you realize, well, I really have to put a lot of thought into what I'm doing because if he goes out and says these things, he's taking responsibility for those positions and I should put as much thought into those positions as he would on his own. So I would say I've gotten access to the trials and troubles of leadership and have an appreciation for not being a leader and not having full responsibility. It's easy to write a speech and say, okay, you go get heckled. I'm just going to hide back in my office.

Of course, there are limits to the ghostwriter's control, which, despite the power of writing, always remains tied to hierarchical arrangements. Interestingly, the CEO just mentioned would sometimes signal displeasure with a ghostwritten message by exposing its status in public and distancing himself from the words. Here we see that when a powerful name withdraws support, when someone "pulls rank," so to speak, writing can be emptied of its power. The ghostwriter recounts:

Early on I was at an event where I had written remarks for him and he stood up front and said, okay, I've got these remarks that somebody wrote for me and I probably should read those but after that I'm going to tell you some other things ... If it [the writing] doesn't sound like him, if it doesn't sound like something he wants to say, he'll often ignore it completely or if he does use it, he'll make it fairly plain that he didn't write it.

In this case, the executive's relinquishing of purported authorship was a way of putting the writer in his place. Control was asserted not by taking ownership of the writing but by re-separating from the ghostwriter and demoting the writing. Such re-separation or demotion of writing perhaps reaches its ultimate degree in the following incident, relayed by the legislative aide:

One of the senators fired all four of his staff last Christmas, right near last Christmas, because they were trying to tell him what to do. And in part they were trying to do that through the writing and he would have none of that.

I have tried to show how the value of writing, its transactional flow within employee–employer relations, and the competing definitions of the author that this value brings into being, manifest in ghostwriters' descriptions of their routine composing processes and their working relationships with client-employers. The subtle and sometimes strange borrowing and lending of status on which ghostwriting depends includes management of the status of writing as a discrete locus of power. Especially important to the success of these transactions, both pragmatic and ethical, is the prestige of authorship, which is central to the mystique of ghostwriting and often important to the satisfaction of an individual ghostwriter. But it is also a power than can convolute and at times compromise the subordinate writer's work. The prestige of authorship, especially expert authorship, is exactly what must be given away in the ghostwriting exchange and yet it seems inseparable from the experience of writing.

Literacy and scarcity

Another aspect of the status of writing that ghostwriting foregrounds is the fact that literacy functions in a system of scarcity. Time is one such scarcity motivating a lot of paid ghostwriting. Political leaders, physicians, CEOs, and other executives are typically responsible for massive amounts of written communication (from annual reports to speeches to correspondence to various kinds of certifications) that are beyond their individual capacity to produce, especially given other obligations. So they outsource to ghostwriters. To the consternation of some observers, writing is even being outsourced these days by people in writing professions, such as attorneys, authors, academics, and journalists. The time-consuming nature of writing is out of balance with the amount of writing required; as a consequence, hired writers enter the breach. Knowledge can be another scarcity. Decision-makers (for instance, state governors) often oversee complex institutions or operations about which they cannot have omniscient or in-depth knowledge even though they have ultimate responsibility. A ghostwriter may serve as a researcher, knowledge producer, and/or knowledge analyst for such a leader – a "ghost thinker" as one presidential speechwriter called himself (Einhorn 1988, p. 125). Knowledge scarcity can also motivate private citizens to seek formal or informal writing help in, say, the filing of legal documents or composing an appeal of an immigration ruling. Skill scarcity is also a major motivator for ghostwriting. To the extent that writing is treated as a talent in this society, and an unequally distributed talent at that, people who need more writing talent than they possess themselves may seek the services of ghostwriters. Knowledge and/or skill scarcity lies behind the success of so-called term-paper mills. And, as communication and publicity have become more consequential to politics, commerce, and many other spheres, wordsmiths have become as vital as attorneys or accountants in terms of the specialized assistance they can render. The high cultural value that writing carries, its capacity to influence outcomes, and its tendency to make its skillful users look good all create incentive for borrowing others' skills. Skill scarcity also results from unequal access to literacy and language education. Many people in society are required to produce writing or writing in a particular language that they are incapable of executing on their own.[12] Scribes, translators, literacy coaches, and ghostwriters often help in these circumstances. Disabilities of various kinds can also impair skills needed to conduct composition on one's own; certain kinds of brain damage, for instance, can make the ordering of textual language impossible or interfere with the mental focus that writing requires. Without the combination of the high priority for and value of writing, in consort with such scarcity as time, knowledge, skill and access (and the power dynamics those scarcities create), ghostwriting would not be such a common practice.

Above all, scarcity of time goes a long way in explaining the economy of ghostwriting, especially because there is also symbolic value in the association between writing and time. When someone takes the time to write, it can signal attentiveness, care, and involvement with the recipients of the writing, which can be important in situations in which social and/or diplomatic relationships matter. Writing is often associated with the writer's thoughts and so being addressed, particularly in private correspondence, is a visible record that the reader was in the writer's thoughts during the time of composing. Likewise, the writer can be held in the reader's thoughts during reading. These exchanges can permit a claim to intimacy; psychologically, reading or writing can be satisfactory substitutes for spending time together. The connection between time and thought also lies behind the perceived effort required in writing: someone who puts time into writing is presumed to have earned something from the thinking, whether that be knowledge, clarity, certainty, or some other benefit. In other words, the writing act itself, given the time and effort involved, can help to authorize the writer and the message. This association among time, writing, thought, and effort can be especially important in written evaluations, in which the writer has been presumed to have taken time to review and reflect on an applicant, a proposal, or whatever is being evaluated. No doubt, the social or organizational status of the writer, his or her reputation or standing, matters to the status of a message, including an evaluation. But the psychological association among writing, time, effort, and attention means that writing itself, its symbolic import, is a value added in any text. In ghostwriting, this symbolic power is recouped for the interests of the employer/client: not only does the client save actual time by employing the ghostwriter but often still gets credit for having put in that time, at least from the psychological perspective of the reader.

One common example of this symbolic value involves the ubiquitous thank-you letters that go out in bulk to, say, donors to a foundation. Such letters are typically ghostwritten, then printed on fine linen stationery, then signed, perhaps by a real foundation president or perhaps by a machine with a fountain pen rigged up to imitate the president's signature, and then, finally, bulk mailed with first-class postage. Such letters can have their desired effect only because they can be read singly and privately by readers primed to treat personal letters in a certain way and thus primed to feel grateful to the foundation president for taking the time to acknowledge their donation. (An executive I interviewed who signs many ghostwritten thank-you letters told me that on occasion he actually re-copies in his own handwriting an entire ghostwritten letter to be sent to a particularly important donor or donors. Handwriting is an extra sign of his presence. The donation of his precious time and attention reciprocates the financial contribution. The value of writing itself is central to the success of this exchange.)

Skill scarcity can have a similar symbolic value beyond its real measure. Because writing in our society is, at least in some contexts, elevated as a rare talent or an expression of unusual intelligence, those who engage in it well (or ostensibly do so) can derive status from that perception. An effective piece of writing can boost someone's reputation or claim to entitlement. Effective writing makes the writer seem more trustworthy, authentic, or deserving. This accumulated cultural association between literacy and intelligence, goodness, and deservingness is of incalculable social value, a value much exploited in the economy of ghostwriting. As with time scarcity, the symbolic value of skill scarcity is recouped in the employer's interest. In the ghostwriting relationship, power is consolidated when the symbolic status of writing joins the organizational status of the employer/client. Scarcity is transacted into surplus.

Before leaving the topic of scarcity, however, I want to explore a more unusual but no less revealing dynamic in which the real and symbolic values of writing can flow in a different direction: to the less powerful. That is, at times, through ghostwriting, the status of writing can be used to reroute power within organizations. This happens when a person with time and skills for literacy lends these resources to someone who has fewer skills. One of the people I interviewed, who was employed at the time of the interview as a translator and interpreter, volunteered his time outside of work helping fellow Southeast Asian immigrants with their necessary written communication. He prepared personal letters sent to family members who still lived in the home country as well as official correspondence with the US government over such matters as immigration, citizenship, employment, housing, or social welfare. Because government bureaucracies presume a level of English written literacy that far exceeds the knowledge and skills of many of the Southeast Asian immigrants, they often did not apply for benefits for which they were otherwise legally entitled, or else they would often be denied benefits because of paperwork errors. As a ghostwriter of family letters and official correspondence, this volunteer explained that his work involved far more than merely transcribing oral messages into written messages or first language into second language. Rather, working in two languages, he needed to lend his neighbors a textualized voice, a form of authorship involving both control and creativity. He often also lent knowledge of government bureaucracy as well as writing equipment and supplies.

In one extended account, this volunteer ghostwriter discussed a particularly consequential appeal that he wrote for a neighbor seeking to reverse a denial of unemployment benefits. Because the volunteer ghostwriter had had experience with unemployment and at one time worked as a case manager for a social welfare program, he was able to use writing to lend an institutional way of thinking to his neighbor. Whereas as we saw in the earlier section how subordinate ghostwriters would glean organizational thinking from the employer/client and use it to guide writing, here the volunteer ghostwriter lends his neighbor the necessary thoughts that will make his case effective. Through literacy, he is able to redistribute institutional power by lending bureaucratic ways of thinking. He explained:

Someone who doesn't know the process, the requirement, and doesn't speak the language, if you don't tell them what they need to say, their case will be denied. [The man I wrote for] *knew nothing. In the letter, I knew what to say to stress the point. I was laid off once so I knew the correct process and procedure to keep records and what to do if something is wrong. Plus, after I was laid off I got a job working as a case manager helping people who were laid off so I had quite a bit of experience in that field. So I knew what points to stress and the correct person to write to directly to get more accurate information. It was fortunate.* [My friend's] *denial was reversed and he received his benefits.*

In this circumstance, ghostwriting serves not to consolidate institutional power but to redistribute it by blocking the negative repercussions that usually come with low literacy. In many contexts in society, judgments are made about a person on the basis of their literacy or language. Foreign identity signaled in language, particularly, can be grounds for exclusion or rejection. But when, through ghostwriting, an outsider can sound as if he were an insider, knowledgeable about the bureaucracy and fluent in English, those systems of exclusion are confused and made less potent. Potential discrimination based on literacy assumptions is blocked. In this case, the ghostwriter volunteers his literacy in service to his neighbors, sharing his resources of language and education in the same way he might share money or food. It is, most would agree, an admirable act. Yet we also can see in this example the potential subversiveness of ghostwriting when it is used to redistribute power, when it harnesses the status of writing to disrupt the social order. As we will see below, fear of disruption to the social order lies behind many critiques of ghostwriting.

Ghostwriting and the social order: cases of controversy

So far, we have mostly examined the peculiar power dynamics of ghostwriting as they emerge in accounts of workaday ghostwriters, people who, as part of their work, draft letters, speeches, reports, public relations columns, and other documents that are published or distributed under someone else's name. These forms of ghostwriting are accepted as necessary to the busy production pace of government, corporations, and other organizations. Ghostwriters function like other assistants who help organizational leaders do their jobs more effectively. Deception is not the goal. At the same time, we have seen that in such routine acts of ghostwriting, tricky negotiations sometimes must be undertaken in order to handle the status of writing as a site of power. Such management engages an ethical response on the part of ghostwriters who work in contexts where the commercial value of literacy and its scarcity press into their considerations. Balancing tensions between control and creativity is a constant rhetorical pressure for ghostwriters. And while deception is not the goal, the mystique of ghostwriting always depends on the way in which the work of writing is transacted into value, including, importantly, symbolic value for the purported author.

Here I set my focus in a different location: on critiques of ghostwriting, where, as we will see, many of these same issues play out in somewhat different form. I must say at the outset that this discussion is not meant in any way as an evaluative gloss on earlier sections of this essay, or certainly on the ethics of the ghostwriters who were interviewed as part of this project. None of the people I interviewed was engaged in the controversial forms of ghostwriting that will be treated in this section. Rather, I examine some of the more flagrant cases of ghostwriting because they bring to the surface certain normative assumptions about reading and writing that ride along as part of institutional practice and wider social life. Critics of ghostwriting, or at least certain forms of it, find the practice deceptive and damaging to the integrity of literacy and consequently to institutions that rely on literacy. Where ghostwriting seems to overstep its bounds, it is seen to threaten social order by surreptitiously seducing and exploiting the trust that people put in literacy, both their own and that of others (Fosko 2012).

Consider first the controversy surrounding legal ghostwriting, a practice that is part of a new movement toward the unbundling of legal services (Walter 2003). Sometimes clients do not need or cannot afford full legal representation for whatever problem they face; so some law firms break down services into discrete parts and offer them for flat fees to clients who otherwise would appear in court *pro se*, that is, as self-represented, without counsel. The writing of briefs, appeals, and other documents is a popular unbundled service (as the scarcity principle might predict). A behind-the-scenes lawyer will ghostwrite court papers for a client to sign and file. However, some judges have responded negatively to this practice, and sharply so. (For a range of views, see Goldschmidt 2002; Robbins 2010; Rothermich 1999; Swank 2005; Weeman 2006.) For one thing, ghostwriting seems to elude some of the bedrock responsibility that lawyers have toward the judicial system, namely candor and accountability. Some commentators worry that by writing briefs without disclosing their authorship, lawyers might be tempted to do a slipshod job and get away with it, never facing the consequences of mistakes, omissions, or malpractice that come with signed work. This concern suggests how the claim to authorship serves as a crucial mechanism for the display and enforcement of professional accountability and candor. Professions such as the law not only borrow from the status of writing to bestow status on members but also have come to rely on writing as a site to enforce and make manifest their professional standards. It is interesting to observe that even though a legal brief is a work made for hire (i.e., clients buy the writing services of attorneys), many courts are reluctant to recognize the transfer of authorship to a (lowly) client. When professionals sell away authorship –especially to the less wealthy or less powerful – they destabilize professional codes and disrupt professional compacts that are carried through institutionalized acts of reading and writing. They also potentially dilute their exclusiveness as a profession.

Legal ghostwriting also collides with the custom of the court to be lenient with self-represented litigants. When lay people serve as their own lawyers, including, presumably, handling their own legal writing, their amateur status is recognized, and if mistakes are made they are overlooked, or repaired, or taken into consideration as part of the administration of justice. Although some judges claim they can always spot professionally prepared papers and so are not bothered by ghostwriting services, others maintain that some degree of uncertainty will always be introduced when the authorship of legal papers is unclear, an uncertainty that is disruptive to the relationships and processes upon which justice depends. According to critics of legal ghostwriting, a professionally prepared piece of writing misrepresents the person appearing before a judge: litigants can appear more legally literate than they really are. This obfuscation can interfere with justice in at least a couple of ways. First, filing professionally prepared papers under one's own name may make a person less deserving of leniency because that person is less than fully pro se, self-represented. In other words, legal ghostwriting may give people an advantage to which they are not entitled. On the other hand, the quality of the writing may make litigants appear more in control of the case than they are, putting them at risk of higher expectations by the judge or other representatives of the court. As a result, they may not be accorded the leniency they need and deserve. In any case, justice is threatened when one appears more literate than one really is. This controversy exposes underlying social values associated with literacy that run tacitly through the judicial system (i.e., high literate skill carries favorable connotations, and low literate skills must be accommodated).[13] Interestingly, those who defend legal ghostwriting do so in part on the grounds that it levels the playing field: first, because unbundled legal services expand access to legal aid; and second, because lending literacy (in this case, specialized legal discourse) to a layperson blunts the usual power advantage that accompanies full professional representation. For instance, Jona Goldschmidt (2002, p. 1207) writes, "If lawyers lose some of their advantage over pro se litigants because of ghostwriting and coaching, that increases access to justice, and the complaining attorneys must accept this new reality." Critics of legal ghostwriting, though, believe that the mystery and uncertainty it creates, the inability to locate power and responsibility in the written representations, makes the practice corrosive to judicial processes (Swank 2005; Weeman 2006). Specifically, ghostwriting is thought to disturb the attorney–judge relationship, which is made manifest through normative practices of reading and writing.

The military is another site of controversy over ghostwriting, especially the ghostwriting of personnel evaluations, a practice that is reportedly on the rise. Marine Lt. Col. Thomas C. Gillespie (2002) is one critic of this practice by which reviewing officers depend on lower-ranking officers to prepare fitness reports on individual marines under their command. The reviewing officers then submit the reports under their own names. Some see this practice as a benign and practical solution to the proliferation of paperwork and argue that lower-ranked officers are better positioned to write the evaluations anyway because they have a closer, daily relationship with the rank and file. But Gillespie regards such ghostwriting as a serious disruption in the chain of command and a dereliction of duty on the part of supervisory officers. To Gillespie, the reviewing officer's signature implies an independent review has occurred when in fact it has not, creating not only a misrepresentation but also a breach in the hierarchy. Through ghostwriting, the words of the lower-ranking officer leapfrog over their supervisor and go straight to another level of command, where they are treated as authoritative. Gillespie cautions reviewing officers to "[w]rite only what you yourself know from personal experience or objective record" (p. 30)." He calls on reviewing officers to use writing to become more involved in direct observation and evaluation of those in charge and thereby reassert their genuine authority. Authority requires the act of writing, including the attentiveness, judgment, and reflection involved. Gillespie's argument is similar to criticisms that have been lodged against judges who are seen to rely too heavily on their clerks to write opinions in court cases (Choi and Gulati 2000; Lerman 2001). There is something unseemly, critics say, about passing judgment on someone else without undertaking the mental wrestling entailed in writing an opinion yourself. Writing does something to those who write: earning them, through the work of it, the authority of their verdicts and thereby the authority of their positions.

A third controversy – the most complex and perhaps the most flagrant one – involves scientific ghostwriting sponsored by pharmaceutical companies. In this case, pharmaceutical companies conduct research on their own products and, when the outcomes are favorable, hire a medical education firm to write a scholarly article based on the company's experimental data. Once the article is drafted, the pharmaceutical company locates a prominent medical professor willing to "guest author" the article for purposes of submitting it to a research journal for publication. Pharmaceutical companies defend the practice as a way of getting important clinical information out to the medical community in a timely fashion. Medical education firms defend the practice so long as their writers get full access to all the data and use rigorous scientific overview. In their view, a rigorous and principled writing process makes the article worthy of publication on its own merits, regardless of the name that ultimately goes on it. Needless to say, however, this practice has met with outrage from journal editors, scientists, and other academics, as well as various professional organizations, the general public, and even Congress.[14] Academics tend to object because guest-authors are credited with publications without putting in substantive effort, creating unfairness in the academic reward system. Journal editors object because the articles cannot, on their face, be differentiated from those that are written with more independence. Because the editors are not privy to the origins of the work, they compromise their relationship with reviewers and readers. On their part, readers just feel duped. Ghostwriting deprives them of the usual means of bringing critical interpretation to data and findings.[15] In this situation, when the prestige of writing is borrowed and lent, the integrity of everybody's literacy is threatened. What may be especially goading is how the commercial drug company commandeers the most prized tools of the academic trade (writing and publishing articles) to insert their interests into the ostensibly impartial institution of science, and do so by stealthy exploitation of the academy's literate habits and values, including trust in the independence of academic writing.

Professional associations of journal editors, medical writers, and scientists have published codes of ethics in an effort to curtail this practice, mostly by insisting on disclosure and transparency among all parties involved. As with the cases of military commanders and judges, reformers call on guest-authors to become more involved in the work of writing as a means of restoring integrity to the process. Robert J. Fletcher of the Harvard Medical School finds a close association between professionalism and *the work* of writing:

The integrity of the published record of scientific research depends not only on the validity of the science but also honesty in authorship. Editors and readers need to be confident that authors have undertaken the work described and have ensured that the manuscript accurately reflects their work, irrespective of whether they took the lead in writing or sought assistance from a medical writer. (Fletcher 2005, p. 549)

Thus we can see through controversies over ghostwriting how deeply writing and writing–reading relationships matter to how contemporary institutions maintain a sense of themselves. Where professional or institutional breaches are perceived to occur, they often implicate authoring and composing practices and/or take advantage of members' usual (trusting) habits of reading and writing. Controversial ghostwriting practices seem especially to disturb normative reading and writing practices that maintain hierarchy or social demarcations, or else condition systems of access and reward. Litigants who appear as if they can write like attorneys, low-level officers whose words carry the weight of their superiors, or commercial writers who can write like professors all pose threats, at least in some eyes, to the ways that order, or justice, or privilege, or integrity is maintained. The remedies to these problems lie either in the redistribution of the work of writing back toward the purported author or in full transparency in disclosing who does what in the composing process. However, despite efforts like codes of ethics developed by medical editors, many observers remain doubtful that the practice of ghostwriting – including the obfuscation of authorship that lies at the heart of its success – can really be curtailed. Writing is just too valuable and scarcities of time and skill too great to stem the tide.

What's presiding?

Those of us who teach and study writing these days cannot help but be aware of how current economic, social, and technological changes are affecting the meanings and values that surround literacy and its practices. This influence, in my view, begins with the deep appropriation of literacy, and particularly writing, into the processes and products of the so-called information age. Writing as a mass practice thoroughly participates now in the trading of things and ideas, and in the competition for attention to things and ideas. While always connected to commercial life, the powers of writing have never been more valuable to more people in so many places, in so many ways, and at so many levels of public and private enterprise. Further, the Internet seems to be favoring a less original form of writing: creation by citation, sampling, cutting and pasting, the blurring of the roles of writers and readers. And in the arena of artistic creation, courts seem eager to recognize the authorial rights of corporations and copyright holders. The idea of the individual author as originator of ideas and expression has been most buffeted, indeed, over the last several decades. Yet, for now, its cultural power, legal standing, and psychological appeal are enough intact that its value can continue to be exploited by agents of change.

The proliferation of ghostwriting, its growing presence in publishing, politics, public relations, and professional services, and in the routine maintenance of complex organizations, speaks directly to this rising value of writing in general. But as I hope I have demonstrated, ghostwriting also constitutes unique grounds upon which current transformations in literacy may be particularly apprehensible. As writing is separated from authorship to be embedded in processes of production and transaction, its political and commercial value – not to mention its ethical integrity in the eyes of many – remains tied to interpretive habits that continue to link writing and authorship. How these competing sets of values will ultimately resolve themselves is yet to be seen. But the fact that ghostwriting is a matter of vigorous debate right now in law, medicine, even textbook publishing (Schemo 2006) indicates that something is afoot and tells of the sense of violation and disruption that changes in literacy can engender.

Especially intriguing is the extent to which so many institutions depend on the idea of the author as originator in order to manage power, even as they depend on the labor of workaday writers to whom authorship is denied. In many contexts, authority rests precariously in the act of writing itself, which justifies the right to pass judgment, to make a decision, to claim entitlement. The high status of old-fashioned writing legitimates power, largely through its taxing effort, its call on a person's time, attention, judgment, and skill, and its capacity to strengthen and improve those who take it up. As writing changes and its status is destabilized, there remains a question: what will happen to the legitimacy of this power? Ghostwriting and its controversies bring our attention to how unconsciously institutions depend on members to invoke normative habits of reading and writing to define institutional relationships and make things run smoothly. My analysis has only scratched the surface of that dependency, but I hope it has shown how deeply our current shifts in literacy could reach.

Meanwhile, workaday ghostwriters will continue to negotiate these transformations one task at a time, as these transformations appear as practical challenges in the lending and borrowing of power and perspective that ghostwriting always entails. So I close this section by returning to the experiences of two ghostwriters whose accounts epitomize the human complexities at stake.

When I interviewed 37-year-old Jason Slager, he was working as chief aide for a high-profile state legislator, a woman who had a prior career in the health profession. He ghostwrote a good deal, mostly in the form of letters to constituents who contacted the legislator's office on issues of concern. With varying degrees of guidance and feedback, Slager would write the letters for the legislator's signature. In the following interview excerpt, he and I explore what it can mean to compose in this form of writing:

DB: *So, this means you are writing as a woman?*[16]
JS: *Well, I write as a woman and a nurse and a legislator and a mother and a grandmother, and I am none of those things. It's not overly difficult. We understand that nurses are very trusted and my boss is very professional and trustworthy. So when somebody* [contacts us] *who is in constant pain because they have no money for treatment, I reach into my thoughts on how as a nurse I understand, I've seen this kind of thing. Also, in the voice of the* [legislator] *there is prestige. I'm the*

[legislator] *and there is prestige in who that person is, a nurse, a grandmother, a mother, a progressive Democrat, that's the embodiment right now.*

DB: *Do you ever go the other way and use your writing to push* [the legislator] *on something?*

JS: *Can I push* [the legislator] *or overlay my own perspectives? Certainly, sometimes. In agriculture, she values the family farm but that's not her issue* [Slager is the grandson of family farmers]. *I have a great deal of latitude with that. I can do a lot within that and I have a great deal of freedom and it's fun. There I can let a little bit of myself out. The flip side of that is that we get calls and letters on things like, well, why won't my insurance company insure my dogs? Well* [and here, to be clear, Slager is talking about himself], *my 2-year-old son was attacked by a Rottweiler. He's going to need plastic surgery. He's fine but he has a big scar on his face and it has impacted him. So we're going through the legal process. So I have an intimate and personal experience there, and I grit my teeth. I don't argue with people because you don't engage in that capacity. It's hard for me to write those letters. I write those letters. I say, I understand. Dog's important to you. So there are two sides to that. So sometimes you have some room and you can say something. Other times, you can't. And you get energy where you can.*

As we have seen, according to law, Jason Slager is a salaried employee engaged in writing that is considered so ordinary, so bound up with immediate usefulness, so ephemeral, so without unique personality that it is considered authorless and ownerless – beneath the threshold of consideration by statutes governing copyright and other matters pertaining to the ownership of writing. So how does work get done under these conditions? How does composition occur? At one level, as Slager attests, it does not appear overly difficult, as we see in this account how a writer can indeed rationally share ownership, produce words that are not his own, and say what he does not mean. Yet if this is what so-called humdrum, ownerless, authorless writing looks like, it nevertheless is embodied in and emanates from the experiences, personalities, knowledge, and histories of the people who create it. For Slager, writing in the name of the boss entails borrowing and lending of powerful elements of personhood and authorship – including knowledge, experience, status, identity, and integrity. Significantly, this writing also creates space for political expressiveness. In fact, where it doesn't, where expression is stifled by the rules, it can inflict hardship on the integrity of the ghostwriter.

Like other ghostwriters encountered earlier in this chapter, Slager tries to compose from inside the head of the employer, the purported author of this correspondence, thus creating the astonishing line, *"I reach into my thoughts and, as a nurse, I understand, I've seen this kind of thing."* This deeply impersonating move seems to purchase the inventional footing needed to compose, especially lending Slager the legitimacy of the borrowed identity with which to craft a letter, including the boost in prestige that is required by an underling. Slager also seems to treat the integrity of the nurse/mother/grandmother/progressive

Democratic as a public image that is being projected onto him as he writes. As we have seen, this move inside the head of the client also seemed to grant the necessary ethical license to perform the sometimes ethically murky work of ghostwriting. If you get inside the head of the purported author, the words you write could have been, might as well have been the words she would have used anyway – it seems like less of a cheat, it allows the purported author to maintain her moral rights to put her name to the words even in the absence of actually thinking up those words herself (that is, actually doing the work). This move inside the head of the employer is part of what people get paid to do – part of the way they satisfy an employee, part of the art in which they take pride. They work on this impersonation over time and measure their success by how little their employer or client changes the words they have written before delivering or publishing them.

Yet we also see how Slager loans back to the employer some of these same powerful elements of embodied authorship – in this case, experience with and knowledge of family farming and the integrity that comes from being the grandson of farmers. From this position, Slager wins back fuller rights to authorship through the authority of his experience, gaining more latitude, more freedom, more self, as he describes it. Still, the ghostwriting relationship, writing under the name of a more powerful employer, actually amplifies Slager's authority as he is able to express his political concerns about family farming through the powerful voice of the legislator – the part, I suspect, that makes it so much fun.

These residues of authorship, what Fisk (2003, p. 2) has called "irrepressible authorship", are an aspect of the workplace writing experience that is unacknowledged and unclaimed by the legal regime that governs it. It is not calculated into the regulation of the work made for hire and escapes its control. But while irrepressible authorship often springs up as an experience of power or moral right – as a claim of ownership no matter how anonymous or authorless or ownerless the text is supposed to be – it also can be a site of pain and turmoil. Where the authorial drive is in conflict with the rules surrounding the work made for pay, the results can be self-distortion, diminished capacity, a corrosion of dignity, a deflation of energy. We see this when Slager's position requires him to validate the view of the dog owner, requiring him to write against himself and those he loves. (*"I don't argue with people because you don't engage in that capacity,"* he says, where "capacity" could mean not only his rank as legislative aide but also the capacity that comes from saying what one really means.) Where this gap occurs, writing hurts.

An even more dramatic case of irrepressible authorship and self-alienation occurs in the next example. Here Cecily Lawrence, a freelance science writer I interviewed, describes the process of ghostwriting a series of academic articles for a professor. The professor had suffered injuries in an accident that affected short-term memory, making it impossible to write. The two worked together over a period of a year and a half, during which time Lawrence turned a series of the professor's talks into articles for scholarly journals. In this freelance assignment (which, incidentally, would be recognized by law as creative and copyrightable production), Lawrence must not merely impersonate the author but take on a way of working that is not her own and an identity that in her view diminishes her commitments and contributions rather than amplifies them. Here we see how a set of personal properties can be aroused and disturbed by the work made for hire, so much so that, when this assignment was done, Lawrence decided to quit ghostwriting:

DB: *Did you get any attribution?*

CL: *I got thanks in the acknowledgments and that was the deal that we worked out. That she would thank me for invaluable editorial assistance and that is a typical arrangement for a ghostwriter.*

DB: *Were there any ethical dilemmas?*

CL: *No, I didn't feel ethical dilemmas with doing the journal articles because although I do think there are ethical problems with ghostwriting in some cases, I guess I felt like I admired that she had found a way to carry on with her career and she did remain substantively involved. I didn't feel like she was cheating.*

DB: *Did you try to be her?*

CL: *Yeah. In the writing I did. I think in some ways I tried to be an improved version of her. I tried to be more rigorous in the reasoning. How do you turn that off in yourself if you are reading an argument that she's made in a talk or in another paper and you just feel like there is a big logical gap here? It has to be filled in or changed in some way. How do you pretend you didn't see that? For pride's sake I felt I had to make it the best that I could. The articles got accepted for publication so I guess it turned out well. But I just felt like a hack. I felt like I was just writing somebody else's ideas and I didn't feel like they were the best ideas in the world. Maybe if I were a ghostwriter for one of the world's best theoreticians who happened to have had a car accident and couldn't write. Say, if Steven Hawking needed me. I felt it was fine but I didn't feel totally inspired by the subject matter and one thing that I could see is that we were rewriting the same paper over and over for different journals, with a little different twist but basically the same material and evidenced by the fact that I didn't have to learn anything new for the second one or the third one or the fourth one. Just rewrote it and organized it differently. It just didn't feel like . . . I just had this moment when I felt like I wanted to do more with my career.*

We see again in this account the blurry borrowing and lending of authorial elements that characterize collaborations occurring within the hierarchy of ghostwriting; on the one hand, the effort to borrow the thinking and style of the client author (again it seems to protect the purported author's moral claim to substantive authorship) and, on the other hand, to lend from the self missing elements – in this case, rigor and logic that Lawrence believed, through her own academic training, belong to academic writing. Yet we also see in this account that these processes of borrowing and lending go on deeply at the level of the writing process where they can become hard to manage. Lawrence is being asked to be a kind of academic writer that she doesn't want to be. An academic writer, in Lawrence's view, should be making a valuable social contribution, should be expending effort to learn and share the learning. Yet that is not occurring for her or her employer in this project. When Lawrence remarks that she wanted to do more with her career, you can't tell whom she is speaking as. Herself? The freelance writer who needs more independent work? Or as the ghosted academic? The fusion of selves required in the ghostwriting experience seems to continue in Lawrence's individual decision to make a change. In any case, we see residues of authorship that are neither wholly regulated nor wholly satisfied when writing for pay.

Conclusion

This chapter has tried to chronicle how some workaday writers navigate the ideological complexities that surround writing as a form of labor, production, property, and personality, and do so as part of everyday acts of composition, as part of getting the job done. That writers can work in environments of such oddly distributed authorship, borrow and lend, ventriloquize and impersonate across differences in status and identity, suppress their speech rights, and at the same time, by necessity it seems, compose from deep within their own set of experiences, interests, and values – all while technically producing writing that they do not own – testifies to why debates about authorship and ownership of writing have been so complicated and unresolved over time. For Jason Slager and Cecelia Lawrence, can we say that the writing is an inalienable property of the person who produces it? An expression of personality? A corporate product? A communal good? A piece of hack work? Does it mean what it says? These are questions about writing that have been deliberated as a legal matter by lawmakers and courts and have been decided differently across time depending on the facts, interests, and exigencies of a case. At any moment in a composing process, the workaday writer must negotiate these questions too, as part of the deliberative work of writing. Depending on the situation, they arrive at different conclusions.

While there are interesting parallels, then, between the legal debates over authorship and ownership and the practical dilemmas of the workplace writers, these accounts expose obvious gaps between legal characterizations of works made for hire and the experience of the individuals producing them, especially when it comes to what I have been calling authorial residue – what's left over in the writer's person as a result of writing, something that is unacknowledged and unaccounted for in legal tradition but clearly implicates the civic and human spirit. The dismissal of workaday writing from serious consideration either in copyright case law or in First Amendment case law, the cut and dried attribution of authorship to the paying employer, all clearly belie the level of emotional and intellectual investment that goes into workaday writing, and the extent to which it serves as a site – quiet and overlooked perhaps – for political, aesthetic, and intellectual stirrings in the people who carry it out. These effects of writing – the effects of writing on the humanity of the writer – positive or negative, exhilarating or humiliating, cannot, it seems, be relinquished, and can be neither disowned nor sold away.[17]

Yet, as Kwall (2001) and others have observed, the effects of writing on the writer have never been much of a consideration in debates about authorship and ownership of writing. Rather, throughout its legal and cultural history in this country, writing has been valued, regulated, and litigated on the basis of its value as a product – on what it can do for readers, which is the source of both its moral value and, ultimately, its commercial value. Where the government has cared about the speech interests of writers, it has been in order to ensure that readers have broad access to information and knowledge. Where the law has protected writing, it has been indirectly through the protections afforded to the reading public. Intellectual property and copyright law – at least at the beginning of the United States – found their rationale through the needs of readers: government provides incentives and protections for creative and intellectual work in order to ensure that the minds of its reading citizens are nourished and replenished. The concern has been with cultivating the reader's humanity by cultivating the writer's productivity. But how does writing productivity affect the humanity of the writer? Those effects will give the future of mass literacy its most uncertain and challenging aspects.

2   Writing for the State

Asked about the voice he uses in the writing he does at work, a long-time policy analyst for a government family-services bureau responded this way:

Generally I'm using the voice of whoever I consider I'm representing, whether that's the tribes, Joe Citizen, or a family, or whoever. Ultimately things may be changed by political decisions but I work for the people. I'm a professional. If the governor or the secretary [of the agency] *has a position, I could sit down and write a really good argument for their position. But that's not my job. My job is to have them question their position, not for me to accept theirs, because if we aren't in there making* [government officials] *defend positions, why are we here?*

As he describes it, this analyst uses his professional workplace writing to precipitate processes of deliberation that he associates with good government. He seeks to multiply the viewpoints out of which public policy will be decided. By writing in "the voice of whoever I consider I'm representing," this civil servant creates what he sees as a critical, productive dialogue between the governing and the governed. Unelected and without decision-making power, he nevertheless positions himself actively as a populist voice within the democratic processes of his government. Indeed, in his view, it is his professional responsibility to do so.

Other civil servants have different ideas about the professional role of their writing in the making of good government. Here is an account from another policy analyst, who works in a state department of administration, describing the approach he uses when researching and evaluating proposed legislation:

You're looking for the best information to support [the governor's] *position. This stuff gets run through the mill quite a lot and sometimes you might think, well, the governor's got a pretty weak position here. I can hope that the Fiscal Bureau or the legislature will point out these problems. I can hope that the governor doesn't get his way. But my job is to make the best case for the governor's position. I'm going to give you the best fight I can. If I'm over matched, if there are weaknesses, I'm going to hide those weaknesses and try to figure out a way to structure my game. I don't serve the process well if I don't. That's the separation of powers. That's the way democracy is supposed to work.*

This analyst also sees an active role for his writing to play in precipitating processes of deliberation. But for him, responsibility derives from his structural position within a system of governmental checks and balances. His professional duty is to put his knowledge and writing skills to work on behalf of his side, the executive side, of government. In his view, the interests of the public (including his own as a citizen) are best protected when different branches of government make the strongest case they can and then seek workable resolutions of their differences.

My aim here is not to defend or critique either of these viewpoints but rather to demonstrate how those who write in the employ of government inevitably represent – to themselves if not to others – concepts of democratic government as part of their workaday efforts. Writers for the State are thrust inevitably into acts of representation – of people to government, government to people, government to government and government to self – that require steady reflections on their own values as citizens and engage them intensively in the political churnings of their society. Public sector writers carry out myriad activities on behalf of government: investigating; rule making; licensing; contracting; allocating benefits; negotiating; adjudicating; researching; and publicizing, to name a few. In the process, they must find ways to embody in their language choices the meanings of laws, rights, democratic processes, and civic ideals. In turn, these compositional demands can affect their own thinking and actions as members of a pluralistic, democratic society.

Considering the ways that routine government writing is civically formative for the people who compose it is an admittedly unorthodox perspective to take on long-accepted relationships among literacy, government, and democracy – relationships that historically have been understood to pertain more to the civic sphere than the employment sphere and more to the reading citizen than the writing bureaucrat. In an ideology reaching back to the early Republic, mass literacy is considered a requirement for an informed and independent voting public. Through acts of reading especially, citizen-voters are expected to develop habits of healthy skepticism, perspective-taking, and truth-seeking, making them worthy and judicious overseers of their elected officials.[1]

To encourage and protect these responsibilities, the Constitution limits government intrusion into the literacy lives of the population. The First Amendment safeguards political expression; secures access to a wide spectrum of published material; and inhibits the government from using its powers to suppress beliefs and viewpoints it disagrees with. Over time, a circle of privacy and autonomy has come to surround adult reading choices. Indeed the right of reading citizens to unfettered access to ideas and information has provided the sturdiest protections for freedom of speech in American case law. As interpreted over time, the Constitution associates the people's literacy with their liberty from government overreach.[2]

But when the gaze turns from reading citizens to writing civil servants, a different set of historical and legal relationships comes into view. With the growth of what Oz Frankel (2006) has called the "modern information state," the writing skills of millions of Americans have been recruited into the daily processes of government.[3] The government needs writing and writers to exert its power, represent its interests, and carry out its responsibilities. While government has long had the mandate to record its official activities and share useful knowledge with the population, its right to broadcast its own viewpoints in "the marketplace of ideas" has also come to be well established over time. Governments cannot use their powers to suppress viewpoints but they are entitled to have and express their own.[4] By the twentieth century especially, as mass communication and public relations came to play an important role in managing power, government turned to writing among other means to maintain its image in society and carry out its work. Today, government is both one of the largest employers in the United States and one of the largest publishers in the world, making it, on any given day, a major appropriator of American writing literacy.[5] Bezanson and Buss (2001) enumerate the wide range of formal and informal speech acts, mostly written, that government undertakes, or to be more specific, that employee-citizens undertake in the name of government:

Modern government is not limited to prohibitions. It is instead a creator of rights and programs, a manager of economic and social relationships, a vast employer and purchaser, an educator, investor, curator, librarian, historian, patron and on and on. Government inculcates values, defines justice, fairness and liberty, and shapes behavior. It assures safety, protects the helpless and uninformed, and prevents injustice. It taxes and spends, subsidizes and penalizes, encourages and discourages. None of these undertakings . . . could be successfully pursued without speech by government. Government *must* explain, persuade, coerce, deplore, congratulate, implore, teach, inspire and defend with words. (p. 1377)

In short, governments have viewpoints, and they call upon the writing literacy of citizen-employees to express those viewpoints. This need creates relationships between government and literacy that depart sharply from the hands-off principles traditionally associated with civilian reading. Not only does government have a right to further its interests in official activities and in certain public forums, according to the courts, but government employees must carry out these interests independently from their own viewpoints. In this regard, government employees are no different from private employees and relinquish their independent speech rights when they contract their services (including their literacy) to their government employers. From this side of things – the writing side – we see a different function for literate citizens: their role in promoting and maintaining State power. From this side of things, civilian literacy has no special protected status. Indeed, as we will see later in this chapter, writers for the State can experience unsparing government intrusion into their language processes in ways that some can find repugnant to cherished associations between literacy and liberty.

Such conditions can have far-reaching effects on the individual writers involved, effects that rarely register in our discourse about literacy and citizenship. On the one hand, as we saw above, people who write for the State can enjoy unusually intense, direct, even heady involvement in the organs of government. From various inside positions, individual employees find ways to use their writing to shape political processes – if not outcomes – in accordance with deeply held views and values, a process that often results in feelings of civic engagement and satisfaction. By virtue of their professional responsibilities, many become quintessentially informed citizens – growing intimately familiar with laws, policies, current events, and history that broaden and inform their own political perspectives. That is, as government writers, they gain the kind of knowledge that can support the exercise of judgments long associated with the exemplary reading citizen. Yet they gain this knowledge and exercise this judgment from their status roles as government-sponsored writers. In these roles, they are not independent of the government but subservient to it, and it is always toward the enrichment of other people's civic life – not their own– that the writing literacy of government employees must bend. So civil servants write in thorny conditions. How they navigate these conditions – with what variation and with what impact on them as citizens – is the concern of this chapter.

Backgrounds

To handle the complexity of the writing conditions that I found among government employees and to account for their active role in negotiating it, I apply a concept of *the State* that comes from *State in society* theory developed by Joel Migdal (2001), who took issue with traditional political theory that treats government as a homogeneous and autonomous source of authority, power, and legitimacy.[6] Rather, government is just one source of influence, competing with or operating alongside other sources (religious, familial, ethnic, commercial, etc.) for influence over people's behavior. As he explains it, the State-in-society model "zeroes in on the conflict-laden interactions of multiple sets of formal and informal guideposts for how to behave that are promoted by different groupings in society" (p. 11). Migdal brings attention to myriad gaps that inevitably open up between literal laws or government policy and the messier ways they are implemented or lived out – including in the decentralized practices of State actors and agencies. This concept of a socially enmired State (rather than a unified, autonomous, and centralized one) fits the reported experiences of government writers I have talked with and no doubt helps to account for the range of postures and perspectives they take toward their official government writing.

This concept also accurately captures the interpretive work that government writers must undertake. Government writers not only compose out of the gaps that Migdal identifies; they also must try to fill in those gaps by way of their language decisions. It is their job to bring government to life through language. The resources they call upon to do it are not limited to official rules, instructions, or precedents that may accompany a governmental writing task. Rather, like any other writer, they inevitably call on their range of experiences, identities, allegiances, and perspectives – not to mention their literacy skills – to figure out how to proceed with a writing task. Indeed, as this chapter will explore, it is when government writers must work the gaps between task and linguistic action that they are most likely to call upon their own understandings of democratic process, their notions of good government, and their sense of their individual roles and responsibilities in it. It is in these gaps that they wrestle with "conflict-laden interactions" of morality and power, and it is in these gaps that they are most apt to find their own political perspectives as well as their literacy tested and altered.

This chapter is based on one- to two-hour interviews I conducted in the mid-2000s with thirty full-time government employees positioned in all three branches of government (executive, legislative, and judicial) and at the local, state, and federal level. The employees ranged in age from their mid-20s to their mid-60s and included Anglo, African, Latino, and Asian Americans, including two naturalized citizens. Their job experience ranged from several months to more than thirty years. Their educational attainment ranged from fewer than four years of college to advanced graduate degrees. Fourteen were women and sixteen were men. Three wrote bilingually at work; others exclusively in English. Among the interviewees were law enforcement agents, a library archivist, social workers, an army recruiter, legislative aides, policy analysts, a housing administrator, court administrators, a licensing manager, an information technologist, public defenders, a revenue administrator, a science researcher, an auditor, human resources managers, a civil rights specialist, health workers, and communications specialists, among others.[7] The vast majority of the people I interviewed were in civil service positions that were insulated from the ins and outs of elected office. However, four of the people I interviewed – two legislative aides and two top-level agency directors – were not part of the civil service system and worked at the pleasure of particular elected or partisan-appointed officials.

A majority of those I interviewed reported that writing engaged them for 50 percent or more of the workday; estimates of time spent writing ranged from a low of 15 percent to a high of 90 percent. Although more will be said about their writing later, collectively they reported producing a wide range of genres engaging a wide range of functions. The genres included: instructions; correspondence; evaluations; fact sheets; policy memos; issue papers;

subpoenas; search warrants; newsletters; press releases; proposed legislation; administrative codes; catalogs; manuals; court orders; pamphlets; statistical reports; legal briefs and case summaries; strategic plans; forms; scholarly articles; grant proposals; flyers; meeting notes; annual reports; feature articles; and speeches. Everyone wrote emails and routine reports. Twelve of the thirty regularly worked on long documents (thirty or more pages in length). Five routinely ghostwrote (mostly for elected or appointed superiors); all but a few primarily wrote anonymously, that is, without author credit. More than half of the interviewees posted information to government websites. Three wrote blogs as part of their work. A handful (communication specialists and legislative aides) used Facebook and/or Twitter to communicate with the public.

Collectively, their writing was addressed to all the major participants in political processes: elected and appointed officials, including governors, cabinet members, and representatives of other governments; state and federal legislators; judges, attorneys, juries, victims, and defendants; public commissioners; compliance regulators; staff in other agencies; the media; and various members of the public, including constituents, educators, the scientific community, lobbyists, parents and guardians, and children. Many of them underscored the public nature of their workplace writing and its migration to wide, sometimes unanticipated audiences (an issue that gets further treatment later in this chapter).

It should be mentioned that during the interviews, the government employees I talked with were asked the same questions as other workaday writers in the overall study. I asked them to describe the kinds of writing they did; the decisions that went into it; the ways they learned it; how they thought about it; how it was or was not regulated; how it related to reading; and how it affected other spheres of their lives. Like other paid writers in organizations, they struggled to find the time to write at work; they worried about clarity and correctness; they negotiated the micro-politics of working in teams or satisfying a supervisor; they made efforts to learn and improve; they experienced satisfaction when they saw the impact of their writing. At the same time, though, their interviews revealed how engaging in government speech routinely put them in – and up against – powerful engines of State, bringing sharp consequence to their writing and precipitating civic reflection as they enacted multiple roles simultaneously: representatives of government, representatives of the governed, and employees with a job to do. It is toward these categories of experience that the following section is directed.

Representing and represented in government writing

If representation, at a fundamental level, entails making present what is not literally present, then all language and writing is inherently representational. Having to represent in words a situation, a problem, a solution, a position, an action, an idea, an argument will consume the energies and attention of any writer. Likewise, workplace writing will always be assumed to represent the organization from which it emanates – its corporate interests, positions, image, voice – and not the individual who stands in to do the writing. Further, as Hanna Pitkin (1967) observed, representing, as commonly understood, can actually entail a range of roles – agent, tool, delegate, trustee, substitute, steward – and involves different degrees of subordination and independence between the represented and the representative. As we will see, different positions within government involve such varying degrees of subordination and independence (or, as the analysts above demonstrated, at least varying interpretations of this relationship).

But at a more fundamental level, Pitkin's probing treatment of the concept of representation helps to illuminate the multiple loyalties government writers experience in their work. On one hand, they must represent in their writing the policies and wishes of their employer. On another hand, they are often expected to use their writing to lend their employer expert, objective advice based on their professional training and affiliation. And on yet another hand, government writers are counted among the citizens who will be affected by the official words that they write and whose interests the government ideally is there to serve. In Pitkin's framework, their authorization (whom they write as) and accountability (whom they write for) arise from and partake of multiple and sometimes conflicting sources. As government writers manage this multiplicity, they engage in reflections about what and whom their writing represents and arrive at strategic decisions about how to proceed. In the process, their civic views and values can be tested and changed.

We will look specifically at the accounts of four individuals who work in different positions at different levels and branches of government.[8] They are: municipal police officer Henry Pine, a 34-year-old African American man with a master's degree in public administration and ten years' experience on the police force; legislative chief of staff Diana Garcia, who is a 37-year-old Mexican-American lawyer and former prosecutor with four years of experience working for elected officials; public policy analyst and government liaison Marvin Marks, who is a 60-year-old European American man with a bachelor's degree in English and thirty-two years of government experience; and Melinda Lucas, who is a 32-year-old European American woman with a bachelor's degree in bacteriology. She has been conducting research for a federal science agency for nine years.

"What you see is important." The police officer

As a patrol officer, Henry Pine works the night beat in a downtown neighborhood of a midsized city, responding to calls that run the gamut from bar fights to domestic disputes, robberies, sexual assaults, and homicides. After responding to a call, he will record an incident report, mostly while sitting in his squad car, often choosing to dictate the narrative part into an audio recorder for later transcription because it frees him from the space limits of the pre-formatted report forms. While he described his reports as *"fact-based"* with *"no editorials allowed,"* he also went on to say that, *"As long as the required information is there, those facts, you can be creative in how it's actually worded. It's based on your ability."* In the following lengthy account, we see how Henry Pine uses his writing ability – including a strong narrative sense and aesthetic sensibility – to inject representations of what he calls *"the whole human element"* into the justice system that he serves. He explained:

I write my reports as if I were writing a movie. I want you to be able to read my report and visualize everything that happened chronologically. I want to write this as if there was a camera at this location filming everything. There needs to be a chronological order to things and events. Order is important from a legal standpoint as you might expect because detectives, district attorneys, they have to construct or at least put all these pieces back together. But I do believe that most people that you deal with, if you approach things from a "tell me what happened next" standpoint, you get everything that you want quote-wise, fact-wise, that you need without having much of an issue. You know how kids tend to learn. Kids replicate what they see. They replicate what they hear. Those senses are extremely important in how we get from what happens to what is written. And I think that's underestimated on the part of a lot of people. What you see is important. So you paint a picture. You are Michelangelo, if you will. There is a whole human element that needs to be communicated. So you have to start off with the facts and the numbers and the specifics of what happened but you can grow if you want to. And I definitely feel like I've grown to be able to include that human part with the factual part. That's where I get my satisfaction of telling the story, telling this other person's story in a way that is usable for that district attorney, in a way that is usable for the command staff who has to review it, a detective to follow up on it, and the jury who has to decide. Also, I won't testify to anything that I don't completely remember. Maybe I'm on the stand and my recollection of that fact or detail is fuzzy at best so I can ask, may I please look at my report. I have some cases that are two years old, five years old. But the way I write, I'm right back there. I can go back five years and I am completely in the moment because I brought more of a human element to what I wrote.

Henry Pine also discussed how his report-writing functions as a form of diary-keeping. Incident reports are a medium through which he captures and processes the sometimes "sensitive" experiences in law enforcement. Pine's report-writing also represents his own growth and learning as a person over time, including his ability to render a broader public representation of what the work of a police officer is really like – despite sensationalized depictions in the mass media. He said:

[Report-writing] is the way I communicate what's happened to me in a given day outside of talking with friends or other people. If it's a sensitive matter I can't go out and talk about those types of things with friends, but the writing is where I draw a lot of the

satisfaction. Because a lot of people think the police thing is beating somebody up or chasing somebody in a squad car. People are obsessed with the part of police work that they show on television. But that's a small part of what you do. A lot of what you are doing is communicating what's happened. I get some enjoyment out of doing that. I like using words that aren't in the spell checker. It helps me. I learn more by doing these things too.

As a first responder to the scene of a crime, patrol officer Henry Pine has the task of documenting facts through observation and interview. How does he proceed? In his account we see how he takes up a cinematic, narrative style of reporting that in his view works for everybody who must rely on his reports for something: victims, witnesses, detectives, prosecutors, juries, and even himself. That is, he invests in a writing style that he considers broadly democratic. He writes in a chronological, sense-based way congruent with how he believes people learn or process experience. Because his "tell me what happened next" approach is universally apprehensible, the form of his fact-gathering and writing is more equitably accessible to the people whose story he represents; the people who must assimilate those representations into the legal process; and the people who must use those representations to render judgments. Because of how he writes it, everyone is invited to read his report in the same way. When Pine says *"what you see is important,"* the *you* is also inclusive of all parties. Seeing refers to the primary sensory experiences of victims, witnesses, and himself, as documentarian on the scene, and so it is important for Pine to represent what he and others see. But seeing also refers to what prosecutors and juries will represent in their minds, how they will make the link backwards from what is written to what was seen and heard. Justice is dependent on what you are able to see, and Pine uses his writing to try to help everybody see the same thing. He uses the narrative powers of the storyteller to try to put everybody on the same plane. Further, Pine's style of report-writing functions as a personal ethical solution to the problem of trial delays that can compromise his memory and therefore his integrity as a witness. His writing serves as a mnemonic device; it allows him to be "back in the moment" and carry out his oath to tell the truth. Finally, in seeking to capture the "whole human element" in his writing, he includes himself, the human writer. He uses his report-writing to process his own life experience and experiment with language in ways that contribute to his own growth. In his hands, the police report becomes a robustly democratic genre that he uses to represent his sense of justice and his own humanity.

"So you are a mouthpiece." The legislative aide

The writing of legislative aides is obviously closely bound to the interests, positions, and often the speaking and writing styles of the elected officials they serve. *"I represent the Representative,"* explained Diana Garcia, a former prosecutor who served at the time of our interview as chief of staff to a state assembly member. *"Your boss has a position and you are representing things in the way he feels about them,"* she said. Unlike the policy analysts introduced earlier, Garcia's primary loyalty is to neither an external public nor a structural position within a system but to a particular individual in a partisan political context. (*"There is no way to get away from the fact,"* she said at one point, *"that what you are doing is working to make sure that your boss stays in the legislature."*) She continued:

So you are a mouthpiece. And sometimes that's hard because sometimes he and I may not have the exact same opinion, which is why he is good at reviewing things because if I insert something of my own, he'll take it out.

Characterizing her job as *"seventy-five percent writing,"* the aide said she corresponds with constituents, does background research for legislation, writes press releases and guest editorials, coordinates activities with other government staff, maintains an official website, and posts news and announcements on Twitter, among other responsibilities. Whether writing under her own name or that of her boss, Garcia characterized her role as writing on the assemblyman's "behalf":

Being that everything you are doing is on behalf of another individual, you have to have a good line of communication to make sure that you are giving them what they want. At this point I've worked for him for almost two years so I know him well enough that I know his stance on most things. I've learned how to write like him.

The legislative aide recalled how she had to go through an adjustment period when she was initially hired because she brought with her the communication style of a different elected official who had employed her previously, a style that she dismantled with the help of her new boss. Speaking of her previous employer, she said:

I had her voice down. She's very intellectual and has a different flow and speaking pattern. Phrases are different. He is more direct in his speech patterns. He would change the writing so it wouldn't sound quite like her. He called it "de-L____ing the letters."

In writing in a way so closely anchored to the political positions and style of a particular individual, Garcia depicts herself as an agent, a proxy, at times a ventriloquist for the legislator, a substitute or surrogate who acts directly in his stead, or at least always in his best interests as she interprets them. But, as we see in the following passage, doing this hired work also can entail going beyond articulating a legislator's political stances and into expressing the broader interests of the people who elect him. Representing the representative means being responsive to a "home district" that is not the aide's home. In this case, Garcia's close adherence to the person she works for thrusts her into a more abstract form of voicing, giving her similar responsibilities and requiring similar perspectives as the elected official:

We're doing things on behalf of [the district], *which I don't have a personal tie to. So there are some things that I really could not care less about. But it's a big deal for the local community. Like the paving of Main St. That's a big deal for the people who live* [there]. *So you are speaking on their behalf. You understand it. You understand how things get done on the local level. So you feel like you are part of the bigger process.*

While Garcia characterized the art of her writing as "morphing" and "*not that you really believe this, but kind of losing your identity*," a more complicated picture emerged when she discussed the writing she did in connection with legislative planning and development. The aide invests much of her time in doing research for proposed legislation. She worked for eight months on crafting a draft of a bill (eventually passed) that protected low-income borrowers from excessive interest charges. She consulted policy briefs prepared by the National Coalition of State Legislatures and researched similar initiatives in other states, assessing them in relationship to local law "*to see how they fit and what could and could not be done here.*" The aide experienced this research process as a site where she had shaping influence on the legislation and ultimately on the lives of the public, as her legal analysis was designed to help the legislator "*figure out what exactly he was looking for,*" that is, to move a general idea and direction into something concrete and actionable. She also described how she served as a "sounding board" during policy formation and decision-making. In the following passage, we see how Garcia indeed brings something of her "own" into the work, as she voices her views and has them returned to her, in a writing task, powerfully distilled through the legitimacy of the elected office:

With my boss, before he does anything, we have discussions and we talk things through. My boss is really looking for a sounding board and somebody to come up with ideas. I definitely feel I get my opinion in before everything is created. You have to just distill it for the purpose. When you see a new law go into effect, you see first-hand how the work you are doing made a difference.

In this brief treatment, we see how, from a subordinate and behind-the-scenes position, a legislative aide not only acts politically on behalf of an elected official but also acts politically through him; in lending her voice to the legislator, she also borrows positions, perspectives, and legislative prerogative that give her "*the feel*" of the representative process. When Garcia observes that her "*boss has a position and you are representing things in the way he feels about them,*" she captures the deeper levels of impersonation entailed in her work, as it is the representation of the things – including the way things are for the constituents – that must be mastered, not simply the representation of the legislator's voice (as much as that is a preoccupying need). In these deeper processes of representation the aide finds her own civic sense expanded. In discussing the hours she spends each day responding to correspondence from constituents, Garcia demonstrates how her writing on behalf of the elected official becomes representative of a wider constituency and alters her own view of government:

What I've mostly found out is that constituents like it when their legislator is available to them and listening to them so a big focus in our office, if a question comes in, we answer it to the best of our ability, even if we don't agree with [its premise] or if it's about a difficult issue. As long as you get that information out then people tend to appreciate that. It has changed my perception about what government provides to people. It never occurred to me to write to my state representative about a very personal issue and it gives you a sense of other people's very direct lives and what they are dealing with because they never contact you when things are going well. It's whenever there is a problem that they need help and by the time they have reached out to their state legislator they have already reached out to everybody they can think of for help and then you are their last resort. So I think it does open your eyes to what other people are dealing with.

As a "*mouthpiece*," this legislative aide serves as an agent of an elected official in a partisan context. Her own political values and views align closely with those of the person she represents. ("*I've never had to work really hard at an issue that I didn't believe in*," she said.) Diana Garcia takes distinct pleasure in seeing legislation passed or having a press release she has written "*gain traction*," when it "*causes other people to listen and think*." In this way, she is a co-sponsor of political action. In some cases she is able to see her own views taken up and distilled back through the power and authority of the elected position, a form of re-representation. But many times as a writer, she must try to fill gaps as best she can, especially when she must write above the name of the legislator. If she fills these gaps too much with her own views, she may find herself curtailed by her boss's deletions or rewrites. But sometimes in standing in for him, especially in correspondence with constituents, she experiences the responsibilities of the elected representative. In speaking for him, she speaks as him and must voice the interests of the "*home district*." In representing the representative, she inevitably must represent to herself the people he serves. As a result, her views of government are changed.

"*So all of that attitude really seeps into the writing.*"
The intergovernment liaison

Marvin Marks, who was quoted at the beginning of this chapter, is a long-time social policy analyst with a state family welfare agency. He played a major role in codifying into the statutes of his state the landmark 1978 federal Indian Child Welfare Act, which secured the rights of American Indian orphans and foster children to be placed, whenever possible, in the custody of their extended families or other members of their tribes. The legislation reversed decades of routine placement of American Indian children into foster and adoptive families outside of Indian nations. At the time of our interview Marks was serving as his agency's liaison with eleven sovereign tribal governments within the boundaries of his state and chaired an intergovernment work group tasked with developing joint agreements on child welfare and protective services, among other matters. In the interview Marks discussed the challenges of writing up from his mid-level position in his government bureaucracy to address leaders of other sovereign entities, a task that is rather uncommon in the top-down bureaucratic system in which he usually operates. These communications sometimes require diplomatic rewording of his supervisor's brusque commands into messages that express appropriate deference. He explained:

One of the hardest things about dealing with the tribes from a bureaucratic perspective is that I work for the secretary of the department, who is appointed by the governor. The secretary will say to me, "I want to meet with the tribal leaders and here's the day and place." And part of my job is to say, "Well, no, you're not their peer. The governor is their peer. You don't tell them where to come and meet." So you have to translate that into language where you're talking about decisions that the department is making or that we are going to have a meeting or that we want some representatives of the tribes to serve on a committee, or whatever it might be. If I need a county representative on a committee, I just write to the county association and say, hey, we need three people to be on this. If I write to the tribes, I go into a whole lot more about what it is, what the genesis of the work is, what the impacts are going to be, why it's important to the tribes, all while recognizing that their staffs are overworked. So it's a whole lot more.

Marks discussed the friction he sometimes experienced with his agency when he wrote as a representative of the intergovernmental working group, a liminal position that he interpreted as belonging neither to the state nor to tribal governments. In the following excerpt, we see how Marks's interpretation of his task required him to resist the hierarchical power relations of his agency (in which it is assumed that he speaks and writes at the behest of his supervisor) in order to maintain the trans-governmental and trans-cultural integrity of the working group. In the process we see how, from this location, Marks arrives at understandings of the relative differences between two forms of government, their different ways of wielding power, their different philosophies of democracy – and the need to find written language that participates in both perspectives. He reflected:

One of the interesting processes is that when you are working on committees internally [i.e., within the agency], *it's collegial but ultimately it is hierarchical. And for virtually every issue there is a vote. It may not be a vote among equals, but there is a vote somewhere along the line in terms of what the position is going to be. Working with the tribes, that is something you avoid. You don't ever want to take a vote in a committee with tribal members because that's just not how things work. The tribes will not argue with each other in public, they will not allow a wedge to be created between them by saying some voted this way and some voted another way. When you are working with the tribes, you go to the wall to do stuff by consensus. Generally speaking, the tribes will all come together at some point. So all of that attitude really seeps into the writing. We spend time together and do everything by consensus and everything is written in such a way that it reflects that consensus and so it is extremely difficult for somebody to attack. What's a little bit more difficult is making sure the department is also in there. So it's kind of weird because I work for the department but as the chair of [the intergovernment committee] I feel it's my responsibility to bring the voice of the work group to both the tribes and the department. If there is some jurisdictional issue we're dealing with, we'll do drafts and send them out to the tribes and to the secretary and the secretary will say, "Change this language." And I'll have to say, "No, it's not my language; it's the work group's language." So there are conflicts because of that. But the nice part is that it really does challenge your use of language because you have to appease both groups.*

As a European American man, Marks said he struggles with the power disparity between tribal governments and the US state government that employs him, including the long legacy of betrayal and distrust that infects the relationship. "*I used to step in it all the time,*" he said of his initial attempts to communicate with tribal officials. He discussed how he turned to reading and writing history as a resource for addressing unequal power relations. In his off-work hours, Marks said he became an avid reader of Native American history and treaty history and said he insists now on including historical context when he drafts legislation or other documents:

I focus a lot more than I would otherwise on history. When we were going through the four years of codification [of the Indian Child Welfare Act] *I must have written hundreds of pages looking at the history of the boarding schools and what was happening to Indian kids... Also, for example, Federal Law 280* [which transferred some federal jurisdiction in tribal affairs to the states] *was written in 1953, the same year that the feds terminated the existence of the Menominee Tribe. Twenty years later the Menominee got the recognition back but the law was written during the termination. It created a whole bunch of issues and the department and the tribes sometimes have different views on it. The logic that Congress used was not good. So the best way to deal with that is to go back to the history. You don't want to say in a letter, well, this was because this was one more time the feds screwed the tribes. You have to say that nicely. But you get into the history of what was going on, the attitudes of the federal government. You've got to interpret it.*

History is not the only genre that Marks cultivates in support of his intergovernmental writing. A lifelong poet who occasionally used to publish, he said the role of poetry in his life began to change as he came to rely on it more "*therapeutically*" in connection with his career. He said writing poetry in his spare time helped him to stay "*freer*" in his writing on the job:

[Poetry] *keeps your brain a little freer. It's too easy in the bureaucracy to find yourself in a little box, writing letters and policy memos, and it's just not expansive enough. For me, poetry style is much more akin to speaking with the tribes. Even their business language has more depth to it, more thought behind it, more history that's caught up in it. So I think* [writing poetry] *actually helps my writing here because it keeps me freer and every once in a while I will write something in a poem and say, wow, with a little twist I could use that in a letter.*

In his official position as a liaison between tribal and state governments, Marvin Marks engages with markedly different styles of government, democracy, and language use. To maintain the integrity of the intergovernmental voice that he has been asked to represent, Marks positions himself at a distance from the hierarchical bureaucracy that employs him and at times must refuse the top-down assumption that what he writes represents the views or authority of his agency. Instead, he makes sure his writing makes visible the sovereign status of tribal governments, whether through deferential address or by embodying consensus values in the writing of joint documents, and he turns to history-writing in his official government texts as an attempt to keep visible the larger context of US-tribal relations. Off-work literacy plays a role as well, as Marks uses personal reading and writing, especially poetry writing, to maintain the "freer" and "expansive" consciousness he needs to persist in his work.

"It's a public trust." **The government scientist**

Melinda Lucas is a bacteriologist who works for the US Geologic Survey, a federal agency that is the largest employer of earth scientists and the largest pro-ducer of maps in the United States. Its mission, according to Lucas, is to provide the public with unbiased information about the nation's lands and waterways, information that can inform decisions about managing natural resources and formulating environmental policy. At the time of our interview, Lucas was involved in the final phases of a thirty-year study of water pollution that had been mandated by Congress as part of the implementation of the Clean Water Act. She was also involved in a newer collaborative government project on mer-cury levels in waterways. Here Lucas describes the parameters of her agency's mission, which sets parameters on her writing:

We're just there to provide data. We can't say this plant is causing a problem by dumping into this stream. All we can say is there are PCBs here and they are not there. Think what you will. And then the Environmental Protection Agency can come in if they want to and say what it really means. We're not told what we can write and what we can't but in the sense that we are non-regulatory, we're not really charged with pointing fingers or doing any of that kind of stuff.

In fact, as part of an extensive process of external and internal review, regional supervisors monitor the writing of Lucas and her colleagues to make sure it does not veer into policy. *"If you start to have an agenda, they don't like that,"* she explained. The review is *"a safeguard so they are not blindsided by papers that are coming out."* While Lucas reiterated that *"data aren't political,"* she did explain how politics of a kind enters into her scientific thinking:

ML: *There are so many vested interests in the mercury issue – power plants, mining interests, everybody has their own take on it. We do think about that when we are collecting data in the sense that we have to be aware of what's out there. So we know where mining sites are because that will impact what we'll get for data. I wouldn't say that we modify what we are searching for based on any kind of politics. We're just in more of an academic sense trying to figure out how things work and how mercury is traveling through the system and becoming an issue.*

DB: *So you are saying that the politics of mercury affect the water that you are looking in?*

ML: *Yes.*

As a government scientist, Lucas must understand how mercury is "becoming an issue" not in Congress or among her fellow citizens but in the life of the rivers and streams she studies. It is that system that she must understand and represent accurately in her reports. To that extent, she must represent to herself the political circumstances around those sites to help her interpret the water samples she reads.

While Lucas knows how to read water–mercury relationships as a bacteriologist, she recently had had the occasion to read and hear about her own research in the news, when a mercury study that she was working on hit the national headlines. In the following excerpt, which serves as an interesting companion to the comments above, we see Lucas reading the politics of mercury differently when her work is re-represented to her through the public press. In these circumstances, she reads as a common citizen and can engage her full critical faculties, looking between the lines for the motives of political actors even as she gains expanded perspectives on the political meanings that her scientific writings can have for other citizens. She offered this observation after being asked whether her research writing has affected other spheres of her life, including her personal views on the environment or environmental policy:

When you deal with data, it's not political. It's just data. But when it becomes political, you look at it differently. Last year we published a report. It was on NPR. It was all over the news. One of the tag lines said that we found mercury in every fish we studied, three hundred species. It was interesting to see the effect of that paper. There was a lobbying group that was really tenacious and they were called something that you would think, "that's nice," but the group was funded by someone else that clearly has an agenda about the data you are collecting. I wouldn't say it made me more cynical but it makes me understand the different weights and balances that people are looking at. They are trying to conserve jobs, they have their own interests in mind, but I don't know. It's just interesting to see the strategies people use to try to further their agendas.

If literacy is a mechanism by which Lucas adjusts her thinking between the biological agenda of streams and rivers and the political agendas of actors around them, literacy also plays a role in breaching what Lucas calls a "disconnect" between her specialized research discipline and the public she serves. The proper role of the professional expert in shared governance has been a contentious topic in American political life, at least since the exchange on the topic between Walter Lipmann and John Dewey in the 1920s.[9] More recently, political scientist Frank Fischer (2009) has written probingly of the tensions between professional expertise and democratic government, as public policy decisions increasingly rely on technocratic knowledge that is often over the heads of most citizens as well as most elected officials. As a result, the capacity of citizens to exert oversight – including the basic will to try – becomes diminished. In fact, environmental policy is often named specifically as an arena in which ordinary citizens are losing a grip.

It was clear from our interview that Lucas and her colleagues experience this tension most directly. On the one hand, because the agency is required by statute to put all of its research in the public domain, Lucas routinely co-authors lengthy scientific reports that go through months of preparation and review before they are published on the agency's website. On the other hand, she knows the reports are beyond the ken of most citizens, accessible instead, as Lucas put it, to "*other people like me,*" scientists in and out of government. From her point of view, it is important for her to invest fully in the paradigms and protocols of her scholarly field in order to carry out what she sees as her public mandate – even though this specialized discourse can alienate the general reader. "*My mission,*" she said, "*is to give the best information I can so that other people who have decision-making capabilities can make the decisions they need to make.*" But who has those capabilities in the end is a real question. In the following excerpt, taken from her response to a query about how she imagines her audience, Lucas addresses the "disconnect" that comes from being a specialist writing in what she calls a public trust:

We have a commitment to publish pretty much everything we do. Anything meaningful in our studies, we are supposed to have that published. All of our data are public. So it's a public trust. [In terms of audience] *I don't see individual citizens. A lot of people won't read my reports. Taxpayers are giving money so we should be able to give them the best information we can. Because we are a federal agency, people look to* [our work] *and maybe give it more credence than something that is less researched. So what I write should be right and I should be very confident in it. I would hate to diminish that* [trust] *in any way by writing poorly. But I think there is probably a disconnect. Typically, we try to write so that a layperson could understand. But it's not in a popular style. It would be really tough for a layperson to understand my reports. Average people are not going to be interested in a technical report. But it's available to them if they are. A lot of people I work with put in extra hours on their writing. Our projects are so expensive that we try to make that up on holidays and weekends. There is a lot of desire to get things right. There is a lot of feeling about the good of public service.*

If average citizens likely won't understand what Lucas writes, at least, she suggests, she can be a good steward of their money and their trust. She cannot represent them by acting as a citizen would, because she sees things as a bacteriologist, and she cannot represent them by acting on behalf of their interests because her allegiance must be to the data (*"I don't see individual citizens"*). Rather, the civic duty is represented in how the writing is done – well and right but also on weekends and holidays, so as not to have it absorb too much of the value of the taxpayer's money. Lucas and her colleagues use their writing practices to fill a gap between two versions of public accessibility: dissemination versus comprehensibility. The gap arises not only between the government scientist and the lay decision-maker but also between the enormous expense of time, effort, and money it takes to write up *"everything we do"* and the lack of information value it will have for the average taxpayer. The gap is filled through overtime, the writing ethos of her office.

Writing and representation

That writing can represent the reach and authority of government is well recognized. That writing can represent, in a symbolic sense, the bureaucratic excesses of government, the proverbial red tape, is likewise well recognized. But what government writing can represent to the people who carry it out is rarely, if ever, noticed. Yet, as we have just seen, for the police officer, the legislative aide, the government liaison, and the scientist, writing is not merely a form of paid professional labor. Rather, through their writing they are recruited deeply into the projects and processes of the government. When they take up a writing assignment, they routinely must find ways to represent to themselves and to others their conceptions of law, democracy, justice, and good governance in ethically satisfying ways. They enact these representations at various levels: in the ways they interpret writing tasks; in the ways that they wield the written genres associated with their positions; and in the ways they assess the consequences of their writing. Thus, the police officer seizes on the narrative structure of the crime report to try to create an equal-access instrument for all constituents in the justice system. The legislative aide perfects her ventriloquism to try to help an assemblyman provide lending protections for poor people. The intergovernment liaison appeals to history-writing as a hoped-for antidote to amnesia around US–American Indian relations. And the government scientist aims to cement the public trust in her adherence to scientific protocols. To the extent that public-service writers inevitably become knowledgeable and think critically about their government in the process of carrying out their duties, the vehicle of their writing literacy informs them in similar ways to how reading is thought to inform the citizenry. Yet, unlike reading, this literacy is not autonomous from or protected from government intervention. Rather, for civil servants, their powers of writing and thinking mingle intimately with powers of State in various degrees of subordination and amplification. The words they compose come back to them in politically consequential ways: from the witness stand; in the authorized voice of an elected official; in the force of legislation; or in the sensationalism of a headline.

All the while, the literacy skills of government writers stretch and grow as they work the gaps between tasks and texts, between this need and that need, between accountability to this entity or that entity, filling those gaps when necessary with the stuff of their lives: experiences, training, knowledge, and belief. These efforts – undertaken on and off the clock – influence their views of government and their understanding of their own positions in the democratic enterprise. These efforts also can motivate and influence the ways they read and write as private citizens. If Migdal (2001) has brought attention to how society flows into State actions, these writers' experiences bring attention to how that process is reciprocal. Through the writing it requires of them, the State exerts its influence on the language, literacy, and thinking of its employee-citizens.

My goal to this point has been simply to establish the extent to which workaday government writing contributes to the civic formation, political consciousness, and language development of those who carry it out. But this writing occurs under conditions that are largely exempt from the broad constitutional protections that surround civilian reading. The legacy of writing as a form of labor offers no special protection to citizens' literacy when it is in the hire of the government. Writers for the State engage their literacy in processes of deliberative democracy in settings where their own First Amendment rights are mostly inoperative and where the autonomy of their literacy is not secured. On the contrary, as we will see in the next section, civil servants find their writing routinely exposed to overt government regulation. Largely these rules are there to protect the civil rights of the reading public. That is, not only do the rights of citizens to read about their government's activities create a lot of work for government writers (remember the bacteriologist who spends hours rendering all of her work as public reports) but also, in order to honor these rights, civil servants must always be ready to submit their workaday writing to public oversight. As we will see, these circumstances infiltrate their composing processes and language habits. That is, the hard-won freedom of citizen-readers to scrutinize the workings of their government is not without consequences for the writing literacy of civil servants. Some of these consequences – positive and negative – are explored in the next section.

"The greatest possible information." Government writers and the citizen's right to know

The government as employer is not the only interest that weighs heavily on the writing of civil servants. So too do the broad civil rights of reading citizens, as they are embodied in the traditions of the American free press and in various open-record laws, sunshine ordinances, and freedom of information acts that are in effect at the federal, state, and local level. These laws explicitly link the public's right to know with their rights as voters in a democratic society. As a practical consequence, almost everything a government writer composes on the job is considered a public record, and by law what government employees write in connection with their official duties must be retained and can, at any time, be obtained and scrutinized by any member of the public, no matter the motivation. While transparency in government is generally regarded as a prerequisite for a healthy democracy, it is worth inquiring into the legal and psychological conditions it creates for workaday government writers. Unlike writers in the private sector, government writers are not only answerable to their supervisors but also potentially to any member of the general public. To ensure that the rights of all reading citizens are legally protected, the writing of civil servants is legally exposed. I do not intend by this discussion to suggest that transparency laws are unwarranted or to minimize problems of government secrecy or abuse of power. Rather, I simply seek to trace how the rights of citizens to read information about government activity enter for better or worse into the literacy experiences of workaday government writers. That is, I seek to inquire into another dimension of how the government's long-standing protection of the reading citizen affects government-sponsored writing literacy. Toward that end, I first provide brief historical background on the public's right to know.

Freedom of information

Historical treatments of the public's "right to know" emphasize recurring tensions between the government and the governed as disagreements erupt over acceptable levels of transparency and disclosure as well as processes for making records available to the press and public. While some scholars suggest that the people's right to know was enshrined in the Constitution, the legislative struggle for meaningful government transparency has been long, difficult, and, for many, still inadequately resolved.[10] Journalists in the early Republic could be – and were – arrested for publishing true but unauthorized reports of government activities, and freedom of the press was not meaningfully secured in US case law until the twentieth century (Lidsky and Wright 2004). Further, US presidents of both parties, including recent ones, have resisted legislative initiatives to enforce government transparency, invoking national security and potential harm to citizens as the reasons. The effort to pass the landmark federal Freedom of Information Act, which set up procedures by which journalists and private citizens could obtain documents and appeal government denials of their requests, was an especially long slog over decades. When the modern Act took effect in 1975, in the wake of the Watergate scandals, it precipitated a spate of new or updated open-record and sunshine Acts at the state and local levels.

Legislation was updated again in the 1990s as governments moved to digital communication. Still, even today, critics point to continuing government foot-dragging, inconsistency, and duplicity in implementing the Freedom of Information Act.

The state of Wisconsin adopted its first open-record law in 1917, at the height of the Progressive Era, and reinvigorated and clarified it in 1976 and then again, with a new law, in 1983. In the following excerpt from the preamble to the 1983 statute, we can see how the rights of reading citizens serve as the rationale for the legislation, even as responsibility for transparency and disclosure is explicitly put on the shoulders of individual government employees:

In recognition of the fact that a representative government is dependent upon an informed electorate, it is declared to be the public policy of this state that all persons are entitled to the greatest possible information regarding the affairs of government and *the official acts of those officers and employees who represent them* [my emphasis]. Further, providing persons with such information is declared to be an essential function of a representative government and an integral part of the routine duties of officers and employees. (Wis. State 19.31 [1981–82])

It is beyond the scope of this discussion to review all the legal ins and outs of open-record laws, which have been a source of ongoing debate, litigation, and revision. But suffice it to say that any document or artifact that relates to the business or duties of a government office, including inter- and intra-departmental memos and emails (as well as visual and audio artifacts), is considered a public record and open for potential civilian scrutiny, unless it falls into certain exempt categories. Common exemptions include: active law enforcement investigations; tax records; privileged communications, for instance, between teachers and students; and some personnel matters. Courts also have established that an employee's personal communications, within guidelines, are shielded from the law, even though they may be undertaken at work on government-owned computers. Further, under Wisconsin law, drafts, notes, or other pre-decisional writings, including the "mental impressions" of state employees, have been declared exempt, although that status has been challenged. As a rule of thumb, if employees fail to destroy a pre-decisional document whose topic pertains to an open-records inquiry, they can assume it will be turned over as part of a request. But the law is complex and ambiguous; and policies and procedures, including procedures for preserving documents and training employees, vary among agencies.

Beyond the technicalities of the open-record law, modern relationships between politicians and the press favor the flow of government information into the public domain. Because the texts of civil servants often are transmitted out of their agencies and into the possession of elected officials, their written work, un-copyrighted and anonymous, can travel far and wide, even at times making its way into print under the auspices of other agents. This is another aspect of public ownership that, as we will see, influences government writers.

Helping the public

For many of the civil servants I interviewed, fulfilling the informational rights of the citizenry was a broad and diffused duty that they considered synonymous with public service. They embraced as a matter of course the legal mandate to supply information as an essential helping function, and their empathy with the citizen's right to know often took their writing and speech right up to the limit of what their positions allowed them to disclose. That is, they took seriously the commitment to provide "the greatest possible information" even when that created challenges in crafting their communications and risked overstepping boundaries. They regarded these balancing acts as delicate and recurring, and the everyday pressure of making these decisions came to influence their overall language habits.

These dynamics were perhaps most fully expressed by a chief appellate court clerk, Cordelia Simmons, a 54-year-old African American woman who at the time of our interview had been with the court system in various capacities for thirty years. She supervised a staff of fourteen and wrote primarily in connection with administrative responsibilities. But in addition she helped staff attorneys prepare and keep updated a citizen's guide to writing an appeal, and she spent a significant amount of her writing time at work answering queries from people – many of them incarcerees – who were seeking to file cases before the court. As she explained the nature of this communication and the effects it has on her, Simmons revealed the constant self-questioning that accompanies her writing:

CS: *I write letters to individuals who contact this office. We are not allowed to give legal advice but sometimes some of the questions that come in, particularly from self-represented individuals, you want to try and give them some direction. It's very important to be very careful about how things are worded. I may know something but I really can't tell them because if they apply it to their situation and their situation is really not how I understand it, it could really be a problem for them. It's important that I understand the little subtleties of the line between legal advice and procedural guidance. If someone contacts me and says they want to file a notice of appeal and gives me a particular scenario, I can maybe point them to a place in the statute where they need to look. But they need to look and interpret that for themselves. Also, with electronic communication growing, we get emails from attorneys and self-represented individuals all the time asking for information and there again you have to be very careful with the type of information that we give. Is this something I should respond to or should this go to a staff attorney? It's very important in the court system to be very neutral with everyone. We can't provide information to one party and not give it to another party. So I have nine deputy clerks that work under me, and it's very important that they understand that concept. But we try to point someone in the right direction. If we have materials we can send, we will do that. I try to keep in my mind, okay, I can't answer this, I can answer that. I try to give them something. I try to do that. I try to be a reasonable voice of the institution. I can't go outside my role. I have to respect the constraints of the institution. But as an individual, I can make choices about how I represent the institution. And I try to do it in as helpful a manner as I can. I try to empathize with people. I can't give legal advice but what I do give them I want it to be truthful and as honest as it possibly can be within the framework in which we have to work.*

DB: *Has this affected how you think about or use language outside of work?*

CS: *It has probably made me a little more conservative in my communications outside of work. Sometimes when I'm away from work I have to remind myself that I don't have to keep doing this all the time.*

Interestingly Cordelia Simmons told me her commitment to public service was the reason she agreed to my request to interview her (even though it took up valuable time on a busy afternoon). *"It's a public service job, which is why I had a hard time saying no to you,"* she said. *"Someone asks me something that involves my work, I try to help them."* In her view, I was a member of the public exercising my right to know about the public position she held, so she made herself an open book to my inquiry.[11]

The tension between fulfilling citizens' rights to know and respecting the constraints of the institution also surfaced in my interview with Kurt Ellison, a 33-year-old European American man who served as the public information officer for a municipal police department. Ellison, who had been on the job for five months at the time of our interview, held press conferences and wrote press releases directed at the local media. He described the main activity of his position as *"building a relationship with the press and the public by releasing information about the department."* *"I write as the spokesman for the department,"* he continued, *"because someone has to get this out."* Asked what values go into being a spokesman, Ellison answered this way:

A high level of integrity needs to be in place here and I say that because you have to admit when you are wrong and not cover up anything. The biggest challenge in this job is knowing information, knowing it's valuable information, and the media asking, "What can you tell me on this?" and you feel bad that you can't tell them, for instance, that you know who the alleged shooter is and he's about to be arrested in another hour or so. But you can't tell them that even though you feel like you want to give them what you know.

Later in the interview, asked what was most difficult about the writing he did and what was most consequential about it, Ellison returned to the wrenching struggle in balancing between disclosing and withholding information, revealing how this struggle leaves a lingering effect on his overall language habits:

KE: *Most difficult would be two things. One, knowing there is more information to be put out and just not being able to put it out. Also most difficult would be if I put something out there that is damaging to the department or the investigation, which I don't think I have done. But I would feel guilty. I'm very cautious. When* [the previous communications officer] *was in here, he had a different style than mine, right or wrong, that's for others to judge. But his style was this: I got the information and I'm going to go with it and give it to the media. When I came into this office, there were a lot of detectives who said in order to gain our trust and get information from us, we don't want a cowboy mentality of just taking it and running with it. So I'm very cautious as far as what I put out. You make sure you put out only what is needed for a homicide or large-scale investigation, only what's needed to put out there but don't put in anything false or misleading. Be very careful what you put out there because* [communicating with the media means] *you are in people's living rooms representing the police department, so if you are giving false information or contradictory statements, you are going to be held accountable or you are going to lose people's trust.*

DB: *Has this affected how you think about or use language outside of work?*

KE: *I am more thoughtful now. I used to shoot from the hip with comments or the way I'd say things or react to things. Now due to the writing, due to talking with the media, whether it's in this job or at home, there is more thought put into what I'm saying.*

The comments by both Cordelia Simmons and Kurt Ellison shed light on "*the little subtleties,*" as Simmons calls them, that surround the general mandate to share the greatest possible information with the public, especially when such sharing potentially jeopardizes institutional interests, violates regulations, or can potentially harm the rights or safety of others. Although not writing from any significantly adversarial positions, both feel a separate, competing interest between the public's right to know and the government's need to limit information. For Simmons, that split registers in the difference between procedural guidance (allowed) and legal advice (not allowed), as she walks that fine line armed with pamphlets, manuals, and the occasional "direction" toward the language of relevant laws. For Ellison, it registers in the struggle between satisfying public media clamoring for news and protecting investigators calling for reserve. The competing urges to share what they know and withhold what they know infuse the writing of these two public servants with care and caution. Both write with awareness that failing to get that balance correct has the potential to mislead the public and damage its trust. Both try to produce that balance as part of performing their chosen communicative styles.

Public ownership

The court clerk and the public information officer control their own messages for the most part and direct them to particular audiences. However, others I interviewed, like the scientist treated above, as well as several policy analysts, discussed the experience of seeing their writing come back at them through public channels as their written products were taken up in wider domains. Technically speaking, texts produced by the government are owned by the public, are not copyrighted, and can be used freely. This free flow of information can create experiences for government writers that are more typically associated with published authors or public figures than with obscure government bureaucrats. Family services analyst Marvin Marks relayed the experience of reading a book on the Indian Child Welfare Act and coming across *"a quote from me"* that was part of a legislative hearing. He continued: *"So you never know when something is going to come back. Generally speaking the general public isn't going to be seeing what we're doing but when you give something to the legislature, you never know where it's going to end up."* An education policy analyst observed, *"We always get a little nervous here when our stuff gets released because we're always worried that what is concluded from it is not something that should be reached from what we did. All the staff feel that way."* And one state environmental policy analyst laughed as she told the following anecdote as we discussed audiences for her work:

Generally the audience is the budget director, the governor, the secretary. We occasionally have to do summaries of things that go out to the general public. One time we had a rather large initiative in the governor's budget to change the farmland preservation program so I created a table that highlighted the main subject areas within the farmland preservation program and compared current laws to the governor's recommendation. That was part of the budget bill. At one point, an interest group gave it back to me, saying it was a really good summary that I might find useful. I wrote it!

Writing in the open

We have seen in earlier analysis how splitting allegiances between an inquiring citizenry and a self-protective institution can make government writers more "careful," "cautious," and "conservative" in their language choices – not only on the job but also residually in their private language habits. Similar concerns with caution surfaced in discussions involving open-record regulations, which potentially expose nearly all government writing to public surveillance. For some writers of public documents, especially those whose race or gender subjects them to potential bias, writing in the open can bring heightened levels of language consciousness. Consider the remarks of Eva Torres, a native of Puerto Rico, who works as a detective for a local police department. Her signed investigative reports are eventually made available to the press, as well as to a wide range of readers in the criminal justice system. Here she discusses how an awareness of how stereotypes operate in society encourages a form of defensive writing on her part in case *"people don't think I can produce"*:

My native language is Spanish. I continue to learn how to express myself in English verbally and in writing. So I will review my report, I will read it again, I will edit it. I make sure if I quote someone speaking incorrectly that I put that in quotation marks, to make sure people don't think I speak that way. I'm very much aware that I'm writing something that somebody else is going to read and maybe criticize me. Some people might never get to see me or know me but that's all they will see and they will judge me. I think I probably write better than a lot of people around here. I study the language. I have to. And I never stop trying to learn.

Among most of the government writers I interviewed, the composing process was affected less by the guarantee of public exposure (as in the case of law enforcement agents) and more by the vague potential for exposure. Open-record statutes empower the press or the public to obtain any routine government documents for any reason within a seven-year window. These regulations create general wariness among government writers, escalating for some into uncertainty about the finer points of open-record statutes. For instance, the open-record law in Wisconsin makes strong but "not absolute" pronouncements about transparency, leaving it up to individual offices to decide how to store or destroy documents according to general guidelines.[12] As a result, many people I interviewed were confused about the law and were more likely to err on the side of caution by simply assuming everything they wrote was a public document. At the same time, some writers found contradictions between the heavy regulations of written communication under open-record rules and the more casual functions of some electronic written communication, especially as it has come to replace face-to-face and telephone exchanges.

Consider the following reflections by a policy analyst for a state agency, who provides backstage advice to the governor. The analyst expresses genuine perplexity over the finer points of the open-record law and thinks that regulations around electronic communication intrude too far into needed give and take. At the same time, the analyst expresses the recurrent theme of care and caution in writing. These remarks came in response to a question about audiences:

ANALYST: *There is a whole open record thing and you always have that in the back of your mind. It's a little fuzzy this whole idea of what are open records. So you're a little cautious, you have to be careful about what you say. Sometimes you want to be a little flip. You gotta be careful. So we talk on the phone and that phone call is gone. I think if I scribble something on a napkin and give it to you, you can say it's just a working document. If I type the same thing in an email and I send it to you, now all of a sudden it becomes an open record. I think those things should be privileged communications. They would be if they were on the phone. If things leave this agency and go somewhere else, even to the governor's office, that can be considered an open record. It's a unique situation between us and the governor. We're advising him but we're a different agency. So the way the law is written, it's crossing agency lines. It's not even clear. I think if [a document] is written within the division it's clearly a working document but if it leaves the division it becomes more problematic, even if it stays in the department.*
DB: *Is that the way the law is written or how people interpret it?*
ANALYST: *I can't really answer that.*

A state legislative aide expressed similar uncertainty and frustration. The aide just assumed that all writing done at work could be subject to public disclosure. Here, the aide articulates a felt contradiction between the consequential, formal status of email under open records and its informal value in helping co-workers let off steam during the flow of work:

In my capacity, anything I put in writing from seven in the morning until five at night can, and I have to believe will, at some point be made public. Email is private with the potential to be widely public, which changes how we write. For instance, I don't use names. I might use a single initial or if, let's say a guy wears a certain tie, I might say something like, "I can't believe Red Tie is saying that." Just to get the tension off. I wouldn't want to spell out that person's name because it could be really debilitating to the office. Humans are animals that communicate and when somebody really mean comes into the office or somebody screams profanities over the phone, we have to let that out somehow. Do we verbalize it or do we write it? Given the age, it's so much easier to write it because if there is a third person in the office that I really want to know how frustrated I am or something, it's all email. You need to do those kinds of things but [open records] *changes the way you do it.*

We can see in all of these testimonies how scrutiny in the form of open records and potential open-records requests alters composing habits of writers who work amid these regulations as a matter of routine. The bilingual, female detective tries to undercut biased readers with her impeccable writing. The policy analyst renders written advice less candidly in writing than in phoning, as a potential outside audience stirs in the back of the mind. The legislative aide adjusts a text to mask the subject of an email, ensuring that the email would not be searched in any future open-records inquiry that might focus on a particular name. Together these testimonies demonstrate how potential public scrutiny of government writing puts civil servants on added guard, in some cases causing expressive attitudes to be disguised or suppressed. The topic of open records came up at least in passing among eleven of the thirty government writers I interviewed, suggesting a palpable psychological presence. The potential for surveillance and unwanted publicity hovers over the very public writing of the public servant. As the rights of reading citizens are encoded in government writing practices, the citizen-overseer looms as a second audience for government writers.

To sum up, we have seen how the duty to uphold the political rights of reading citizens bears on the writing processes of government employees. On the one hand, aligning themselves with the public's right to know is central to government writers' sense of public service and can propel them to be as responsive and open in their communications as they are allowed. Understanding that their writing is ultimately the property of the public helps government writers appreciate that the texts they write may travel widely without attribution and take on meanings far beyond an immediate context. Writing open documents can motivate some to use their literacy to subvert dangerous stereotypes. At the same time, writing in the constant "sunshine" of open government can create legal and psychological pressures that make civil servants more nervous and guarded in their written communications, including with their fellow citizens. (As a municipal property appraiser put it, *"I think I'm a little less nice to a taxpayer in an email than I am in a phone call."*) A mistake of language has the potential of becoming widely public, bringing embarrassment or worse to a government writer and their agency. In some cases these ingrained habits of caution have residual effects on civil servants' overall thinking and language use, even beyond the job.

"Tone down the voice." Government writers and the right to free speech

In this section the focus reverses, to consider how writing for the State affects the ways that public servants experience their own First Amendment rights, on and off the job. The literacy of ordinary citizens is protected as a critical medium for freedom of speech, especially freedom to criticize the government. But the same cannot be said of the literacy of government employees. Across a number of recent First Amendment decisions, the Supreme Court has been expanding the powers of government to control the speech of its employees on the job and, in some cases, off the job. The Court has set out criteria by which to determine when the government can discipline or terminate employees on the basis of speech and when employees can invoke First Amendment protections. One criterion involves the substance of employee speech. If it deals with a topic of internal management (for instance, the government's decision to reorganize an office), employees enjoy no First Amendment protection, according to the Court. If it is on a topic of general public concern (for instance, a referendum on school spending), the Court is more circumspect. In these cases, a second criterion is applied: is the speech disruptive or not to the morale or mission of the government? If a public employee expresses viewpoints in the workplace or in public on matters of public concern and in a way that does not compromise government morale or mission, that speech is usually (but not always) protected. We see in these criteria an attempt to find balance between the needs of the government as employer to run a tight ship and the value to the citizenry of having robust discourse about government policy.

Recently, however, in a 2006 case that has attracted considerable criticism, the Supreme Court moved decidedly in favor of the right of government as employer to discipline workplace speech that it deems insubordinate. In this case, a deputy district attorney wrote an internal memo critical of shoddy police handling of a criminal arrest. After this government attorney wound up being called as a witness for the defense during trial, he was transferred and denied a promotion. He sued on the grounds of First Amendment protection. The Supreme Court ruled against him, deciding that the speech rights of government employees, like those of private employees, are not protected when they are carrying out the duties of their position. The First Amendment protects free speech undertaken as a private citizen. But, they ruled, salaried speech is bought speech and so is not free speech.[13]

A slightly different line of reasoning has been applied to First Amendment cases involving the off-duty expressive speech of government employees on topics unrelated to work. These cases have tended to involve sensational or controversial speech by people in sensitive roles – for instance, police officers who launch pornographic or pro-Nazi websites in their off-duty time. In these cases, the Court has considered the damage of that speech to public perception of government and the potential erosion of public confidence. In their decisions, courts are moving toward identifying classes of government employees whose individual professional viability is so dependent on the public trust (for instance, police officers or teachers) that First Amendment protections can be trumped.[14]

In this discussion I do not intend to try to adjudicate these issues. Rather my interest is in examining, against this legal background, how everyday civil servants experience First Amendment tensions as part of their literacy practices on and off the job. Interestingly, what the courts debate as legal matters – especially the thorny issues of who or what gets represented when civil servants express themselves and how or what gets undermined when they do – appears palpably to workaday government writers when they contemplate their First Amendment rights. When the title of a recent scholarly article asks: "Whether an employee speaks as a citizen or a public employee: who decides?" (Fabian 2010), the phrasing captures a question that is not only debated vigorously before the courts but also is debated internally by civil servants, as a practical and often heartfelt matter. That government workers are aware of these constitutional controversies was most evident in the comments of Althea Nixon, a 64-year-old African American woman who heads up an equal opportunities department in a municipal government. Here she discusses what happened after an employee under her supervision spoke out in a public meeting against the mayor's plan to reorganize the civil rights office:

The staff opposed the move. So one of my employees got up [at a council meeting] *and criticized the mayor. So the next day the city attorney was calling me telling me there are certain things you can't do and we have court decisions to prove it. I had to call the employee and tell him to cool off. You might not like what the mayor is doing but you can't speak out.*

In fact, several government workers I interviewed addressed free-speech issues during the course of our conversations. As individuals, they differed in how they said they resolved the issue, in part because of the positions they hold and in part because of who they are. Paradoxically, as we will see, even as civil servants gain through their workplace writing the very kinds of knowledge and perspective associated with the quintessentially informed citizen-critic, they can be among the most circumspect, if not the most restricted, citizens when it comes to expressing their own political viewpoints in public. Many in fact find it difficult, even impossible, to extricate and exercise an unencumbered citizen voice.

The most radical example arose in my interview with Phillip Richter, a 46-year-old European American who serves as an experienced auditor with a non-partisan legislative service agency. The agency conducts financial and administrative audits of government-financed entities, often at the request of the legislature and sometimes in connection with politically controversial events and issues. The reports must be scrupulously objective and are written according to strict protocols. Throughout our interview Richter emphasized how the integrity of the agency depended on its independent judgment and partisan neutrality. In the following portion of the interview, in which I asked a standard question about whether any regulatory agencies oversaw his workplace writing, Richter provides this rather hair-raising account of how his civilian freedoms are explicitly restricted as a condition of his employment:

In terms of our written work [on the job], *regulation just wouldn't really come into play. But in terms of our private lives as non-partisan legislative service agency employees, it is made clear to everyone that there are strict boundaries that we cannot cross. You have to agree to this. You are basically giving up your constitutional rights. We discourage any type of external correspondence that would be published anywhere. We discourage all of our employees from providing any public comments related even to issues that might typically be associated with one party or another. It's something an employee has to agree to limit. But we would have no credibility whatsoever if we were associated with a particular partisan issue or, God forbid, a party itself. We would lose all of our credibility and I assure you the legislators look at us very closely. An example I like to give is when the legislature was involved in securing funding for the renovation of* [an athletic field] *and there were a number of public meetings and hearings that were held. I happened to be in the area and I attended one of these meetings* [i.e., not on work time]. *A legislator, a member of the audit committee at the time, was participating in this meeting. Afterward she told the state auditor* [i.e., Richter's boss] *that she was watching me during the hearing to see if I was giving any visible signs of whether I approved or disapproved of the funding. But I believe these restrictions are absolutely essential. I really don't think we would have the credibility that we do if we were viewed as having a personal opinion. Everybody has opinions about some things. It's impossible not to. But in terms of how we conduct our work, we do a very good job of not allowing that to influence how we portray ourselves.*

Richter's account demonstrates how well the government understands that the subjective voice of the public servant mingles with the voice of the institution – or can be easily perceived that way in the public mind. This mingling – a crucial ingredient, as we have seen, in the production of government documents – becomes a potential problem when government employees express their personal views in public because they may implicate the government in potentially compromising ways. For Richter, exercising his First Amendment rights would risk exposing his agency to charges of partisanship, potentially weakening its claim to independence and crippling its effectiveness in the eyes of the legislature and the public. As his agency operates in a highly partisan environment, appearing neutral becomes a necessary political strategy for legitimizing the agency's work and making it less vulnerable to charges of bias. But as a result, an extraordinary level of prior constraint bears down on the public expression (indeed, facial expression!) of its employees – a level of constraint that is inconsistent with First Amendment protections. The range of topics that potentially could come before this agency is so vast that employees simply can leave no "visible sign" of their opinions on any issue – just in case. It is not surprising that expressive writing addressed to other people comes under especially severe proscription in these circumstances. Writing is highly incriminating because of its association with the innermost subjectivity of the writer and its capacity to travel and endure. These qualities create potential dangers for Richter and his agency.

As an interesting comparison to Richter, consider the case of Ben Rollins, a 60-year-old European American who has served as a long-time attorney with his state's public defender's office. Over his tenure, he developed a reputation as a skilled and lively writer and an experienced court observer. At the time of our interview, Rollins had recently been recruited by his supervisors to launch a daily blog on the public defender's website, a blog that provided summaries of current court decisions and tracked issues pending before the state Supreme Court. The summaries were livened up in the emerging tradition of blog writing (Barlow 2007) with Rollin's own analysis and commentary – some of it quite droll and biting. If the state auditor was required to shut down his expressive voice outside of work, the public defender/blogger was invited to develop an expressive voice at work that would make the blog readable and attractive, not only in order to help overworked staff attorneys stay current on relevant rulings but also to improve the public visibility of a state agency that struggled for respect. Indeed, Rollins was taking some pleasure in the fact that judges and private attorneys were becoming subscribers. Of all the thirty government employees I interviewed, he seemed the most authorial, enjoying considerable creative license and developing an avid readership. Yet his foray into a new form of social communication – one that is explicitly associated with an individuated, even opinionated personality – brought him to the same representational worries as Richter. He explained:

If this is a [state] *public defender site, at what point is somebody going to throw back into our face a position that is promoted on the blog? It hasn't happened yet but it could. I may take a position on some point of law or promote it there, and down the line it may be contrary to the interests of some individual litigant represented by a public defender. And at some point the state representative on the other side, the district attorney or the attorney general, might ask, "Why are you taking this position when on your sponsored website you've taken the opposite position?" It gets into some interesting problems. Someday when I am gone, that stuff may come back to haunt the agency.*

Despite the association of blog writing with individuated voice and despite the fact that Rollins takes the extra step of setting his commentaries apart graphically from the decision summaries, he is not confident that his voice is sufficiently segregated from the agency that sponsors him – at least not enough to protect it from the adversarial conditions in which it must operate. His writing, he recognizes, could cause a chink in the case of a future defendant that prosecutors might exploit, thereby undermining the agency's fundamental responsibility to its clients. Where, Rollins wonders, might his speech rights hurt the system of rights? Interestingly, in both the case of the auditor and the public defender, adversarial conditions (for Richter, partisan politics; for Rollins, the agonistic legal system) put the most pressure on their expression. Politics and dispute may enliven the civilian voice, but they quiet (or disquiet) the government employee voice. In any case, Rollins recognizes, like Richter, that the capacity of writing to linger and endure beyond its immediate moment can threaten the integrity of his agency. He also recognizes that his voice is not easily freed from the larger collective he represents (including the citizenry).[15]

Typically the civil servants I interviewed did not have their speech explicitly regulated as a condition of employment. Rather, they had to figure out on their own what may or may not be appropriate, what may or may not be safe, when it comes to expressing civic views in and beyond the workplace. Here I discuss the topic with Alba Tabora, a 51-year-old Latina who serves as a financial management director for a revenue agency:

DB: *Do you ever feel you are curtailed in your ability to write to a government official or write a letter to the editor because of your role in the government?*
AT: *No, I have never felt that way. But internally, I see things I don't agree with, that I think is an abuse of power or a waste of taxpayers' money. But I don't feel that I could call* [the local TV station] *or the papers. There is, I know, whistleblower protection, but to me that's really not a protection. I don't feel that would protect me if I would go outside. So I guess the way I deal with that, I just try to express my concerns in a productive way. But then when you don't see anything changing, then, okay, this is not working so what do you do?*

In the next interview excerpt, Leah Serinsky, a 37-year-old European American, discusses how, early in her tenure as a public affairs director for a state benefits agency, she learned the limits of her free expression at work:

I had never worked before at this level for a state agency that reported directly to the governor's office. So I was gung-ho to get out my first press release. It was critical of the government – very mildly so, but just enough that everybody else said, "I can't believe she said that." And we had a call from the governor's office saying, "Oh, is that how it's going to be now?" I had come from the non-profit sector, more like a private side, where it was okay to be an outsider, pointing fingers, saying this could be done better. Can't say that any more. Even if it is the truth and even if your agency is not happy with how things should go, you really must tone down the voice and you don't send out a critical press release. Fortunately it wasn't a horrible gaffe but it was a wake-up call and you dial down, click over, tone it down a bit more.

All in all there was general reticence among the government writers I interviewed to risk writing publicly as private citizens on public issues. While displeasing the political higher-ups was a common source of reticence, government writers most of all worried about the tricky business of representation, the difficulty of having personal statements follow them back into their workplace, where they potentially could bring added and unwanted scrutiny to the work of their agency. At the same time, they worried that their institutional affiliation compromised the integrity of their citizen voice. (That is, they worried that their viewpoint could be interpreted merely as so much shilling on behalf of their agency.) This strong representational interdependency of personal voice with institutional voice – which writing notoriously signifies – was expressed in the comments of Alice Johns, a 45-year-old European American woman who served as a program manager for a county human services agency. Her remarks came in response to a question about whether she had ever written a letter to an editor or to an elected official:

This job would limit that. There would be a lot more scrutiny because of how you are representing the agency out in the community. If you're a citizen voice out there and somebody finds out what you do, well, that's just going to be automatically linked to you as a person.

Not all the civil servants I interviewed were so reticent about exercising their speech rights.[16] Perhaps unsurprisingly, Marvin Marks, the policy analyst who appeared earlier in the chapter, was in regular and vociferous contact with his elected representatives on public issues of concern to him. But even this outspoken citizen, who was willing to withstand push-back from the higher-ups, modulated his citizen voice when he felt it could interfere with the larger mission of his government agency. Asked if he ever wrote letters to the editor or to elected officials, he said:

Oh, yeah. I'm a regular conveyor of my ideas to my legislators. Just because I work for the government doesn't mean I don't have rights as a citizen. I pay taxes like everybody else. I have a right to my views. I think there was one situation when there was a little fluff up when some legislator called about something I wrote to them. Well, I didn't write it from here. So somebody is going to be ticked off every once in a while but the legislator should know better than to bring it up and whoever it is that it is brought up to should know how to deal with it. So I don't worry about it. I have First Amendment rights like everyone else. Now, there have been times when I haven't exercised them. I really cut back on my external communications with legislators when we were doing the Indian Child Welfare Act because that was just so critical. So I did back off for a little bit because we knew we were going to need bipartisan support. I didn't want anything to screw that up.

Conclusion

The testimonies of these thirty government writers demonstrate the considerable power that government exerts over the speech of its citizen-employees as it depends on them to articulate its viewpoints, even as it exposes what they write to strict regulations and broad public scrutiny. The government intrudes into the literacy apparatus of the writing public servant in ways that are simply not experienced by the general citizen. At the same time, as we have seen, government writers infuse government documents with aspects of their own subjectivities in the form of language resources and life experiences that bridge the gap between task and text and address the multiple authorizers and overseers of their work. So we can also say that writers for the State intrude into the literacy apparatus of government in ways that are simply not experienced by the general citizen. But as a result of all this meshing, the subjective voice of the public servant cannot be easily disentangled from the voice of the government: one seems unable to express without the other. Of course, government writers are not the only ones who must navigate boundaries between the private and public, the professional and the civic, the politically wise and the politically unwise as part of their everyday writing at work. But it is worth appreciating how differently elected officials treat the expressive speech of their employees from the expressive speech of their constituents. It is also worth appreciating how sensitive government writers can be about potentially compromising the rights and well-being of their fellow citizens through their writing. So difficult do some civil servants find it to separate their own voice from government that they will perform a civic duty by staying silent rather than speaking up.

These irregular relationships between the government and the writing bureaucrat have played little role in how we think about and talk about literacy, government, and participatory democracy, a discourse in which the citizen is invariably cast as the autonomous and constitutionally protected citizen reader rather than the considerably compromised government writer. The recruitment of mass writing into the projects and processes of government has been poorly considered in relation to the overall health of the democracy because of how mass writing in general is subordinated in legal and civic conceptions of literacy and freedom. As a matter of legal tradition, mass writing simply does not enjoy the same robust ring of protection afforded to mass reading when it comes to government intrusion, and as a result the issues of its intrusion are simplified or overlooked. When the courts deliberate on the First Amendment rights of government employees, they keep a steady eye on the rights of the general public but do not seriously consider the effects of government speech policies on the civic literacy of writing employees. Rather, the debate centers – as it does with open-record legislation – on a proper balance between the interests of the government to pursue its missions efficiently and the interests of the public to keep its leaders accountable. In this debate, the expressive rights of citizens who write for the government are squeezed from both sides.

Even critics who argue that government control over employee speech has become excessive and dangerous do so in defense of the general public – that is, readers and reading – rather than in defense of the civil servant – that is, writers and writing. Legal scholar Helen Norton, one of the most astute thinkers in the area of government and speech rights, regards the 2006 Supreme Court decision involving the district attorney's critical memo in this way:

[T]he government's political accountability to the electorate for its effectiveness may well be undercut by the carte blanche [this case] gives government to discipline workers who truthfully report irregularities and improprieties pursuant to their official duties . . . [This case] reflects a distorted understanding of government speech that overstates government's own expressive interest while undermining the public interest in transparent government. (Norton, 2009, pp. 90–91)

Likewise, when the Supreme Court decides that when public employees write in connection with official duties they are not speaking as citizens, the justices treat workplace writing as a form of transactional labor, a clean exchange of human mind and language skills for salary. Absent from this conception are the messier conditions in which the real work of government writing is done, and the ways in which it depends on the civic values, experiences, and expressive skills of public servants to articulate the meaning of democratic government to others and to themselves – not to mention the sacrifices and side effects entailed in doing so. Most intriguing is how government, including the courts, readily recognizes the intimate intermingling of writer subjectivity with institutional mission as the dangerous mix that potentially undermines the government's voice when employees speak out in the public domain and political arena. Yet the courts remain incurious about how this dangerous mix affects the citizen voices of the millions of Americans who must write every day on behalf of government. The weak civic tradition around the people's writing literacy provides few avenues for such reciprocal thinking. There is no Occupational Safety and Health Administration for literacy! Nor does a strict transactional model of salaried writing pay attention to what government writers create for themselves, as citizens, as a by-product of their work, how they develop civic viewpoints and understandings that affect their lives and language in both expanding and constricting ways. In the transactional model, these by-products go unrecognized, undervalued, constitutionally unprotected, and unredressed. Unlike for mass reading, we lack robust civic and legal theories of mass writing, and we lack them increasingly at our peril.

3   Occupation: author

Writing over reading in the literacy development of contemporary young adults

The belief that writing ability is a subsidiary of reading ability runs deep in American society and schooling. *You can only write as well as you can read. The best way to learn how to write is to read, read, and read some more. Reading is the best way to exercise the mind.* Commonplaces like these are easy to find in the advice of teachers and often well-known authors as well. Reading is considered the fundamental skill, the prior skill, the formative skill, the gateway to writing. Students' poor writing will often be ascribed to their lack of reading experience. When writing is taught to very young children, it is often in order to introduce or reinforce reading. As schooling progresses, reading becomes the pump that primes writing assignments and assessments. At minimum, reading is thought to teach the techniques of textuality, the vocabulary, diction, spelling, punctuation, and syntax that any aspiring writer must master. Even more profound, reading is thought to shape character and intellect, and provide the wisdom and worldliness that make one worthy to write. In every way reading is treated as the well from which writing springs.[1] We need only try to reverse the commonplace advice to appreciate the superior position that reading holds. How many would readily agree that *you can only read as well as you can write?* Or that *the best way to learn how to read is to write, write, and write some more?* Or that *writing is the best way to exercise the mind?* These assertions may seem less intuitively true, if not wrongheaded, even though literacy researchers emphasize the interconnectedness and complementarity of reading and writing, and how the two emerge from a commonly developed pool of linguistic resources.[2] Logically there can be no reading without writing and no writing without reading. Yet writing has never attained the same formative and morally wholesome status as reading. Indeed, writing unmoored from the instructiveness of reading is often considered solipsistic and socially dangerous (Keen 2007). We honor the well-read life and perhaps the well-written text. But the well-written life? The phrase has little meaning. Through most of the recent history of mass schooling, writing has been forced under the wing of reading, domesticated as a school-based subject, and made to function companionably within and in support of the ideological projects of mass reading.

Yet in the longer history of mass literacy, reading and writing were not so amiably conjoined. Rather, they have their origins in sharply different, even competing, pedagogical contexts and cultural histories. These differences relate to the different functions with which each came to be associated as well as to the sponsors who promoted them. Mass reading emerged in America through the eighteenth and nineteenth centuries, largely through the sponsoring agents of church and State. Reading was critical to salvation in the ideology of the Protestant church and to the promise of citizenship in the ideology of the Republic. In the initial project of mass literacy, however, writing held no great sway. Harder to teach, messy to learn, not as suitable a vehicle for religious and social control, and especially dangerous in the hands of the oppressed, mass writing emerged separately from mass reading and more slowly. It was promulgated not through church and State but through artisanship and commerce. Those who wrote depended on patrons with power and money to subsidize their efforts. First linked not with worship but with work, not with reading but with mathematics and accounting, writing was rarely central to the doctrines of salvation and assimilation. The association of writing with the worldly domains of art, commerce, craft, and mercantilism helps to explain why writing instruction in colonial America was largely excluded from the literacy campaigns of churches and Sunday schools as well as from the traditional grammar school, at least initially. Writing was taught instead in separate, private-pay settings, almost exclusively to non-enslaved males, and found its value in the budding communication trades and service economy of the new nation. Reading and writing instruction also proceeded differently. In reading, the book was treated as the main instructional element. The person who taught reading mattered less than the canonical text. As a result, the teaching of reading often fell to families or to a wide variety of instructors. But in writing, the person of the writing master mattered a great deal. The teacher was the significant instructional element as writing was taught as a craft and an embodied technical skill.[3]

Interestingly, even as mass writing was culturally associated with labor, it developed a political "subtext," as Monaghan (2005) has observed, one that connoted freedom, personhood, self-possession. An intimate, irreducible connection pertains between writing and human presence, writing, and human will. Signatures and other written marks make palpable the agency and action of the ones who inscribe. Thus, writing as a universal skill posed more of a challenge to the political and social order. Access to writing was more controlled than access to reading, especially when it came to the enslaved and other subordinated members of society. Knowing how to write not only could enable financial independence but also was a skill for subversions such as forgery, impersonation, or conspiracy. Here Monaghan remarks on how these associations took on meaning within the fraught regime of slavery:

It is striking how universal the assumption was, even among those prepared to offer enslaved Africans some education, that it was legitimate to teach reading but not writing. This assumption illustrates the unstated but deeply held belief among colonists that writing acquisition was somehow the hallmark of the free. Quite apart from its potential for forging a pass, it marked a person's identity in a way that the skill of reading did not. And it did so in a context in which writing was viewed pedagogically, as just another vehicle for conveying the ideas of others by copying them. (p. 271)

I have briefly invoked the history of what Furet and Ozouf (1982) call the "cultural dissociation" between reading and writing in order to reopen that gap as a gambit for this chapter. How might such dissociations persist to this day and why do they still matter? How do long-standing differences in the cultural projects of mass reading and mass writing challenge traditional assumptions about literacy and how it develops? In what follows, writing-based literacy will come out from under the dominance of reading to be explored as an independent and legitimate route to literacy experience and development, one that is worthy of understanding on its own terms. Simply defined, writing-based literacy is a literacy driven primarily through engagement with and orientation toward writing instead of reading – a literacy that develops by way of emphasizing and embracing the social role of the writer rather than the social role of the reader. If, as this book is arguing, writing is now becoming the more prominent grounds of mass literate experience, it is imperative to gain clearer insight into how writing might drive literacy development. If economic and technological conditions continue to insist upon a new relationship between writing and reading in contemporary life, schools and society need to be better positioned to understand and respond.

Toward that end, this chapter develops contemporary pictures of writing-based literacy. It rests on interpretations of the lifelong literacy accounts of thirty young adults who have strongly oriented themselves to writing, in most cases from their earliest years. (More about the study design below.) The examination is attuned to how the long sponsorship history of writing, including its association with craft, labor, commerce, art, and artisanship, still matters to the acquisition of writing, even though these legacies remain largely suppressed and attenuated within the confines of a reading-privileged, school-based literacy. Further, this chapter attends to *what is different* about a writing-based literacy from a reading-based literacy, including in terms of what it demands. Specifically, this chapter will consider the contrarian possibility that in order to flourish, *writing requires separating from reading*, detaching from the far more societally expected role of the reader and claiming affiliation with the enterprises of authorship – a move that is not always made easy by the reading-insistent environments of school and society. As we will see, examining literacy from a base in writing enlarges what rightly belongs to literacy and to the formative experiences we associate with it.

When I refer to *reading* in this chapter, I mean to invoke the common sense notion of taking up words that have been written down by someone else. *Writing* refers to the common sense notion of producing and inscribing words. For purposes of this analysis, reading one's own words during acts of writing and knowing what to do about them are considered part of writing, as belonging to the skills of writing. I will not deny in this discussion that reading and writing flow together in the exercise of literacy in ways that are hard to differentiate at times. But I will argue that it is useful to push on their critical differences as a way to bring writing out of the shadow of reading. As we will see, writing's strong counter-heritage to reading is still relevant to the experiences of writing-oriented youth, and writing can just as easily inform reading – and be part of the reading experience – as the other way around.

The inspiration for this chapter began with an interview I conducted with a young adult we can call Evan Davies,[4] whose experiences epitomize what I am calling a writing-based literacy. By the time he was 20 years old, Evan had published his first book. This is how he said it came about: as a young boy, he started collecting exotic amphibians and developed a passionate interest in caring for them. Through the Internet, he began participating in forums with fellow amphibian lovers, swapping information and experiences. When he was about 14, he set up a website on which he began to write on this topic, creating a series of care sheets that he posted to the website, along with notices about amphibians he was willing to sell from his growing collection in order to cover the cost of keeping his dot-com address. By the time he was in high school, Evan was spending an hour or so each morning answering email enquiries from people all over the world who wanted to know more about how to feed their amphibians and care for them when they got sick. As this teenager's website gained in authority, it came to the attention of a major publishing house for pet care books. When Evan was 18 years old he received an email, out of the blue, from the editor, seeking his interest in writing a traditional print book about one of the species he knew well. Instead of starting university, which had been his plan at the time, Evan took a deferment and devoted himself full time to writing the book. When it was published, the book was distributed nationally through pet supply chain stores and sold 10,000 copies in the first year. The success of the book led to an invitation to write two more books for this publishing company, which Evan has done, earning money to help pay for school. All of his titles remain available for sale in pet supply stores and through Internet book outlets, where they earn enthusiastic ratings by reviewers. As a result of this experience, Evan began writing and selling freelance magazine articles about amphibians as an additional way to earn money. In 2007, when Evan filled out his federal income tax return, he listed his occupation as author.

In his interview with me, Evan talked about an event that had reinforced this authorial stature in an unexpected way:

*My girlfriend and I went to Pet Smart the other night to buy a lizard and there was
a magazine stand. I have two articles out right now in two magazines. So there was
one magazine, the other magazine, and my book behind them. It was really funny. My
girlfriend took a picture with her cell phone.*

As I talked with Evan about his literacy development, I asked him what role
reading had played in helping him learn how to write a book. He confessed that
he did not like to read and did not read books very thoroughly. This is what he
said:

*I wasn't one of those kids in grade school who read all the time. I didn't even read the
books assigned in school. I rarely ever finish a book. I will read a couple of chapters. I
just don't remember ever getting sucked into a book. Most of the time, I'd much rather
be writing than reading. I like the process better. When I'm writing, I'm thinking really
deeply. Sometimes I will forget to eat. It focuses my mind. It clarifies my ideas.*

Asked if he thought a person needed to know how to read in order to write,
Evan responded uncertainly:

*Probably. Maybe not. You need to understand basic principles so that what you write
makes sense to other people. But it may actually limit you more to read because then
you get conditioned and you just start writing the way other people write.*

I offer Evan's experience here not because it is typical but because it illustrates how writing literacy may flourish in cultural dissociation from reading;
how from certain angles writing and reading can be antagonistic toward one
another; how the powerful socialization and integration functions of reading
pose risks when you have to compete with other writers on the basis of dis-
tinction. Evan's experience also suggests how getting lost in a book can be
that much more pleasurable and intellectually generative when it is your own
book. Above all, Evan's account demonstrates how his literacy has been pulled
along by the economic and social arrangements around writing in the larger
society, and its status as: a transactional product; a form of paid labor; a vocation or avocation; a social exchange; a declarable occupation; a recognizable
form of cultural contribution; a ubiquitous companion to buying and selling.
This long-standing status of writing, its active association with the engines
of publication and commerce – revved up now by the powerful potentials of
digital communication – propels Evan's literacy development. Over the course
of four or five years, he moves from a chat participant, to expert hobbyist, to
published author, a developmental arc sponsored not by formal schooling nor
credentialing – and not by the instructiveness of reading – but by commercial
interests associated with the so-called knowledge economy. These days, one of
the main functions of writing is to congregate, educate, and cultivate consumers
(Burton-Jones 2001). The more informed pet owners become, the better chance
they will frequent the pet supply store. That's the idea. When Evan writes, he

finds his literacy is in circulation with these larger functions of writing, its connections to commerce, production, profit, and service to others. In this case, a publishing house locates, captures, and reorganizes the knowledge he created through an amateur hobby and turns it into a commercial product, as Evan's established rapport with his Internet audience serves as an attractive asset in the bargain.[5] Through this process, Evan gains the socially recognized status of the author. It is a role, interestingly enough, that he did not intentionally seek, yet saw reflected back to him through responses to his forum posts and care sheets, through the public nature of his website, the overtures of the publishing company, his books and articles, and such other material artifacts as the tax return and the magazine stand. In Evan's literacy development, this connection to the broader industries of writing matters more than reading.

A research study is born

So intrigued was I by Evan's account that I wondered if other young adults took similar directions in their writing development. Was it common to write intensively while eschewing reading? Could I find other instances of writing-based literacy development? To find out, I went in search of thirty young adults, aged 15 to 25, who said they engaged in regular, substantive writing outside of school (i.e., not required by courses) and/or professed a preference for writing over reading. I was deliberately interested in finding young people who wrote the kind of texts that society tells them they should be reading. These included book-length projects of any kind, literary texts, or texts that reported or analyzed current events. I also sought participants who engaged in what might be considered high-stakes or consequential writing beyond school, having to do with entrepreneurship, employment, or civic, political, or governmental participation. Participants that I sought could be writing on or off the Internet, in traditional or digital genres, and in any language. Their writing could be published in any form or not published at all. They could write in forms accompanied or not by non-textual elements like images or sound. Of less interest to this study was the kind of writing that has been characterized as "talking with your fingers," that is, intimate, ephemeral, conversational discourse by phone texting or other social media. Social media writing was of interest in this study only when it was linked to or otherwise helped to sustain the other kinds of writing (which it sometimes did). While I sought participants who said they wrote outside of school at least twice a month, most of those who joined the study said they wrote nearly every day.

Participants were sought in the community around where I live through a number of channels – through contacts with teachers, counselors, youth groups, and community leaders, and through my own searches through websites and local publications. I sought inclusion in terms of gender, race, and class.[6]

Fifteen participants were female and fifteen were male. Seventeen were European American. Eight were African American. Three were Asian American.
Two were Latino American. Twenty were living in middle-class households.
Eight were living in working-class households. Two were living in poverty
households. Seven were attending high school at the time of their participation.
Nineteen were attending two- or four-year colleges. The rest were out of school
and working either full- or part-time. As it turned out, sixteen of the participants
were engaged in creative writing (i.e., poetry, novels, short stories, spoken-word
performances, songs, plays, scripts). Eight wrote primarily in connection with
entrepreneurial enterprises or paid or unpaid work, including writing for student
newspapers. Three wrote as part of political/civic/governmental involvement.
Finally, three others were engaged in life-writing in the form of personal journals, private essays, or blogs.

Participants were reached through email, text, or phone and, where necessary, parental permission was secured. I interviewed each participant singly,
face-to-face, for about one hour, at a time and place convenient to them. In the
interviews I asked participants about the writing they did, how it got started,
how they learned to do it, how they thought about it, and how they said it
affected other domains of their lives. We also explored their reading experiences and how they thought about relationships between reading and writing.
I digitally recorded the interviews and transcribed them. Then I coded line-by-
line as a way to build a grounded theory of what I am calling writing-based
literacy. Especially pertinent in the analysis were all patterns relating to the
sponsorship legacy of mass writing as it surfaced in the accounts, particularly
association with craft, commerce, and publishing; what might be thought of as
the vocational or avocational industries of writing. I also looked for explicit and
latent dissociations and differences between reading and writing in participants'
reported experiences (what I came to call separating), as well as connections
between reading and writing. I also coded for evidence of the impacts of writing
on those who undertake it.

As I suggested earlier, this study was inspired by the guess that I might find
that a high proportion of the participants, like Evan, were devoted to writing
and diffident toward reading. But this did not turn out to be the case. Rather, as
I will discuss further later on, a range of writing–reading relationships turned
up in the accounts. Some of these young adults were voracious readers from
their early years; others hardly read and did not care for reading; and still
others came to reading post hoc, through their writing. However, despite these
variations, as this chapter will progressively demonstrate, these young adults
shared an orientation to what I came to call *writing over reading*. This is a
phrase that is meant to capture a set of significant and interconnected patterns
that emerged strongly from the analysis and will be illustrated and developed as
the chapter proceeds. First, the phrase *writing over reading* is meant to indicate

a simple preference for writing compared to reading, liking to write more than liking to read. This was a preference that was prevalent although not unanimous among the research participants. The phrase also indicates how writing is given priority over reading in the participants' often busy lives, as the two might compete for time, attention, and mental energy. But more substantively, the phrase *writing over reading* is meant to capture how participants pursued their orientations to writing in instructional and other social contexts where they were being construed (along with everybody else) as readers. Although occasionally invited to do so by adults in charge, these individuals more often had to "write over" the reading bias in their environments as a matter of individual initiative, sometimes violating expectations even to the point of reprimand. And finally, *writing over reading* will be explored as a strategy that these participants routinely invoked *during reading*, a strategy whereby they separated from the readerly role expected of them by the circumstances and used the occasion to cultivate their writing. As they reported it, these individuals would abandon the expected duties and pleasures of reading (i.e., comprehension, response, critique) and begin writing in their minds as they sat over a text written by someone else. It is in these moments where the reading–writing relationship is at its most intimate – and where no doubt the adages about learning to write by reading have their origins. But it isn't exactly reading or "reading like a writer". Rather it is a set of strategies that requires deliberate separation from the rules of reading. In order to contextualize these strategies of *writing over reading*, the discussion begins with a look at how the vocational and avocational status of writing in society mattered to these writing-oriented young adults.

Occupation: author. The salience of writing as a vocational pursuit

In the opening pages of *Cultures of Letters*, a book that examines nineteenth-century American literary works in relationship to the forms of community life from which they sprang, Richard Brodhead (1993) recounts how novelist Theodore Dreiser, as a newly arrived blue-collar worker to the city of Chicago, was seized with an inchoate desire to write about the urban life around him. But, as Brodhead put it, quoting from Dreiser's later autobiographical writings: "though he 'seethed to express himself,' this desire remained almost wholly 'nebulous' – unactable because too vaguely imagined – until he acquired a more specified concept of writing as worldly work" (p. 1). It was a concept Dreiser fleshed out only after taking a job as a newspaper reporter. This strong interaction between the desire to write and the vocational formations through which that desire takes hold is the interest in this section, as we look at how the societally-recognized status of writing in terms of occupation, vocation, avocation, and career path matters to what I call writing-based literacy. As we will see, "writing as worldly work" functions aspirationally in the lives of the young writers I interviewed, exciting dreams of their future selves and inviting them into precocious engagement with some of the most powerful genres of the culture. Further, the worldly work of writing and publishing – activities that are normally associated with the production and support of readers – creates nodes of contact where aspiring writers acquire "a more specified concept" of the (a)vocations of writing.

Cultural and literary historians have documented how the career writer emerged in society out of such enabling factors as publishing technologies, rising literacy rates, commercial markets, and intellectual property regimes. While most of the scholarly attention focuses on literary authors, some have studied a wider stratum of people who, by the latter half of the nineteenth century, were finding ways to support themselves as journalists, magazine writers, technical writers, and freelancers. Still others have documented how the rise of the professional study of journalism, creative writing, technical writing, and other related fields at the post-secondary and graduate level contributed to the production of career writers.[7] Together, these histories underscore the shifting economic, technological, and cultural contingencies upon which the social meanings and social possibilities of writing and authorship depend, including, as Adrian Johns (2010) has impressively argued, arduous evolution in how societies learn to ascribe meaning to texts and to the people who produce them – a process that is again up for grabs as the so-called age of print is overturned by digital communication.[8]

These histories of authorship serve as a reminder of how – in order to support mass reading – the material productiveness of career writers comes to extend deeply into everyday social structures. As we will see, the productivity and social activity of career writers created opportunities for those I interviewed to construct ideas about the writing life. Many of them relished personal contacts with working writers and, as they came of age, they sought out work in the ancillary industries of editing, publishing, and selling writing. In addition, these histories of authorship illustrate how ideologies about writing and the writer enter public consciousness and thicken over time. The equation of *writing* with *literary writing* exerts a particularly strong hold on the popular imagination, carrying with it all the contradictory meanings that have accumulated around the figure of the literary writer: romantic genius, social seer, dissipated rebel, bestselling celebrity, and so on. So for the young adults I interviewed, taking up writing (of any kind) often meant grappling uncomfortably with social images of the writer or having those images imposed on them by others. In any case, the (a)vocational and commercialized status of writing – a status that makes it different from the other language arts of speaking, listening, and reading – proved highly salient to the young people I interviewed, affecting, among other things, their motivations, the ways they took up the genres in which they wrote, the jobs they sought out, and the ways they made contact with writing-based resources, supports, and regulations.

Aspiration

Learning to read is an expectation and a rite of passage for children in this society. But the idea of *being* or *becoming* a writer has more profound aspirational power. The high prestige of the published author, the literary artist, or the trusted journalist was not lost on the young people I interviewed, and neither was the (iffy) proposition that they might someday make their living as writers. Even as very young children, many of them experimented with the vocational and avocational potential of writing as part of their engagement with written language. Further, the connection between writing and career paths helped caring adults in these youths' lives to interpret their precocious interest in writing. In the following remarks, which peppered the interviews, notice how writing is wrapped in yearning and sometimes titanic ambition, tantamount to chasing a dream:[9]

I always wanted to be a writer, ever since I can remember.[10]

I really, really want to become a published author. It's a dream. Some part of me wonders, what if I get a book published before I graduate from high school? It's a fantasy.[11]

I have a hope that something I write will turn into a movie. It's my ultimate dream.[12]

I want to make new forms and new ways of talking and new ways of writing. I want for my writing to be respected in a way that comes along with the connotation of the poet.[13]

In high school I decided I wanted to be a news anchor. Through different tragedies that we have had it's always the news anchor that has been in our living rooms and telling us the story and being with us every step of the way. And I wanted to be that person.[14]

I'd love to publish a novel or two and poetry books. Ideally my profession will be involved in creating art for the rest of my life. It would be the ideal.[15]

I really wanted to write a book really badly. It was a dream of mine. I just knew that was what I wanted.[16]

I don't want to be the person posting gross photos to Facebook. I want to be the [journalist] *people look up to, someone who will see both sides.*[17]

By sixth grade I was heavy into poetry. I knew I wanted to become an artist or a writer.[18]

I don't really know a whole lot about the publishing process or anything, but I just know I want to.[19]

My Dad always said I would be an author.[20]

When I tell people I want to write as a career it's almost revered in a way.[21]

I've thought about being a poet, and a lot of my mom's friends told me that when I grow up they are going to pitch me as a poet. When I look in the mirror at myself I see that as well.[22]

These comments certainly suggest how the highly regarded social figure of the writer can be a meaningful and motivating force in youthful writing experiences. At the same time, some of those I interviewed told me they were deterred from pursuing writing, at least certain forms of writing, because they felt they fell short, a feeling they frequently arrived at, ironically enough, through reading. The figure of the professional writer proved too high a standard of comparison:

For a while when I was way younger I thought I wanted to be a writer. But I don't think my writing is where it needs to be to pursue it professionally.[23]

I would read a book by a professional author and just get discouraged. I couldn't put together that, hey, you are only 13 and only trying this for the third time.[24]

I was just some untrained teenager trying to write poetry. It wasn't any good. I knew it wasn't good.[25]

I wanted to be a songwriter. I wanted to be in a super group. I liked the process [of writing songs] *but once they were done, I would read them and didn't like them. So I gave that up.*[26]

Just as these young people were well aware of the high prestige afforded the successful artist or published author, they were also well aware of the precariousness of the occupation and the difficulty or unlikelihood of making a viable living as an independent writer, as well as some of the negative connotations and dangers that are associated with writers or the pursuit of writing. Sometimes parents transmitted these messages:

It would be so awesome to be an author. It would be the ideal thing. But there is always that insecurity of not being able to find the right story to publish. I'd be nervous to rely solely on that.[27]

I don't tell people I want to be a writer. If you do, they judge you in a certain way.[28]

I like writing fiction more than writing poetry. There is a whole sort of cliché about poets that they are dark and they are depressed and I don't feel part of that.[29]

I got more disheartened as I got older, although I definitely want to keep [fiction] *as a side occupation.*[30]

I wanted to be a rapper at one time. But my parents didn't really support me on it. I don't think they see me becoming a rapper any time soon. They want me to have a good job.[31]

I still think about it [becoming a writer] *but I feel like my mom wouldn't take it seriously. She's very, "you need to be able to support yourself," because she wants us to have everything that she didn't have.*[32]

My parents worry as any parent would worry. But they have gotten used to having an artist in the house. I think my versatility makes them feel better because I'm not just writing. And it makes me feel better too. If I were just a writer trying to sell short story collections, it would put me in a hole financially.[33]

I said, "Hey, mom, I think I want to go to college for journalism." And she said, "You are not going to the Middle East." That's the first thing she said.[34]

It is worth noticing in all of the above comments the extent to which the status of writing as a vocational pursuit and a craft, the writer as someone you can be or become, invites early-life consideration of such matters as training, publishing, publicity, commercialism, reputation, fame, social contribution, risk, nervousness, social disapproval – all of them aspects and onuses of "occupation: author" and all of them relevant to how these young people think about and engage with their writing. While gaining the social designation of reader can certainly be a harrowing and in some cases unattainable desire for some members of society, aspiring to the designation of writer is more broadly daunting and ideologically laden, dependent as it is on many forces and vulnerable to many deterrents beyond one's control. These young people knowingly pursue their writing-based literacy in a culture where permission to be a writer is more hard-won than permission to be a reader.

At the same time, (a)vocational desire encouraged precocious engagement with whole, culturally powerful genres, from surprisingly early ages. By the time they had reached late adolescence or young adulthood, many of the aspiring writers I interviewed had produced hundreds, even thousands of pages of novels, poems, stories, songs, essays, and journal entries, which they kept in suitcases, plastic bins, dresser drawers, bookshelves, and computer files. Alexis Harrison said she started writing poetry at the age of 7, *"realized I could market my work when I was 12 or 13,"* and started drafting her first novel at 15. Carla King, who was named a "Promising Young Writer" by the National Council of Teachers of English when she was in middle school, said she started making up stories at the age of 2, stories her graphic designer father would transcribe, illustrate and make into *"little books."* Nick Barrington said that at the age of 7 he wrote his first poem, entitled "Horses Are the Dreams of Children," and submitted it unsuccessfully for publication. (*"I had writer's block for four years after that,"* he added.) Robert Jackson, a poet and gospel songwriter who wrote his first poem in the company of his cousin when he was 8, said he was composing rap songs by age 9. Amanda Costner said she *"really didn't start writing what I would call good writing until maybe sixth grade."* Verdell Fisher began writing poetry on a nearly daily basis beginning at the age of 8. Marissa Fernandez became a writer of raps in middle school. Shameka Howard was *"heavy into poetry"* by the time she was 11. Kaitlin Rieser said she started writing her *"first legitimate stories"* at age 10. Lela Shao, who as a young teen self-published a bilingual fantasy novel, first started writing books at the age of 6. David Platz said *"I wrote comic books from an early age but I didn't write novels, full length prose, until sixth or seventh grade."* Akira Burkes saw her first poem published at the age of 8. Alison Cabot had completed two novels by the time she started high school. Annie Mack became a lifelong diarist beginning at age 5. Valeria Rojas was the youngest member of her school TV production team in her native Colombia, serving as a news writer and anchor at the age of 11.

Aspiration was not merely future-oriented but was expressed through a present-tense pursuit of publication. Twenty of the thirty young adults I interviewed had already published one or more pieces of poetry, fiction, journalism, or other non-fiction work in some form. Three had authored traditional print books.[35] One had published more than twenty-five poems in print and digital literary journals. Two had published op-eds in campus or community newspapers. One was a regular contributor to a collaborative political blog. Four were news and feature writers for school or campus newspapers. One had a poem selected for display in the subway cars of his hometown. One had recorded a poem for a CD that was issued in commemoration of a local educator. Four performed poetry or original gospel music in public venues on a regular basis. While traditional print publishing was surprisingly high among the young people I interviewed, some also published and performed via the Internet, in digital journals, on one of the many websites that now solicit writing in all forms, on YouTube, and, in a few cases, on personal Facebook pages. One used Twitter as an outlet for material that was not going to make it into formal poems. In addition to posting original work to the Internet, many of these individuals also were engaged in actively publicizing themselves and their work via the Internet. One had a biographical entry in the digital directory, "Writers and Poets." Several had websites on which they provided biographies, listed publications, and blogged as part of self-promotion or promotion of a business. The names, images, and bios of those who performed or emceed in slam poetry events were circulated in promotional materials, both textual and digital.

Occupational aspiration also figured into the critical thought these young people gave to managing their interests, responsibilities, and reputations as future career writers, including reflections on the technologies and legal regimes through which writing is disseminated. In some cases the competitive and proprietary environments that regulate the enterprises of authoring and publishing entered intimately into their composing choices and processes.

Due in no small part to the long memory of the Internet and the easy ways it can be searched, some hesitated to leave a public record of their early writing. Otto Rivlin, who was incoming editor of his high school newspaper at the time of our interview, planned a career in broadcast journalism after college. He said he shied away from writing editorials, sticking instead to "hard news," and he said he kept a deliberately low profile on Facebook:

I don't do a lot of editorials because if I do one day get into journalism, I don't want people digging up all those past editorials. With Facebook, it gets back to the same thing. I use it for communications more than I write status updates. To establish a career in journalism, you have to stay impartial. I'm taking it pretty seriously.

Other individuals I interviewed were highly reluctant to disseminate their work on the Internet, where venues for sharing and self-publishing abound, for fear they would lose authorial control. Partly these fears involved letting go of writing that was not yet mature enough, writing that might display too big a proficiency gap between where they were and where they aspired to get to as writers in the future. But more frequently these fears had to do with the potential of having their work stolen or misused. Amanda Costner, a prolific 16-year-old novelist, was one individual who expressed such reservations:

AC: *My aunt introduced me to a site called Figment, which is especially for writers to put their stuff out there. There's tons of stuff out there. But I didn't really stay on it. I don't want to put my stories online because then everyone can look at them. I really would prefer if one day I could publish a book because then it's much more perfected. It's copyrighted. They can't cut and paste it. I'm very reluctant to put anything that I'm serious about online.*
DB: *Because it could get stolen?*
AC: *I hadn't really thought about it before but I think that's probably why.*

Expressing similar reticence – along with keen awareness of intellectual property regimes – was Justine Strater, a 20-year-old college student who has been performing spoken-word poetry since high school. Asked if she had shared or published any of her poetry online, she responded:

As someone who is trying to do art for a living, I try not to so much because it risks my work being manipulated or exploited or not credited. When I was younger and I didn't value my stuff as much maybe I would put some things out there for feedback on different artistic websites. But now my poetry is only for the work I do physically in the world. If I write something small just for fun, maybe I'll put it on Facebook and let my friends see it, but I don't value it as much. The work I put a lot of effort into, I don't put on YouTube or post on Facebook because you don't really own that work. It's taken away, that value, because it can exist without my permission. I don't know if you are familiar with Brave New Voices. It's a high-school level poetry slam. A lot of their work is online. But it is credited back to BNV and then credited back to the artist. So the artist is definitely given credit for that piece of work. They are just not dismissed. Or the opportunity to really abuse that work is not out there. It has some sort of protection. Otherwise, someone can take [your work], steal it, and make magic with it and you won't reap any benefits from it. It also can be manipulated and turned into something disgusting that wasn't your intention for that work.

The comments by Amanda Costner and Justine Strater are interesting in light of how often the Internet is lauded as a place where writers can gain instant reading audiences for their work. But artistic websites are populated not only (and maybe not mainly) by regular readers but also by other writers, who can "look" (an interesting substitute word for *read*) and potentially poach or manipulate. As unaffiliated writers, without agents, publishers, sponsors, or copyright protection, Amanda and Justine see their writing as vulnerable in the public arena of the Internet. Their concerns also demonstrate how aspiring writers inflect their own reading (and viewing) habits with vocational awareness, affecting, for instance, what they consider credible in their own writing or the writing of others.

Copyright laws also played on the writing processes of fiction writer David Platz, but in a different way, because to him copyright connoted the need to protect a proprietary relationship between self and creation. He especially did not feel ownership over his fictional characters, even though the public rules of authoring made him feel that he should. Here Platz raises the topic of copyright during standard questioning about his writing processes, saying:

Other writers are obsessed with the ideas that this character is kind of like me. I distance myself as much as I can from my characters. It's very truncated. It's the space between me and a mural, rather than my being in the mural. In an ideal world I wish there were less copyright infringement because I don't have a personal stake in my work as other people do.

In other words, David Platz feels the negative pressures of copyright as part of the composing process.

Another way that occupational aspiration was expressed was in the kinds of work, paid and unpaid, that many of these individuals undertook outside of school, positions that called upon their writing and writing-related skills. This work allowed them to learn more about what I have been calling the industries of writing and to develop social relationships with other writing-oriented people. Four were editors or members of editorial boards for student-founded magazines, either literary or style magazines, where they planned issues, evaluated manuscripts, and occasionally contributed writing. One of these editors also maintained a blog on the journal website. Another individual wrote occasional articles for a national, online men's style magazine (where he also was able to promote his streetwear business) and maintained a word-and-photo blog on his business website. Two worked as copywriters, one for a press and one for a corporation. One, who belonged to a writing collective, was helping to produce and edit an anthology of the group's work for eventual publication. Three designed and managed websites for small businesses, two of whom blogged for the sites. One wrote special-occasion poetry for money. One was a chief writer and communications advisor for a couple of political campaigns. One live-blogged and did sports reporting for her university's athletic department and also held a paid position with an online, writing-based peer support service. Two were correspondents with online national and international youth news sites. Two wrote gospel songs and poems as part of a religious outreach group. One held a summer internship with a local television station. One was in the midst of applying for a year-long internship in the story development department of a national game company. Several of the spoken-word poets were hired to perform or emcee at various poetry slams or to appear at special events, ranging from youth leadership meetings to store openings. Several had won contest money or college scholarships on the strength of their writing. Some of these scholarships were substantial; four of the college students I interviewed had received full tuition scholarships to a highly competitive hip-hop arts program at a Midwestern university. All in all, two-thirds of the college students I interviewed held part-time jobs that used their skills as writers.

We have been exploring how the worldly work of writing – its association with vocation, avocation, publishing, publicity, and property – asserts itself in the literacy experiences of the writing-oriented young people I interviewed. The status of writing as an occupation, the idea of the writer as a culturally valued figure one may *be* or *become*, can lend aspirational – as well as intimidating – power to literacy learning from the earliest years. The explicit relationship between occupations and text types – the fact that poets write poetry; novelists write novels; reporters write "hard news" – lends permission to aspiring writers for productive, even precocious engagement with the deep properties of whole, culturally significant genres. While learning to read in this society is largely regarded as child's work, learning to write is associated with the adult world, entitling youth to experience the arduous arcs, rewards, and risks of authorship – from the glory of publication to the despair of writer's block to the concerns over intellectual property. Above all, we see in these accounts how the economic and cultural activities that organize around writing, performing, and publishing infiltrate the social structures in which many aspiring writers circulate, creating opportunities for learning, earning, and development. The scrappy efforts these young people exert to publish and ply their skills are a special reminder of how much writing-based literacy seeks to be transacted in responsive systems of labor, service, value, and reward. These efforts have obviously been helped by the role of the Internet in lowering barriers and expanding capacity for writing, publishing, and publicity on one's own – conditions that these young people do recognize and exploit. Yet most of those profiled here simultaneously seek to engage as writers through organized enterprises and recognized auspices – in arts, news, religion, sports, politics, fashion, entertainment – structures that bring social validation if not remuneration to their efforts. In the process their understanding of the worldly work of writing is expanded.

Writing masters

Writing masters, also known as penmen, figure centrally in the vocational histo-ries of early mass writing. "Penmen" epitomized the physicality of the writing act, its reliance on control of the body and the tools. As pedagogues they showed their tutees how to hold the head, the elbow, the hand, how to whittle pens and blot mistakes. As need for their services proliferated, writing masters helped to lay down economies of writing and writing instruction that have persisted – in dynamic form – well into the era of print and beyond. Writing masters were entrepreneurs, copyists, typesetters, and in some cases authors of copybooks, who often opened schools and competed with each other for students on the distinctiveness of their styles. They used public demonstrations and contests to gain reputations for their skill and authenticity and, by exten-sion, to attract apprentices or students. Yet it was the inky, hardscrabble status of writing masters that banished them and their craft from the more cerebral and morality-based world of the school, where books, not people, were considered the models of writing excellence and where the crass physical work and com-mercial values of writing were well sublimated (Monaghan 2005, especially Chapter 10; Nash 1959).[36] This banishment had far-reaching impacts on the contours of mass literacy instruction. Today, in the reading-dominant domain of public education, the teacher is merely the mediator between texts and students. The writing master is almost exclusively the disembodied, canonical author. The apprentice is the attentive reader.

Yet in the accounts of many of the individuals I interviewed, writing masters of various sorts do appear in direct, embodied form and often in close physical proximity to writing aspirants, functioning in evocative ways like the writing masters of old. They may no longer be penmen and copyists, but neither are they teachers of reading nor always canonical authors. Rather, these figures dwell in the (a)vocational, entrepreneurial world of writing and connect apprentices to it through the distinctiveness of their personhood and style. Their presence, their attentiveness, their mentorship prove critically instructive to aspiring writers. And what they teach goes well beyond the techniques of textuality, extending to the broader character of the writer and the writing life.

Who are these writing masters? In some cases, they are living relatives, who pass along something like a family artistic tradition or at least confer the continuity of desire onto aspirants. Nick Barrington's grandmother made her living as a writer in New York. Kaitlin Rieser's father, a civil servant by day, wrote short stories and songs as an avocation at night. Verdell Fisher's mother had been an aspiring creative writer when she was growing up, and Otto Rivlin's mother had considered a career in journalism. Kaitlin Rieser discussed what it was like to have a creative-writing parent in the household:

I definitely think my dad had a huge influence on my writing. I guess it might have happened otherwise but it's kind of nice to have someone who understands what it feels like to write. You know, "Don't bother me, I have a great idea." And it's, "Okay, I understand." Or if you don't have quite the right way to say something, you can ask, what's another word for this? You can get help in different ways. We exchange ideas. He's had plots in mind that he has told me about. And there is this writing contest we enter together every so often.

Verdell Fisher looked to his mother's interest and skill in writing as validation and motivation in his life, even as he recognized that her wish to pursue a writing career had been thwarted by other obligations:

My mom doesn't write poetry but when she was young she always wanted to be a creative writer. She writes a lot. I read a paper she wrote and I knew she was a creative writer. It's just that she doesn't take the time to sit there and write. She doesn't take the time to do that because she worries about me, my brother and my sister all the time, and my grandma. My mom and my grandma are always saying, [Verdell], *you are going to be good, you are going to be a novelist or a poet when you grow up.*

At the time of our interview, diarist Annie Mack said her cousin was in the midst of writing a memoir: *"Yes, she is a writer. I went and stayed with her for a couple days and every day she wakes up at five o'clock in the morning and just writes and writes and writes all day. Smokes cigarettes and does the whole deal."* Justine Strater's relatives were mostly visual artists, whose deferred art careers served as both validation and motivation for her writing:

I come from a family of artists. My generation, my cousins and I, are more outspoken with it, in really embracing the talent. My grandpa on my dad's side is a painter, a really good one too. He didn't pursue the profession but he darn well could have been a really amazing artist. My great grandmother on my mom's side was also a painter. My sister does animation. I took up writing. Art is a huge part of my life.

Besides relatives, writing masters also appeared in the form of local teachers and mentors who were active practitioners of the craft of writing. Nick Barrington was enrolled in an urban arts program called Young Authors, in which he took Saturday morning workshops with community-based writers he described as *"brilliant artists, all grown artists,"* several of whom he considered his *"favorite poets."* As an intern with a local television news station, Valeria Rojas said she studied and sought to blend the styles of three different reporters she worked around, one whom she considered a great storyteller, one who was *"fact, fact, fact but made it so interesting,"* and one who was the *"strict teacher."* She said she was *"always talking to them about my writing."* In a pre-college summer enrichment program, Wren Roberts was exposed to the spoken-word performances of her poet-instructor, from whom she learned that poetry could address public issues. *"He was so engaging. He had the most powerful pieces,"* she explained. *"He did it to share injustices that are happening and he made spoken word connect with that for me.*" Tracey Copeland, a 25-year-old lifelong fiction writer, was the youngest member of a collective for gay and lesbian writers, where she said role models were helping her find the resolve to write non-fiction pieces about lesbian experience, something she had avoided as a younger writer. Alexis Harrison, who was a prolific teen novelist but did not know much about the publishing industry, began attending commercial writing institutes that were offered in the city where she was raised and then, as a college student, she sought out writing institutes offered through the extension unit of her state university. She explained:

I went to a writers' conference and it was helpful. Afterwards I sent [the coordinator] *a few pages of my novel and she critiqued them and mentioned different things I could do, and so I started a dialogue with her. It was so helpful because I had read so many things* [about being a writer] *and tried to be the best I could be but it really did take an expert opinion to give that final push.*

Three of the individuals I interviewed received Saturday-morning writing instruction as well as performance opportunities under the auspices of Turner Brothers Entertainment,[37] a non-profit production and promotion enterprise founded by two creative-minded brothers as a venue for spoken-word poetry performances and gospel music. These two brothers, one an avocational poet outside of work and the other a graphic designer, had grown up in the African American community of the city to which they returned after college. Through various joint sponsorships, they arranged spoken-word events at libraries, community centers and arts arenas, literally connecting teens and adults with stages, microphones, amplifiers, and large, appreciative audiences. As gospel songwriter, poet, and spoken-word performer Robert Jackson explained it, the Turner brothers *"are key to pretty much everything I do right now. They are my company in some ways."*

In a few instances, well-established and canonical writers did appear – in person – in the lives of these aspiring writers. These personal contacts, while brief in some cases, were highly charged, enabling important insights and validating ambitions. As a young child, Marcus Gleason met Judy Blume, his sister's favorite children's author, at a book signing at his local library. In that encounter, he said, he realized that a book had an *"actual author."* While attending a national poetry slam, Nick Barrington found himself in conversation with slam champion Anis Mojgani, a figure, he said, from whom he learned that poetry was allowed to be funny. Carla King was working for a campus literary magazine when she landed an in-person interview with one of her idols, Nathan Englander, an author who, over a conversation about one of his short stories, convinced her that *"it was practical to be a storyteller."* Alexis Harrison initiated a correspondence with poet Nikki Giovanni, who willingly commented on one of Alexis's poems:

I actually wrote to Nikki Giovanni and she responded. It was the craziest thing. I was excited. She is teaching at Virginia Tech so I wrote to her. I had no idea if she would respond. I said I really admired her work and I asked if she could give me advice or feedback on a poem I sent her. And she actually wrote back, not once but twice, in handwritten little notes. That was a surreal experience to actually have a letter correspondence with her.

Brave New Voices teen slam artist Chinaka Hodge made several critical appearances in the poetic life of Akira Burkes, first in the form of an HBO video, "Can You Spit?", which was shown in a summer school class that Akira attended between her ninth and tenth grade high-school years. It was the first time Akira was exposed to spoken-word poetry and it changed her life. Of Chinaka Hodge she said:

I saw her spit. She was gorgeous, she was beautiful. I'd never been around this before. The way she delivered her stuff, it just touched me. This is poetry. But she is saying it. I didn't know you could perform poetry like that. I remember being so excited. As a matter of fact I had this yellow wired notebook with me at the time, college-ruled, and I had been writing in it and I'm looking around class, like, I write, I write poetry. I can do the same thing too.

Before the summer was out Akira performed at (and won) her first poetry slam, held at her neighborhood library, and soon qualified to compete in a citywide slam affiliated with the national organization, Youth Speaks. To her surprise, the featured performer and host for the event was none other than Chinaka Hodge:

It was time to slam and I do remember seeing her walk through the door. I was starstruck. Oh, my God. Does anyone know her? She called me up [to the stage]. *I did my poem. And* [referring to the judges' scoring] *it was ten, ten, ten.*

Within the next year Akira had competed all the way to the national competition. Excited but also profoundly intimidated by what she perceived as many more polished and experienced poets around her, she spent a nervous night in a Los Angeles hotel with team-mates from her hometown:

We went up to the room. I was looking around, seeing all these different people from everywhere. We didn't know what to do. It was the night before the competition and here comes Chinaka Hodge walking along the [inner hotel] *balcony. Our patio door was open. We called, Chinaka, come here, please, please help us. We don't know what we are doing. She sat on the bed and gave us an hour-long pep talk.*[38]

These accounts underscore the powerful influence that writing masters, as embodied, charismatic figures, can play in a writing-based literacy. Beyond what they write, these figures show aspirants how authors hold themselves in the world. It can't escape notice how the *hand* electrifies several of these encounters – the author's signature in the book, the intimacy of an author's handwritten notes, the astonishing classroom scene in which a ninth grader's handwritten notebook of poems is metamorphosed by a poet's "touching" performance.[39] Above all these accounts illustrate how the long, entrepreneurial traditions of the working writer project into contemporary social life. Signing books, sitting for interviews, making videos, competing for performance titles, headlining literary events, maintaining interactive websites – all of these are ways by which contemporary career writers promote themselves, cultivate followings, and expand readerships. But for the writing-oriented aspirant, these activities provide important extra-textual clues about how to be a writer.

Where personal contact with working writers was missing, some individuals I interviewed turned to biographical and autobiographical accounts of writers' careers. Lela Shao was one of them. *"I just started looking at paths to follow to become a writer,"* she said. *"It's interesting to see how successful writers get to where they are today. You just really have to stick with it."* The 17-year-old poet Marissa Fernandez closely followed the life of rap artist Eminem, whose work first inspired her to start writing. *"The more I learned about him – how he wrote everything that happened in his life ... and created a song out of what recently happened – I was able to relate to him in that way,"* she said.

I have made a point of chronicling the presence of what could be called modern-day writing masters in the lives of these aspirants in order to further establish the worldly work of writing as a central underpinning in writing-based literacy. In much of the conventional wisdom, aspiring writers are advised – often by well-established authors – to apprentice themselves to the master texts of their societies. Francine Prose (2007), for one, begins *Reading Like a Writer* with the observation that: "Like most – maybe all writers – I learned to write by writing and, by example, by reading books" (p. 1). This advice is based largely in the belief that writing is a text-based skill that develops in a synergistic relationship with reading and that writing know-how is best passed from one person to another through the language of an exemplary text. But the reading-to-write theory of transmission underestimates the direct, person-to-person role that practicing writers play in the support of writing-based literacy – those who model, instruct, mentor, or inspire writing through their embodied presence and who do so in contexts of production and reproduction.[40] This person-to-person contact provides sources of knowledge, validation, and insight that are not confined to textual strategy and in fact cannot easily be transmitted through texts. When aspirants realize that *"I can do that,"* the *that* is not always and not mainly about text-making but, more broadly, is about ways of occupying a desired form of life. And if they call out, *"please, please help us, we don't know what we are doing,"* a human answer from someone who does know seems most satisfying, most likely to provide that *"extra push."*

The spoken-word and hip-hop poetry movements are especially interesting in this regard. The extraordinary growth over the last two decades in the number of young people who participate in spoken-word events is often attributed to how this literary movement honors oral traditions, is racially and ethnically inclusive, foregrounds social justice concerns, and connects to community – all worthy attributes (Fisher 2007, 2009; Somers-Willett 2009). But it is also important to observe how the arrangements of spoken-word/slam poetry events evocatively recuperate some of the original conditions of writing teaching and learning: person-to-person transmission through the physical performance of signature styles. Based not in liberal arts education but in workshop and performance, organized around contests, and quasi-commercial in nature, it is a movement that privileges the heritage of writing over the heritage of reading.[41]

To sum up, aspirants I interviewed often encountered writing masters in their inky element, at work, or teaching the work, as living, breathing role models. Like writing masters of old, many were positioned outside of school or at the margins, in afterschool or extracurricular, elective or alternative spaces. Now, in some cases, writing masters appeared as part of regular schooling. Two people I interviewed attended high schools for the arts, where faculty members were active writers. One was taught high-school journalism by a former newspaper reporter. One recalled her fourth grade teacher as being *"quite a writer herself."* Four of the college students I interviewed were enrolled in creative writing programs in which faculty were active, publishing writers; four others were enrolled in a well-regarded hip-hop arts program in their university, whose instructors came from the professional world. But even in school, writing masters could appear at the margins. Wren Roberts, a poet who also was a star athlete at her high school, told me she started receiving writing guidance from two of her athletic coaches, after they disclosed that, like her, they participated in the spoken-word poetry scene. Wren was following the poetry blog of one of those coaches. Another spoken-word poet, Shameka Howard, described how, after performing a poem at an assembly at her school, she was approached by a security guard, also a poet, who had seen the performance. *"After the show she came and got me and said we should read our poems back and forth,"* Shameka explained. *"I had a little notebook where we kept in contact with each other so she could see how I was doing. She also introduced me to a website for urban poetry and we wrote each other there."*

On the whole, as I mentioned, contact with writing masters was occurring not only and not mainly through traditional academic channels but in extracurricular, off-site, or alternative school spaces. Even the highly prestigious hip-hop arts program, in which four of the college students were enrolled, was housed not in an academic department but in the university's office of multicultural affairs. To the extent that writing teachers of any kind are associated with vocational practice, they occupy lower rungs in the liberal-arts university; so in that way, we can say that writing masters continue to be marginalized by the "common" school. But even more marginalized in the history of writing masters are parents and other family members. The reading parent is an iconic figure in the history of US literacy, the epitome of the responsible, school-oriented caregiver. But the writing parent remains decidedly missing from this cultural tableau. While a few of those I interviewed recalled parents being recruited into their elementary school classrooms as scribes to record the narratives of children too young to write on their own, this connection between parents and writing otherwise went unrecognized. The role of families in passing along writing skills and values remains a hidden, even suppressed vein in school-based, reading-privileged literacy ideology.

Before moving on, one more aspect of the vocational power of writing needs to be explored – how "occupation: author" can be recruited even into projects of private self-development.

Leveraging the vocations of writing

When massive protests against a controversial governor broke out one winter in the town in which he grew up, 22-year-old college student Thomas Janosi put a camera around his neck and headed to the central square, where protesters congregated. He was not a reporter, was not an editorialist for any news organization, and was not planning to post a report online. Rather, Thomas was a private essayist, someone who used writing to develop his opinions on current events and reflect on the progress of his life. He knew the camera around his neck would help him get to the front of the crowds:

I thought I was pretty clever. I dressed up in very nice clothes for me and took my camera down there and tried to let people think I was press and not necessarily tell them any differently. In any case, it worked and I would get right up on the front line of every speaker. Even on the Republican side, when the Tea Partiers came down and had a bunch of speakers, I was right up there with a CNN camera guy, snapping pictures of Herman Cain. I would go down [to the protests] *not to get involved but just to inject myself into the situation and try to expose myself to it.*

Thomas was among several young adults I interviewed who wrote enthusiastically outside of school, often with great daily discipline, but did not plan to pursue careers as writers. These individuals did not submit work for formal publication or perform their work in public. They did not pursue or plan to pursue writing degrees in college, and did not hold writing jobs or internships. Rather, they wrote in obscurity, for only intrinsic rewards, sharing their work with no or few other people. I came to label these individuals tentative or unaffiliated writers, to signal their relative social isolation from the kind of vocational aspirations, social structures and resources that were emphasized in the earlier parts of this discussion. In some cases, this social isolation had to do with individuals' young ages or socioeconomic straits or the way they were tracked in school – or all three. In other cases the disaffiliation was simply because these individuals had other goals, or were not sure where exactly writing stood in their lives, or else they regarded their writing as too inadequate to ever turn pro (even though they may have liked to). But their experiences are of interest here because of how these individuals nevertheless would leverage vocational "props" as part of their exploratory engagement with writing. In the case of Thomas Janosi, he knew he could use a camera and a journalist's demeanor to exploit the public's deference to the press and get close to the action that interested him. But he also used the role of the news reporter to give himself the kind of objective stance he sought in working out his views of current events. The pose gave him permission to "inject" himself into the situation while also obligating him to hear and represent both sides – a move that was important to the private, contemplative value writing held for him.

Thomas tried on "occupation: author" not so much for the purpose of claiming it but more for the purposes of trading on its socially recognized properties and resources in order to carry out a project of self-edification. Critical to such a project are popular genres that carry socially shared understandings about the worldly work of writers. Popular genres often come to be filled up with the routines, social responsibilities, and epistemologies of their best-known public pliers. Taking over these genres – seizing them not as means of reception but as means of production – commits unaffiliated writers to these well-recognized stances and responsibilities, and they become grounds of self-development. Another chief resource in these endeavors is the Internet, as it provides casual publishing opportunities – for example, Facebook and blogs – that allow experimentation with the feel and look of public authorship. In any case, these experiences demonstrate how the vocational apparatus associated with the writer remains relevant even when the writing is meant mostly for self-consumption. Taking a turn toward the responsibilities and rewards that society accords to the figure of the writer opens critical spaces for growth through writing.[42]

Marissa Fernandez, a 17-year-old high school junior who was born in Mexico and moved with her parents to the US as a baby, traces her awakening to writing to hearing the rap artist Eminem. She explained:

I have been interested in him ever since I heard one of his songs on MTV. The more I heard his songs and the more I learned about him – like he wrote down everything that happened in his life and would make a beat for it and create a song out of what had happened to him – the more I was able to relate to him in that way. It all started in sixth grade. My friend and I were both addicted to his music. So we were rapping to one of his songs and I said, oh, let's make our own. So we started writing down some random words that would rhyme and singing them back and forth and laughing about it. At first I took it as a joke but over time it became more serious.

When I met her, Marissa was writing raps on a nearly daily basis, keeping these handwritten compositions mostly to herself, stored in a bedroom dresser drawer. Like Eminem, Marissa used rap to express the pressures of her political and socioeconomic situation, pressures that registered most directly in her social isolation. Here Marissa illuminates how her own writing came to take over the functions that Eminem's songs had been serving in her younger life, rerouting her loneliness through the public, legitimized powers of the rap genre, and delivering solace through its feedback to her future self:

My mom and dad are overprotective of me. They don't like it when I leave the house. They are afraid of who I hang out with or where I go when I leave. So I'm usually at home in my room alone. And if there is something wrong going on I don't talk to my mom about it because her background is very different from mine. She was born and raised in Mexico and I was raised here. I know if I talked to her the perspective would be different. So when something happens to me I write it down. I let out my emotions and what I am feeling and let all my stress out on the paper. I hold on to it. And later on if I feel the same thing I can reread what I wrote. At least in my eyes I am not alone.

Marissa told me that at one time she kept a diary but it was too unmediated for comfort. In fact, after her brother discovered and read her diary, it created tensions in the family. "*I was pretty depressed and I didn't want anybody to worry,*" she explained, "*I didn't want to cause any conflict with the words I said.*" So the stance of the rapper became a compositional solution, providing a more mediated set of cultural permissions and audience relations – as well as an outlet for creativity – that allowed Marissa to overcome the constraints in her situation. Marissa's raps often address political issues like undocumented immigration, street violence, and discrimination. Although most stay in her bedroom drawer, if they are "*motivational*" and "*not too personal*" she will share them with close friends when they visit her. ("*I don't carry them around with me,*" she explained.) Or she will post them as statuses on Facebook. She likes the genre of the rap because "*it is just about getting the point straight across*" without "*all those similes and metaphors*" she associates with the indirectness of other kinds of poetry. Rap also is a genre that she finds well adapted to the literacy conditions of her society, giving her writing the potential of wide reach (even if shared only with a few friends). Marissa observed:

A lot of people listen to their iPods. People always have earplugs in. They don't read as much. So if I'm feeling something I will write it down as a rap on Facebook to see if people can relate to what I said. Most of the time people say, oh, that's a really good rap. So I think making a song is a good vehicle to make people listen to what I have to say and that's how I can get more people to hear me out.

Interestingly, like Marissa, Thomas Janosi keeps his essays mostly to himself, saved to a computer file named "Writings." He described the genre he writes in as "*almost editorials for newspapers that nobody reads.*" Occasionally he too will post an essay to Facebook *"for no other reason than to see what people think,"* he said. *"I'm sure nobody reads them except for one or two of my closest friends who might say, 'nice piece,' or something like that."* Despite having no wider audience, when these essays deal with high-profile current events, Thomas will research them scrupulously. *"I don't want to have an uninformed personal feeling that somebody could just throw out the window,"* he explained. Going through this process helps him to clarify his thoughts: *"I find myself writing when things are unclear, when I am trying to navigate through things."*

Being accountable to an audience that could be there (but usually isn't) also was important to 21-year-old college student Nellie Hanks, who at the time of our interview had been maintaining a blog for more than two years. The blog is a new and still evolving public genre, protean in form and function, accessible for low cost and relatively low stakes (*"all you have to do is register and suddenly you have a website dedicated to you,"* as another blogger put it). Yet its interactive potential, its published feel and look, its circulation in a broader blogosphere along with professional writers, allows leveraging of authorial status and social reach and accountability.[43] In the following, fascinating reflection, Nellie Hanks demonstrates through the blurred and fluctuating use of "you" and "I" how creating a publicly responsible text functions for private ends:

Yes, I actually go back and read [my blog posts] *a lot because they always make me laugh. My first post was about how hard it was to study in the library because there were so many people around. I will try to throw in a joke or something like that. I don't know if it is entertaining to anyone else but it's entertaining to me. I don't know how often* [my posts] *are read but it's more just for me. I notice that in a lot of my blog posts I don't necessarily give advice to people but just provide overall generalizations about life and about how to go about things and I always try to listen to myself and actually do this myself because I'm thinking, I'm telling somebody else to do this, I probably should do this myself. So sometimes where bad things happen in life, like somebody dies or you have a traumatic experience and I'll write a blog post about how, yeah, these things happen but you need to be able to move on and do something with your life that will make you happy. And then usually I will put a song or something at the end to inspire you.*

Later Nellie remarked, *"I don't have a specific audience for the blog but when I write it I feel there is an audience."*

I have been trying to demonstrate how occupying authorship – stepping into the public role of the writer, using vocational props, and engaging the apparatus of publication – can serve in private projects of self-development. These elements are leveraged to maximize accountability and create social values that are then recouped for self-understanding and self-soothing. We might say that the unaffiliated writers profiled here experience their authorship most productively when they return to dialogue with their own texts. That is, they engage in processes of self-authoring by composing texts they need to read. In doing so, they appeal, often cunningly, to what they know about the vocational workings of writers and their tools – for instance, the objectivity of the reporter, the social consciousness of the rapper, the equanimity of the advice columnist. These appeals lend parts – sets of routines, responsibilities, and public worth and accountability – that encourage and validate self-strengthening. It is not so much what they know about reading but what they know about writing that scaffolds these experiences.

That the vocational heritage of writing contributes so importantly to literate growth is a fact too often subdued and sublimated in liberal-arts education, where reading is privileged, the practical world of work is eschewed, and the text is extolled as the best teacher of writing. However, the foregoing discussion of "occupation: author" documents how a residual heritage of writing-based literacy – one that grew up outside of the school and in connection with work, apprenticeship, professions, art, commerce, and publication – persists in the experiences of school-going, writing-oriented youth of today. This heritage lives in their professional aspiration and ambition, in the effects of intellectual property regimes on their writing processes, in the social arenas in which many of them choose to perform or publish their writing, and in the kinds of employment many of these youths seek out. This heritage also registers in the presence of modern-day writing masters, often liminal figures who instruct through direct modeling and validate aspirants by embodying the writing life. This vocational heritage can manifest subtly whenever properties of authorship are leveraged, even in circumstances with no ostensible vocational ends.

This heritage is also pertinent for interpreting reading–writing relationships in the lives of writing-oriented youths – the subject to which we now turn. How do writing-oriented youths make their way in a reading-dominant environment? How do competing loyalties and values that adhere to the heritages of writing and reading manifest in their life experiences and with what kinds of resolutions? Most important, how does *being* or *wanting to be* a writer infiltrate reading experiences? These questions are taken up in the following section.

Writing over reading

When Akira Burkes was in elementary school, she and her mother attended a school-sponsored book fair, where Akira came across an unusual-looking book that captured her attention. It had a lock on the side. She explained:

It was blue. It had a cat on it. It was very short and square. I remember opening it up, looking at the blank pages. And I got kind of apprehensive. Now what do I do? I felt awkward. There was nothing there, but there should have been something on the pages. I needed to fill them. So I convinced my mother to give me money to buy this diary and I just started to journal.

Book fairs are designed to promote reading and to bring parents and children together around books. They reinforce the idea that reading is a wholesome pastime; that good parents provide their children with books; and that reading enhances school success. Here, the diary, tucked in among the book displays, is a physical reminder of the minor role that writing plays in such official promotions of literacy. If anything, the lockable diary, a place where a child can hide private thoughts, does not exactly suggest the same kind of family togetherness or wholesomeness as a book. So it is a culturally disruptive presence. But this scene also demonstrates how the diary is a cognitively disruptive presence for Akira. She approaches this book from the expected reading stance, noticing the shape and the cover and trying to operate it as a book. But reading fails to serve. To imagine writing, Akira must abandon reading.

Now, some might argue instead that this scene shows how seamlessly reading and writing intertwine and how much Akira's prior experience with reading ushers her into writing. How else would she know what to do with a blank page? But I want to draw attention to the dissonance, the break, the gap that is expressed in Akira's sense of apprehension and awkwardness. The reader's way of thinking is not absent from this occasion but it proves inadequate for the occasion. It fails to operate. Something else is required of Akira, namely, an embrace of the enterprise of writing, a decision – made here privately and on her own – to take the authorial position. These reported acts of realignment – what I came to call *writing over reading* – routinely occurred in environments where reading was being promoted and where participants were being constructed or treated as readers. Indeed, as we will see later on, such ruptures often occurred during reading itself.

When situated in early childhood especially, writing over reading could have a precocious, excessive, even transgressive quality, rearranging customary power dynamics and giving youngsters a feel for the heady social role of the author. Bill Watson, now a political blogger, described how, one day in his kindergarten classroom, he took up ink stamps that children were supposed to use to label their drawings and used them to compose a six-page narrative. His teacher was so taken with this precocious act that she walked him and his story to the principal's office to show them off. *"It was the only time I ever went to the principal's office in my entire school career,"* he explained. *"She showed my story to the principal and they talked about it for a little while."* Novelist and poet Carla King had similar memories of being singled out by surrounding adults on the basis of her compositions:

In the early grades, like second grade, I was allowed to be the one to quiet the kids because they would let me tell ghost stories I had made up. Or I would do this over at my friends' houses. My best friend's mom always said she loved it when I would come over because I got everybody to be quiet with my stories.

In several memories, early writing was recognized by its excess, by going beyond the expected bounds of school assignments. Akira Burkes recalled:

When we'd have these tests [in elementary school] *there was always a portion where you were supposed to write a little paragraph-long answer. I always would fill up the whole page and some of the back. And the teacher was like, okay, she's a writer. She likes to write. And the teacher started to push me.*

Novelist and poet Alexis Harrison had a similar memory: *"In seventh and eighth grade I guess my teachers always knew I was going to be a writer. I intrinsically knew it because they would ask for a story, maybe a two-page story or a five-page story, and I would give them a fifteen-page story."* Not all teachers were appreciative of these precocious excesses, however. Amanda Costner recalled:

In first grade we had these tables groups and we were given little easy-readers about famous Americans, and we just had to write down what we knew about them. I was brainstorming about Abraham Lincoln and just started writing a story about him. But I got in trouble and had to erase it all because I was too far ahead.

The compulsion to write puts these youngsters "far ahead" of the developmental stage prescribed or expected in the instructional contexts around them, where students are constructed as readers (or listeners) first and where writing is primarily used as a check on reading. Early expressions of elective authorship can be valued when they rise up in these settings, but they are treated as precocious, singular, atypical, maybe even worrisome (*"I remember reading my elementary school report card,"* high-school novelist Kaitlin Rieser told me, *"and teachers said they would see me writing by myself."*). In reading-privileged environments, orienting to writing manifests as excess that spills beyond page lengths, overtakes tools, defies expectations, and marks one as different. It also gives very young children the heady experience of communicating one-to-many (a position usually reserved for older authorities) or having their writing discussed by others (a position usually reserved for official school texts).

Such authorial assertions at times could lead to social awkwardness and even, at times, academic difficulties. Amanda Costner, a prolific and serious 16-year-old novelist, recounted an occasion when she decided to seek a response from her teacher on one of her fictional pieces in progress – a piece in which the teacher happened to be one of the characters. *"I had put the teacher in the story as a character,"* Amanda explained, *"and I think it just weirded her out. She was supposed to email me over the summer but I never got the email."* Amanda also recalled how a classmate in middle school, knowing that she wrote fiction, asked if he could read her latest piece. But when she tried to hand him over a forty-page story, he changed his mind. *"I was just tearing all these pages out of my notebook. And he was like, 'Wow, I didn't realize it was this long.*

Maybe another time.'" Aspiring news correspondent Valeria Rojas recalled exasperating family members with her incessant attempts to interview them:

I knew I wanted to be a journalist since I was little. I would pretend to be a reporter and interview my family. My uncle would say, "Stop it, stop it. You are doing too much." I would get mad when they tried to stop me because I liked doing it.

At the time of our interview, 16-year-old Verdell Fisher was taking a year-long break from involvement in an afterschool spoken-word club on the advice of family and school counselors. *"Last year I was writing and writing, and academics went out of the way,"* he said. *"But now academics come first, then poetry."*

Several of the individuals I talked with said they wrote surreptitiously in the classroom, under the guise of taking lecture notes or doing homework in study hall.[44] *"I'm constantly writing, even in classes,"* said Carla King. *"I'll suddenly just know I have to write and I'll do it while I am taking notes."* David Platz said, *"I'm not very good at paying attention in class so I did some of my writing there."* Others used classroom discussions and debates to spark ideas for their writing. *"The best place to get ideas is always in class,"* said Robert Jackson. *"I will get a couple of lines and write them down, words that are not my own and that I have not yet digested, and then I'll go home and work on them."*

In fact, it was during a lively literary discussion in one of his high-school English classes that college student Graham Fletcher made a life-changing decision to become a fiction writer. In the following account Graham shows how, like Akira Burkes at the book fair, in the midst of being constructed as a reader, he overtakes the situation and claims the pleasures of writing over the pleasures of reading. Here is how Graham described his awakening as a writer at the age of 17:

We were sitting around discussing the novel, discussing elements of it with our teacher, who would add different comments to help guide our discussion. It really connected me to the world of literature. Such engaging discussions about ideas. And I really wanted to put on paper the kinds of ideas that were swirling in my mind. I wanted someone to read my short story or novel and take something away from it and not necessarily be changed immediately by what they read but walk away with their mind brewing with ideas. That's how I felt in that class. Just because those fifty minutes of discussion were over didn't mean the discussion would end. Now, when I'm in the zone of writing, it's as enjoyable putting a scene on paper as it is reading a beautifully crafted scene. Holding or advancing some kind of meaning is the way that I most strongly connect to the ideas of whoever it is, whether the author is an historical author, a contemporary author, or the author is myself.

Inspiring students to become literary writers is rarely an explicit goal of a high-school literature class. Rather students are trained to be readers, perhaps active, responsive, and critical ones, but readers nevertheless. Discussions and writing assignments that accompany such classes are almost always analytical or critical, with an eye toward rendering interpretation. But Fletcher blasts through that position, not so much on the power of an exemplary literary text but on the power of what is going on around the text, realizing that rather than engaging in discussion, he could produce something for others to discuss. In his final remark, this young man suggests the deeply satisfying experience that the act of writing gives him, including allowing him to treat himself as an author while engaging with his own writing (a common pleasure among those I interviewed). Though this scene puts us close to what I think Francine Prose (2007) and others mean by "reading like a writer," it would be more accurate to say that Fletcher had to make a break with reading to arrive at this position. The insights came not through analyzing and emulating the language of a masterful text but by appreciating the wider social impact of authorship itself.

Indeed, several of the young people I interviewed appealed to their writerly experience to resist the readerly role they were expected to fill in literature courses, especially when it came to what they saw as over-interpretation of texts. Justine Strater was typical of this group. A voracious lifelong reader, Justine regarded reading as one of her ethical and professional responsibilities as an aspiring literary artist, yet she expressed occasional impatience with having to read analytically in school:

Sometimes I just want to enjoy the work. You can't analyze everything. It's really odd to me in academics. We have to analyze, dig apart everything, which is great because you should be able to find out things. But sometimes taking something at face value can have more of an impact than trying to tear it apart. Sometimes I feel that we start making up things that we see [in a text]. Maybe it wasn't meant to be that deep. Maybe it's just what it says and that's all there is to it. You'll never know unless you ask the artist and have them answer every question you have. But even artists don't know why they wrote that particular thing.

Kaitlin Reiser, another constant reader and prolific and serious novelist, was more blunt as she described her English classes:

Of course we do the what-do-you-think-of-the book thing. But then we will start looking at the themes, the hidden ideas of the author. I just don't think the authors meant for some of these things to be there. It is just the way it turned out. I don't think there is all this hidden stuff they want us to write essays about. It's the only time I really haven't liked writing.

Space does not allow a full accounting of all the "writing over reading" incidents that arose in the interview testimonies. In general, orienting to writing in contexts that were constructing them as readers was a common, ongoing effort of the young adults I interviewed, affecting their experiences in school, at home, among friends, and in the wider society. But before moving on to consider how such an orientation to writing manifests during private acts of reading, I want to share another memory of the indomitable writer Akira Burkes. This memory from early schooling fully epitomizes what it takes to gain an authorial position that resists and exceeds the literacy routines of a reading-dominant environment. Akira recalled a homework exercise that occurred frequently in her schooling. After reading a chapter from an assigned trade book, students were given a list of vocabulary words taken from the chapter and told to compose individual sentences that used each vocabulary word appropriately. Such an assignment, like so many in school, uses writing as a check on reading comprehension.[45] To the extent that the assignment supports writing development, it is in the area of reading-based vocabulary building, a skill classically associated with a text-transmission view of writing. But, as we will see below, Akira transgresses the presumptions of the assignment. Like Bill Watson with the kindergarten stamps, she infuses the materials at hand with excessive narrative drive. She explained:

We had gotten to the Berenstain Bears books, and I would have to do my homework, and I would go ride my bike. It was over on the south side near Moreland Rd. and there was nothing but hills in between the apartments, and I would ride my bike down the hills, and I would just imagine myself going somewhere. So I would make up these adventures in my head and then I would go and write my homework with the vocabulary words in it.

It is interesting to note how the first sentence of this memory (*"We had gotten to the Berenstain Bears books, and I would have to do my homework, and I would go ride my bike"*) coheres only when understood as an account of how Akira went about assembling elements of a composing process strong enough to address yet overtake the assignment. By imagining herself as author, Akira allows her adventures to ride over the meanings of the official text. The assigned words are torn completely from the reading context and given a new narrative origin. This is how writing triumphs over reading.

Attention now turns to how reading–writing relationships are perceived by these writing-oriented youth and how an orientation to writing affects the reading experience. All of the thirty young adults I interviewed said they thought they had learned to read before they had learned to write, primarily because reading was "pushed" at home, most commonly when parents read to preschool children or took them to the library or bought them books. The high cultural priority afforded to reading, its association with learning, language development, and school readiness, means children are much more likely to experience reading first and writing later. So the perception that writing flows from reading may be the phantom effect of a normative social practice more than it is a developmental necessity.[46] Be that as it may, several young adults I interviewed did believe in the indispensable role of reading in writing development. As poet and novelist Alexis Harrison remarked:

I do believe you cannot be a writer without being a reader because reading is where you get your knowledge base from. I was a very voracious reader when I was younger. It was all that I would do really, is read, read, read. The writing started a little bit later. For me, being a reader drove me to write.

Novelist Lela Shao took a similar view:

Without reading I would just not know what to do. You read a lot and these things go subconsciously into your mind and when you are writing your own stuff, you can pick from everything you read and it all comes out together. I read a lot more than my brother did and I don't want to sound pretentious but I'm a bit better writer than he is because I read a lot more.

Political blogger Bill Watson sees a direct connection between limited reading and limited writing:

I think reading is essential in order to become a good writer. The way that you are exposed to good writing affects the way that your writing comes out in the end. You see vocabulary you might not be exposed to. You see writing styles that look appealing. And so I think for a long time I was really good at writing. I was above the curve because I did a lot of reading when I was younger. Now [as a college senior] *I get the feeling other people have caught up with me because they have more time to read the higher level books that I haven't had the opportunity or time to read. So I think there is definitely a direct relationship between the reading you do and the writing you produce.*

But not everyone I talked with held the view that writing flows from reading. It might be fairer to say, for instance, that for Nick Barrington, writing drove him to read, and that the more direct relationship was between the writing he produced and the reading that he did. *"The more I started writing, the more I started reading,"* he explained, *"so I was just reading poetry all the time."* Verdell Fisher also found reading through writing. *"I was playing around with rhymes,"* he said, *"and then went to the library and asked the librarian to show me the poetry books."* Journalist and blogger Claudia Baum believed that her reading only began to develop after she started publishing articles in her student newspaper. Here she inverts the usual reading-to-write formula to show how reading can be well learned through writing:

When I became a writer, I got to understand that I could make somebody think this way or that way depending on how I positioned words. So then I realized how other authors must be challenging readers in the same way. So now I find myself wanting to read more challenging books.

Otto Rivlin, another student journalist, also noticed how writing enhanced reading:

It's like when you ride in a car you don't pay attention, but as soon as you get your driver's license you are much more attentive. I used to read the paper and think nothing of it. Now I might read and say, hmm, that was editorializing or maybe they should have gotten a different interview.

Not everyone in this study liked to read or called themselves avid readers. Not everyone saw reading as a necessary foundation for writing. As with pet-book writer Evan Davies, some individuals avoided reading. Or they found reading paled in impact when compared to writing. Or they preferred the cognitive engagement that came from reading their own writing instead of someone else's. Or in some cases they lacked the physical surroundings that supported reading. *"I write, I don't read,"* explained David Platz, *"This is what I tell* [my creative writing professor] *when he asks me if I have read this or read that. And I say, I don't really read, actually. I play video games more. I watch movies more."* Poet Shameka Howard considered herself much more skilled in writing than in reading. *"You can't always read what you want to read,"* she said, *"but you can always read what you want to write." "I have never been much of a reader,"* said Marissa Fernandez. *"I like to read but it irritates my eyes. The lighting in my room is not as I wish it were and there is no area for me to sit for a very long time."* Cordelia Tanner was an avid and successful writer who mostly avoided reading. A college senior who worked as an outreach coordinator for a medical research center, Cordelia spent several hours a night doing personal writing and blogging, primarily in connection with her entrepreneurial plans to develop non-profit programming for the educational and social uplift of African American girls. Her elective reading consisted almost wholly of doing research for her own writing. Of the relationship between reading and writing in her literacy development, she said:

I can read fine. I just don't like to read. Reading makes me sleepy no matter when I do it. Even with leisure books I won't finish them unless they are super interesting. I'm a crazy multi-tasker so when I'm writing I can have other things on the screen that spark my mind and help me write. But when you are reading, other things around you don't really coincide with it. Also, I'm a big picture type of person, so when I do research, I am always skimming. I get the big picture and move on. But I don't skim when I am writing. I read what I write over and over to make sure that it's clear in my mind, to make sure that I really understand what I am writing. With reading, I feel very distant from reading.

Thomas Janosi, another individual who preferred writing over reading, expressed similar distance from reading. While acknowledging he has picked up *"utilitarian"* information from reading (*"I'll probably subconsciously use things that I have seen, and I have no trouble spelling or with grammar for some reason"*), he went on to observe:

I'm less engaged when I am reading. If it's fiction, then it seems not applicable [to what I write]. *It's hard to become engaged in it as deeply as a real-world idea that I want to explore. And if it's non-fiction, it's after the fact. The discussion has already happened as opposed to something that I can contribute to or feel like I am exploring.*

Journalist Otto Rivlin expressed a similar view. *"Writing is more active, more interactive,"* he said. *"Reading means somebody else has done it and you are seeing what they did. In writing, I am making my own mark, doing my own thing."* Then there were individuals like clothing entrepreneur, college student, and published book author Sean Kelly, who was a lifelong reader but saw reading and writing as different from each other: *"I wouldn't associate reading and writing with one another or tie them together. I've been an avid reader but at the end of the day you get more out of writing."* Even reading advocate Alexis Harrison thought writing was a more complete literacy experience than reading. *"When you are reading you are internalizing things and you are building worlds and expanding your imagination,"* she said, *"so the experience you get from reading is your own. But the words aren't. With writing I could have ownership as well as the reading experience, so it was all mine."*

As we can see, reading–writing relationships among the writing-oriented arise from a complicated range of experiences and attitudes – well beyond what might be implied by the pat belief in the ameliorative powers of reading for writers. Many of the individuals in this study did develop their writing through reading, but others developed their reading through writing. The engaging power of writing drew some of these individuals away from reading just as, as we saw earlier, reading could intimidate fledgling writers and draw them away from writing. Some of those I interviewed made a point of reading or listening to the same genres in which they wrote. Others told me they never read or heard the kinds of texts they wrote.

At the level of lived life, the relationship between reading and writing is not smooth.[47] The two often can be at odds with each other or compete with each other. Certainly this is true when it comes to time. Reluctant reader David Platz was typical when he observed: *"It's a time thing. That's why I write so late. And reading suffers because of that. I have to take time to sit down and crack open a book, and I'm less motivated to do that than to write."* In fact, some of the biggest defenders of reading as a support for writing said that the more serious they became about their writing, the less they read, especially when they had to juggle school and jobs as well. *"Already I do read less now that I am a writer. I will say that,"* observed Alexis Harrison. *"I miss it but it is a time issue. Especially because you are revising your work a lot, you can't read as much as you want. I have almost given it up."*

"Now that I am a writer" is a key phrase that can carry us into consider-ing how an orientation to writing infiltrates the experience of reading itself. Whatever different stances these young adults adopted toward the practice of reading, evidence abounded that when they did read, they affiliated with the

enterprise of authorship.[48] As we will see below – in what by now is a familiar theme of this chapter – this affiliation went beyond a narrow, text-based focus on reading to learn technique or craft. Rather, this affiliation favored forms of reading that engaged broad social, cultural, and vocational dimensions of writerly consciousness.

First, however, it is important to note that many said they did indeed attend to stylistic technique or craft during reading, a strategy long advocated and practiced in school-based writing instruction. But, interestingly, attending to technique served many functions for these writing-oriented youth beyond expanding a stylistic repertoire. Some, for instance, attended to technique in order to compare their own styles to other styles (often favorably). Others attended to technique out of a sense of collegiality, in much the same way that an actor might appreciate the performance of another actor, with a sense of belonging to the same group. Additionally, reading for technique was seen by some as a dangerous compromise to originality – a trap they worked to avoid.

Beyond technical awareness, however, an orientation to writing entered the reading experience at a more fundamental level – one that connects more broadly to the vocational heritage of writing. Just as we saw earlier in this chapter how the longing to be or become a writer could permeate writing from an early age, so too could it permeate reading. From very early childhood, many of the individuals I interviewed associated reading with the urge to write. This early merging of reading into the writing orientation reveals that what matters is not so much what is taught by a text but what is brought to a text – a resolve that "I can do this too." These experiences – widespread among the young adults I interviewed – suggest that what manifests as an early interest in reading could just as well be described as an early orientation to writing. Here are some typical remarks:

Whenever I read something I want to be able to write.

When I read I think, well, this is really cool. I could do this too.

So I met this lady where I live and she introduced me into poetry, just reading it, and then I thought, hey, I could write it.

The teacher would read these amazing books and I would try to mimic them.

I would feel so energetic about [what I just read] *that I would just write.*

I would be reading something that is really sweet or really sad and I'd turn that emotion into something else.

I would flip around a story when I was reading it to make it how I wanted it to be.

Interestingly, several of the individuals I talked with believed that authors explicitly design their work to encourage others to write. *"Part of the reason writers write is to inspire other people to write,"* said Lela Shao. Poet Matt

Gagen talked about how reading made him realize *"my passions are similar to other people's passions"* and that *"what I wrote wouldn't be Shakespeare but it would be my own thing."* Blogger Nellie Hanks said that when she reads other peoples' blogs she yearns for a wider audience for her own. She also talked about her drive to pay forward the indebtedness she felt toward other authors. *"I want other people to understand how I feel when I read,"* she said, *"and I guess the only way to do that is through my own writing."* Poet and novelist Carla King expressed a similar sentiment:

I grew up really poor and books did make my world better. So if I can write something that can transport somebody to another world, even if it is just for the space of the reading, that is making the world better.

Especially intriguing were the individuals who seemed to read out of a sense of solidarity with a larger writing community to which they felt they belonged (see Wegner 1998 for relevant validation). For them, reading was a direct way to support the enterprise of writing, socially, economically, and artistically.[49] Perhaps not surprisingly, this perspective was expressed most fully by spoken-word performers I interviewed. Justine Strater said she purchased chapbooks of poets she knew who lived in or visited her community. *"I like to buy their work to support them,"* she said, *"because let's be real – a lot of artists don't have a lot of money. That support is what keeps the community alive."* She also named four practices that she associated with being a "professional" artist: writing every day; getting criticism on one's work; reading and listening; and sharing one's work with the world. These processes sustain the community of writing. She elaborated:

If you want to be a successful artist, you have to be someone who grows. You are going to stop growing if you stop receiving what people have to say or listening to certain things or reading certain things. It's a conversation. I'm learning from other people. Then my writing in response also enhances the others.

Another spoken-word performer, Nick Barrington, rendered a subtle and fascinating account of how his style of reading is nested within broader styles of social interaction that help him locate himself in a network of writers. A frequent traveler to poetry slams throughout the country, he said:

If you go to the adult poetry slam, you now know someone from every state who does poetry and you have their book or they have your email. You can start a thread, you send a poem, they write back a poem. Or I always like to read authors' acknowledgment pages. You start to see that it's a whole world out there.

Believing that both reading and writing were *"insanely important,"* Nick described how recouping his responses during reading helped him *"test the limits"* of his writing, then went on to suggest how the publishing industry and even a library can sustain communities of writers:

Poetry publishing is getting pretty exciting in the States. People have been able to follow it more in the way that these publishing companies publish poetry from your community and that connects you. Or you connect through the poetry slam library and the chapbooks that [adult poetry slam] *artists bring home to you, and you just explore from there. These brilliant changes that can happen within me* [when reading] *have happened in the state of mind that makes me change the way I am or the way I act or the way I want to write poems from now on or what I gauge to be funny or what I gauge a funny poem can do. So it's seeing something and doing something else.*

Taken together, these accounts of writing–reading relationships among writing-oriented youth demonstrate the radical possibilities of a writing-based literacy, a literacy in which reading would primarily serve writing by serving the lives and development of those who write. It would be a literacy in which, to quote Otto Rivlin, everyone would get a driver's license. It would be a literacy in which institutions originally organized around mass readerships, like publishing houses or libraries, would maintain communities of writers and connect writers with other writers at every age. It would be a literacy in which the quality of texts would be gauged by how well they "inspire other people to write," to quote Lela Shao. If such a vision seems far-fetched, it is in part because of how a writing-first literacy would, to use Amanda Costner's words, "weird out" reading-dominated environments, including schools, by un-quieting youth and disquieting authorities. At the very least, these accounts of how a writing orientation enters the reading experience challenge narrow conceptions of what it means to read "like a writer." In fact, the young adults I interviewed did not read *like* writers. They read *as* writers. So when they read they attended not merely and not always to micro-level, sentence-level craft technique (a matter inordinately emphasized in writing instruction and guidebooks) but rather to larger spheres of social interaction, craft membership, aspiration, and ambition. Indeed, these larger spheres motivated and buttressed technical reading by showing these young adults writers not how to imitate but how to stand out, how to situate their own writing better, or how to act responsibly toward a community of other writers. Most instructive, they were able to overhear in a text an author's encouragement to join in. Poet Verdell Fisher was one such youth whose reading – with a little help from his teacher – homed in from an early age on the enterprise of authorship:

In the third grade, my teacher told us that for every book that you guys read, somebody put in the hard work to write it, to make it interesting, so that you can learn from it. So I took that as a wow. This writer got this book published because they knew what they were doing was going to help somebody else's life. And that's when I started writing poetry.

So far, this chapter has been building a theory of literacy based in writing, one that would be in tune with the communicative arrangements of our time, in which one-to-many modes of information and knowledge-sharing are being replaced by multi-directional, active, responsive networks of voices: a time, in short, when everybody must write. These shifts require us to go beyond laments about the ruination of reading to grasp the rise of writing and to acknowledge the important ways that writing in its own right differs from reading. This shift requires a confrontation with the gritty vocational heritage of writing and its association with work, competition, artisanship, commercialism, apprenticeship, performance, publicity – a heritage that, as we have seen, continues to catalyze the literacy experiences of writing-oriented youths, even as it remains muted in reading-dominant, school-based literacy instruction. A writing-based literacy also requires a better understanding of how reading itself is recruited into the writing orientation – how being someone who writes can shape the reading experience. As we have seen, a writing orientation can create wariness toward reading, particularly toward its association with passivity and conformity. At the same time, a writing orientation can invite strong forms of reading that organize around the enterprise of authorship – so strong that acts of writing can erupt during acts of reading and overtake them.

To complete this theory, one more main component needs to be explored: how the rise of writing can expand – and complicate – what we understand to be the formative experiences and effects of literacy. Through most of its history, mass literacy has meant a reading literacy. The value of literacy has rested in the perceived powers of reading to develop mind, improve character, and expand knowledge, among other attributes. Reading has long been associated with moral and civic uplift in the United States because of its sponsorship heritage: namely, evangelizing Protestant religions which made contact with the Good Book foundational to salvation; and the influence of Republicanism, which made reading critical to exercising the rights and duties of the informed citizen. Both these ideologies associated reading with goodness, providing cultural mandates for a universal reading literacy. This association only intensified as the society industrialized. Reading came to be treated as a mechanism for improving productivity and efficiency, and for integrating more rapidly into urban economies.[50] So the association of reading with self-improvement is built deeply into beliefs about the effects of literacy. This association lingers today in empirical studies that link reading to higher levels of political engagement as well as to personal attributes like empathy and social intelligence.[51]

But writing has held a tangential position, at best, within this belief system. Certainly writing has been associated with devotion and self-disciplining, although commonly in conjunction with the contemplative study of canonical texts or with the close observation of nature. We can see traces of this legacy in the connection that is made between writing and learning, the instrumental role that writing serves as an aid in retaining and synthesizing knowledge, and discovering, recording, and clarifying thought. In fact, the strong belief that writing improves learning has become a chief justification for assigning more of it in school, perhaps because it maintains a comfortable tie to reading (National Writing Project and Nagin 2006). Beyond school, the association of writing with devotions and self-discipline manifests in its use as a tool of psychotherapy; writing is used in informal and informal ways as part of trauma recovery and self-healing. Certain forms of expressive writing have been experimentally shown to reduce stress and promote mental health.[52]

Writing to learn and writing to heal both focus on what writing can do for those who carry it out. But these are minor avenues in the history of mass writing, where the value of writing primarily registers in its receivers, not its producers. What matters in writing is its rhetorical value, its projective and transactional value, its effects on others. Even in writing, then, reading is what counts. Nearly all of the energy in writing theory, research, and teaching has been devoted to understanding how writers create rhetorical value. The goodness of writing is understood in terms of its material impact in the world. In rhetorical theory, the goodness of the writer is not irrelevant, but usually matters only as an ingredient – rarely as an achievement – of writing. So as a consequence of these trends and traditions, writing has contributed little to defining the values, meanings, or effects of literacy and literate experiences. Today, in most minds, literacy remains synonymous with reading. As a result, we have developed little understanding of what writing does to writers. These influences are largely unexamined, even though they are in full throttle. Developing writing-based literacy requires expanding what we typically associate with or attribute to literacy by displacing reading as the defining experience and thinking about what is unique to writing experiences in comparison to reading experiences. So here the discussion turns to the following questions: what has an orientation to writing done for and to the thirty youths in this study? What kinds of literacy experiences has writing given them that reading cannot? And how might attention to these writing-based experiences expand (and even trouble) what we think of as the value and impact of literacy? That is the concern of this final section.

What writing does

Self-improvement – the project most commonly associated with elective reading in studies of mass literacy – also showed up as a major rationale for elective writing among those I interviewed. *"When I'm writing I'm talking to myself,"* said poet Verdell Fisher. *"I'm helping myself be a better person. I can be more."* *"Once I found a way to write about my troubles and not get so mad about them,"* said poet Shameka Howard, *"I thought it was a big accomplishment."* Thomas Janosi used life-writing to *"clear my head"* and find a career direction. Spoken-word artist Justine Strater said her writing helped her to *"dialogue with different parts of myself.*" Fiction writer Graham Fletcher said writing was a way that he opened himself to the world and "*changed my relationship to my own mind.*" Entrepreneurial writer Cordelia Tanner used blog writing to "*express goals in a creative way*" and as a way to manage her perfectionism. Fiction writer David Platz called writing a form of "*self-empowerment,*" continuing: "*It's an activation of everything I am interested in. It is an assertion of who I am, everything I know, and everything I love.*" Several study participants said they turned to writing to improve communication with parents and other loved ones or to let off steam that they feared could damage themselves or others. "*I am never the person who wants to look weak,*" said Wren Roberts about her uses of private writing for self-soothing.

Perspective-taking – a self-improvement skill widely associated with reading – also was considered a benefit of writing. News reporter Valeria Rojas said she tries "*to be the people*" in her journalism, by which she meant both those she writes about and those she writes toward. She also talked about meeting the challenge of covering news events "*where people are saying things you don't believe in.*" Otto Rivlin said writing news "*requires compassion*" because of the need to hear the stories of others. Then he went on to observe:

This kind of writing really allows me to educate myself. I'm living in [a liberal college community]. *I was pretty liberal and I still am. But I find myself thinking is that fair? Is that a fair conclusion to make? Or if I asked the other side, what would they say? I'm constantly thinking to myself, if I were to write an article on this, what would both sides say?*

Blogger Maury Lowell said he took special care with a blog post he composed during an overseas trip that took him to Palestinian areas of Lebanon. "*I spent a lot of time perfecting that blog post,*" he said, "*because the issues are complicated and I didn't want to misrepresent anything.*" "*I have to see other viewpoints and have my point of view shown,*" explained Shameka Howard of her poetry. Several fiction writers discussed the challenges and rewards of developing characters that were different from them by life experience, including gender, race, or sexual orientation. "*I end up writing about things I ordinarily wouldn't think about,*" said Carla King. Alexis Harrison said the need in fiction to manage small details and big ideas at the same time helps in other areas of her life, including her work in leadership positions.

Gospel songwriter, rapper, poet, and spoken-word performer Richard Jackson spoke in the most depth about the role of writing in strengthening the self, an exercise in truth-seeking that was connected to his spiritual life. Caught up unhappily in his younger years writing only about the prototypical themes of commercialized rap ("*that wasn't me*"), he eventually realized that "*my ideas* [in my writing] *could be as big as I make them,*" a realization that brought a sense of "*unlimited power.*" He continued:

All the ideas you associate on your own can come together and you create something new. That's how writing becomes a check and balance on who you are. If you don't explore yourself, you don't know yourself. If you don't know yourself, you can't write about yourself. You can't be true to somebody you don't know. So writing helps form who I am and helps me stay consistent with who I am.

In addition to self-improvement, many of the individuals I interviewed also associated their writing with social uplift. If, by cultural legacy, reading can be associated with *being* good, writing can be associated with *doing* good:

Anybody who writes a poem is doing a good thing.

When you make something memorable for someone, you are doing something right.

It would be awesome to live behind the legacy of doing something good and making the world better than when you entered it.

There is so much emotion that you can evoke with words and it can be used for good or evil.

When you are reporting on what happens you are not making things happen. But on the other hand, you are, because you are educating people and that's an important thing to do.

Writing is having responsibility for a whole world.

These testimonies together confirm that, like reading, writing often involves forms of internal and internalizing experience that are felt to expand, strengthen, educate, or improve the self. This experience no doubt accounts for the deep engagement so many of these young adults associated with writing. Both text-making and text-taking can develop perspective (on self and others) and new mental models (referred to as inner worlds by several of those I interviewed), and both are aspects of literacy that researchers link to social and intellectual growth. We might say that whatever writers eventually do for readers by way of their texts, they have first done for themselves. Or, to put it in the words of Shameka Howard, *"My poems have saved me and they have saved others, and so I continue to write."*

But in keeping with the mission of this chapter to focus on what makes writing-based literacy *different* from reading-based literacy, my interest is on formative experience that comes to these young adults uniquely from the authorship position. That is, my interest is in experiences connected to the writing of texts that have no equivalent in the reading of texts – at least in degree if not in kind. Adopting the social role, and the often public role, of the author has effects on you, but these effects are overlooked when literacy is defined and valued only from the reading or textual perspective. Particularly because writing is an externalizing as much as an internalizing experience, its most consequential effects are delivered back to writers through social contexts by actual (and not just imagined or anticipated) responses of other people. These worldly impacts of writing on the writer can bring great personal rewards in terms of social recognition or remuneration. But they also can bring great personal turmoil.

These tumultuous experiences might be called the social predicaments of authorship – situations experienced through authorial enterprises. Valeria Rojas, for instance, related what happened one day after she agreed to hastily complete her friend's homework for her. In this case, the assignment had been to write a poem. Valeria *"wrote a poem really fast"* and later had to listen silently as the teacher chose the ghostwritten work to praise in front of the class:

The teacher stood in the middle of the class and said what a great poem it was. She liked it more than my poem [i.e., the one she had written for herself]. *I was so mad. I wrote that! But I couldn't say anything.*

Earlier chapters have explored texts and ghostwriters in relationship to transactional systems of value and evaluation – systems certainly well understood in the laboring world of students. But I offer this anecdote here to demonstrate a more fundamental lesson attached to writing-based literacy: how letting one's own words loose in the world can set off impacts that do not merely register as textual meanings in readers' minds but also as consequences for you in the social circumstances in which you live. Learning to write, in part, means learning that your own texts can have impacts on you and others beyond what they say or mean.

These lessons were most pronounced – and not particularly light-hearted – for two college bloggers who used writing as part of their political activism and student government participation. After being elected to student government, 22-year-old Bill Watson began contributing to a right-leaning blogging collective because he wanted to separate his personal voice from his institutional position as chair of a high-profile, highly sensitive budget committee. *"The blog allowed me to put into my own words what exactly was happening on campus,"* he explained. However, he soon had the uniquely authorial experience of discovering a parody of his blog had sprung up on the Internet. *"You have to have an iron will to maintain that level of scrutiny,"* he observed. Left-leaning 21-year-old Maury Lowell started live blogging after being elected to student government in his first year of college. For him, blogging was an experiment in political process, enacting his values of transparency and inclusion. He would live-blog from student government meetings, providing running accounts of actions being taken, and he would simultaneously upload a link to Facebook and Twitter to draw in more readers. After meetings, he would prepare longer, more opinionated blog posts on issues of particular importance. But it wasn't long before his blog began to be visited by political adversaries. *"I was called out for being a Communist,* he said. *"They charged me with libel and threatened to sue me. If you Google my name you will see some pretty detrimental things."*

False attribution, libel, parody, ruined reputation – these are all social for-mations and phenomena associated with the consequences of writing, yet are rarely associated with the people's literacy.

Another predicament of authorship, which showed up especially among the poets and fiction writers I interviewed, had to do with managing relations between one's life and one's work. *Write what you know* is the most common advice given to beginning creative writers, an encouragement to draw on a familiar social world. But several of the writers – especially younger novelists who were teaching themselves to write by trial and error – wandered into some emotional difficulty on this point. Amanda Costner provided this account of her first novel, undertaken when she was 12:

In seventh grade I started a novel and made the mistake of using real people as characters. I had three of my closest female friends in it and then four guys. I had a huge crush on one of the guys at the time. I was the hero and my character was going through some hard times, and he was concerned about me and came in and helped me, which wouldn't have happened in real life because I only admired him from afar. It was my idea of what I wanted from him, a caring sort of mutual feeling. The plot was terrible. It was terrible. Also, I would try really hard not to write when I was mad at one of my friends because it would distort the story. You could tell when I was mad at somebody because I would make the character more annoying.

But even among the more experienced writers I interviewed, and even when they wrote non-personally, authorship could bring a heightened sense of confusion and vulnerability, especially in the vicinity of friends and family. College student Carla King, a fiction writer and well-published poet, said, "*My family loves to read my stuff probably more than I want them to.*" Asked to explain, she continued:

Mostly because I feel it's not completely connected to me so I feel odd having people read it. With poetry a lot of people assume that the poet is the speaker. With fiction they don't necessarily but I'm sure there is a part of me in it so that feels naked when people read that, and when it's people you know it's more awkward than when it is a stranger.

Entrepreneur and college student Sean Kelly was surprised by a similar sense of vulnerability that followed the publication of his advice book on how to start a small business. He explained:

I have sold a lot of t-shirts. If someone tells me they bought one of them, I say, hey, thanks for the business. I don't wonder what they are going to think. But when somebody tells me they are going to read my book, oh, man, I feel more naked. I'm out there. They are seeing my thoughts. [After I gave a copy of my book to my parents] *I was like, don't read it now, read it later.* [That feeling] *was kind of unexpected. I just don't know if I want everybody to know what I put there. But it's final.*

And then there is this authorial realization by the usually private essayist Thomas Janosi, who had second thoughts after posting a rare reflective essay on his Facebook page:

Every once in a while I would throw [an essay] *up on Facebook. I wrote one at the end of the summer that was on the feelings of being a seasonal worker and pulling the piers out and closing out and boarding up for the season. I guess the essay was really dark. One of* [my friends] *who works in a similar setting sent me a private message asking if she could share the essay with some of her friends. I got scared and pulled it off immediately. I pulled it off public access. This time it wasn't an idea in my head; it was an emotion that I was feeling. I could just see one of my friends asking me, "Are you okay? Do we need to talk?" I now understand why some people have pen names.*

To sum up, misattribution, parody, estrangement, charges of libel, self-exposure, the need for a pseudonym – these are all uncomfortable experiences that can attach to people who write yet rarely enter writing instruction as a focus for exploration and learning. Mostly students are taught year after year about the pitfalls of plagiarism, not the consequences of taking action through writing.

Because reading is largely an internalizing process, the effects of literacy have been sought mostly on the inside: in the formation of character, or the quality of inner life, or intellectual growth. These personal changes, developed by internalizing texts, are then supposed to bring changed action in the world. But writing per se *is* action in the world. It is an externalizing experience, and so its effects, as we have seen, can come back at writers from the outside. Thoughts can stay private during reading, but they are relentlessly externalized during writing. How literacy develops by way of a relentless broadcasting of thought is a critical question for teaching and research. But it can be expected to bring more wear and tear, more trouble, more risk. Writing risks social exposure, political retaliation, legal blame. It requires a level of courage and ethical conviction rarely cultivated in school-based literacy and rarely measured in standard assessments of writing ability.[53]

Conclusion

Throughout this chapter I have argued for a full return to the heritage of mass writing as a basis for advancing a genuinely writing-based literacy. It is a heritage, occluded but still robust, that has flourished not through liberal education but through the worlds of art, commerce, apprenticeship, vocational pursuit. It is a heritage in which the dependency of writing upon reading is not assumed, and in which reading, when pursued, serves to connect one who writes with others who also write. It is a heritage that compels us to search the pleasures and predicaments of everyday authorship for the meanings and effects of mass literacy. My argument has been based on evidence drawn from testimonies of thirty young adults who pursue literacy predominately through writing; individuals who elect to write on a nearly daily basis and in genres long considered bulwarks of a thoughtful reading literacy; individuals who have found ways to orient to writing even when the environment around them tries to orient them otherwise. It might be tempting to dismiss their experiences as belonging only to a gifted set of born writers – and therefore irrelevant to a wider population. But to do so would be to miss the radical possibilities that their example offers for imagining, before it is too late, a viable future for mass literacy: one that rides, instead of resists, the rising tide of writing.

4   When everybody writes

There was a time in the not-so-distant past when illiterate citizens were a protected class in the US justice system. Throughout most of the nineteenth century, being unable to read did not disqualify individuals, for instance, from serving as jurors in court proceedings.[1] Further, if their illiteracy led them into financial exploitation by others, those others could be held liable. Illiteracy was understood as a potential vulnerability yet not a stigma. By the early twentieth century, however, as Edward Stevens (1988) has demonstrated, the obligation to read had become thoroughly structured into social and legal relations. Illiterate people became ill-fitted to the practices of the court, and if they signed a contract without knowing what the words said, it was too bad for them if things went wrong. As illiteracy slid into stigma, the inability to read became increasingly punishing. Instead of being accommodated, illiterate people had to accommodate to the risks of living in a reading world. We might understand this shift simply as an inevitable outcome of rapidly rising literacy rates and expanding education. But Stevens shows the deeper churnings in the relationship between literacy and justice, as the presumed condition of universal literacy helped to fuel a buyer-beware way of doing business that altered the legal security of illiterate citizens.

Stevens captures a change in what some might call a literacy *mentalité*. *Mentalities* is a concept developed by sociologically oriented French historians of the mid-twentieth century who sought relationships between social structures at any given time or place and the shared understandings that people in that time and place used to get along in life. Dissatisfied with traditional historical research with its focus on wars, politics, big events, singular individuals, or intellectual elites, they set about illuminating the past in terms of the collective representations that organized and rationalized social life in different times and places. They especially were concerned with the sense-making practices of everyday people. Mentalities could limit a culture's horizon of understanding but at the same time could be the grounds for contestation, innovation, and transformation. Early proponents of the mentalities approach, Lucien Febvre and Marc Bloch, drew from the sociological thought of Emile Durkheim to focus their early research on long-term socioeconomic processes and structures. Over time, as various scholars took up the concept of mentalities, it gained different emphases, in some cases weighted, for instance, toward social psychology, or symbolic anthropology, or the discourse-centered critical approaches of Michel Foucault (Burguiere 2009; Darnton 1978; Hutton 1981; Tendler 2013).

In the study of mentalities, literacy – specifically reading – became interesting because of its role in developing and spreading shared beliefs. But some scholars have focused directly on literacy mentalities per se, especially their confluence with such conditions as material access and distribution, political formations, print economies, and legal regimes around texts. William St. Clair (2004), for instance, demonstrates how copyright laws in late eighteenth-century England played an almost inadvertent role in stratifying access to texts and knowledge, even as the practice of reading was expanding across classes.[2] William J. Gilmore (1992) studied how rural dwellers in post-Revolutionary New England incorporated new reading habits into their lives as they themselves were being incorporated into new political and economic affiliations. Not surprisingly, studies of literacy mentalities have focused almost exclusively on reading and not writing, although Roger Chartier (1995) has considered how people's understandings of writing and authorship matter to the ways they read. In the field of writing studies, an affinity with the mentalities concept can be found in the focus on discourse communities and their regulation of particular styles of reading and writing. Affinity can also be found in the recent work of Phillip Eubanks (2010), who shows how systems of interrelated metaphors organize the ways that everyday writers talk about writing as a social and psychological phenomenon.

Inevitably, encountering this scholarship invites one to think about the mentalities that are emerging as part of the transformation to digital, globalized reading and writing – how society has absorbed the facts of these shifts, including: abrupt changes in writing tools and environments; the rise of new genres and vocabularies; and new norms around work, time, privacy, and sociability. So now, for instance, in the twenty-first century, citizens are more likely to run afoul of the courts not because they are able to read too little but because they choose to write too much.[3] Prosecutors and defense attorneys scour the online writing of prospective jurors, including blogs, Facebook entries, and tweets, to look for predispositions and biases. Several criminal convictions have been overturned in recent years after jurors were discovered writing online about their jury experiences (Grow 2010). Freewheeling personal expression associated with social media is in friction with the court's traditional ways of protecting the rights of defendants by controlling the speech of jurors. Contemporary mass writing habits are proving ill-fitted to court traditions; literacy has become as disruptive to the justice system as illiteracy.

In this chapter I use the mentalities concept in a generative way to consider how the conditions of mass writing enter into the thoughts and actions of the people in my study.[4] My conceptual preferences here are socio-historical and aligned especially with Durkheim's (1982) notion of social facts. Social facts are not so much forms of cognition as they are forms of cognizance – a sense of what everybody takes to be the case, the conditions that people notice and work with as they notice others working with them too. Although social facts take the form of acting, thinking, and feeling, they arise from shared social structure and have what Durkheim has called coercive power. Social facts are not spontaneous creations of individual psychologies. And they are not necessarily what we believe or agree with. Social facts are what we are compelled to acknowledge as part of getting around, getting along, and getting by. Social facts matter to everybody, even though how they matter – and especially how they work for us or against us – will differ by social location, circumstance, or attitude.

It is important to remember that mentalities structure not only the daily habits of individuals but also institutional policy, practice, and investment. Mentalities manifest in a society's tools and technologies. As one limited example, I recall observing over a period of several years the slow demise of the physical card catalog in my university's library, beginning with the installation of computer work stations in an adjacent anteroom, followed by the steady expansion of the library's digital database, as the staff manually entered titles from newest to oldest; the shifting of more librarians closer to the computer work stations, which continued to multiply with each new budget year; the incremental improvements in the ease of using the database; and then, one day, the disappearance of the old card catalog, leaving a strangely empty room in the midst of bustling library activity. Mental and material structures change together.

In this chapter, the interviews of all ninety participants in the study, young and old, are brought together to analyze how mass writing manifests as a fact of shared living. Although the analysis is limited to the semantic content of interviews, it will focus less on the discourse level and more on sociological evidence available in these reports – the presumed shared worlds that underlay participants' answers to my questions, especially their interpretive appeals to mass writing as a given fact of life. As we will see, writing among others who also write – at work, at home, at leisure – is treated as an especially salient social fact among participants in this study. How is this cognizance absorbed into people's sense-making practices? How does this awareness structure actions and feelings? How do literacy mentalities become incorporated into individual literacy histories? And how does taking writing for granted raise risks and vulnerabilities associated with literacy?

See and be seen

The most repeated social fact among the participants in the study is that writing is scenic: it is an observable, nameable, and recognizable activity. Other people can see and make sense of the fact that you write and you can see and make sense of the fact that they write. The scenic quality of writing – comprised of its settings, its materials, and its postures, not to mention its products – is obvious. Yet its very obviousness is what sediments the activity of writing into larger routines and relationships of life. Through the scenic quality of writing, people learn something about how writing is treated in the world and how they might be treated when they write. These understandings can be shot through with affect and values that fluctuate with situation. *"My parents love to see me writing,"* related one high school fiction writer, *"especially now that technology is starting to attack society."* *"So I would write at work sometimes when there was nothing to do,"* recalled a college-aged poet, *"and the boss would come up and say: 'You're not supposed to be writing right now. You're supposed to be doing your job.'"* *"The sergeant came in one day,"* recalled a Vietnam veteran, *"and said, 'Private G___, we see you have this degree in journalism.'"* *"People would come to my father with problems,"* a middle-aged man said of his Mexican immigrant father. *"'How do I file the papers to become a citizen?' 'How do I get assistance that I need?' 'My son is in trouble with the police.' People turned to him for stuff like that. So I saw what he did for people."*

Where writing is explicitly performed, as in the case of slam poetry, its scenic qualities are central to textual meaning. *"Slam poetry is a hard thing to explain to people,"* said a 20-year-old practitioner. *"You have to see it to understand it."* *"I actually got to sit down and watch all these acclaimed poets, the best in the region, and I got to watch how they performed,"* recalled a 19-year-old poet and musician. But even in more implicit circumstances, the visibility of writing as a performance can communicate understandings, for instance, about writing skills (*"After watching my mom as a legal secretary,"* one man told me, *"she blew me away by how many words she can type a minute."*). Its visibility communicates that writing is a form of labor (*"My children often saw me writing for work,"* said a mid-career attorney, *"lots of times late at night or on weekends."*). The economic meanings of writing, including its connections to stratification and productivity, also could become conscious through observation (a young animal caretaker on a high-tech research farm said, *"I have an uncle with fifty cows and on his farm everything is done in handwriting"*).

As was stressed in earlier chapters, the proximity to other writing people can be important for developing collective consciousness and expression. Here a young member of a LGBT writing collective discusses the effect of being around other writers like herself: *"Seeing examples of other people throwing caution to the wind is really inspiring."*

That other people are on the lookout for your writing skill was a ubiquitously available message. *"I was in the youth ministry,"* explained a college-aged poet, *"and the pastor heard I could really write. So he asked me to do a poem for Juneteenth.*" A freelancer, recalling her first job, said, "*I saw an ad in the newspaper for a writer at a publication called* Everybody's Money." A college literary editor recalled walking across campus with her best friend when "*we saw a notice that the Campus Women's Center was looking for someone to take over the magazine.*"

Seeing and being seen, knowing and being known – these everyday events form a broad undercarriage for awareness about how writing fits socially, politically, economically, aesthetically. In its scenic dimension, what is noticed is not what the writing says but what it shows, although what it shows can differ sharply by situation. To the observers above, for instance, the activity of writing might be taken as valiant, derelict, desultory, courageous, skillful, validating, potentially exploitable, potentially transferable, or revealing of one's economic situation or position toward the times. No matter the form or function, writing as an activity is visible. It registers. The activity is treated as informative in itself.

While visibility is strongly associated with physical proximity to others, the Internet especially serves as an abstract force in making writing activity manifest. Asked how he decided to start a website, an amateur herpetologist responded, "*I guess I saw other people making websites.*" A member of a political blogging collective said to me: "*If you search for us, we'll come up on Google.*" A continuing adult educator who offered courses online said about the enrollees: "*I never saw those people. All I saw was their paperwork.*" Such comments suggest how humans and their activity can be inferred from textual constructions and how the web can be conceptualized as an encounter with (other) writing people. Contact through the Internet can support the belief that more writing is being undertaken now than in the past: "*The Internet is forcing people to write more and more,*" said a retired banker. "*In this day and age everyone has something they put on the Internet,*" said a college-aged political blogger. "*If you add up all of the postings, that's a whole lot of people who never wrote a letter to the editor or a letter to their grandmother. So I think it is fostering writing,*" said a librarian. These statements suggest how – in its sheer volume, cacophony, and interactivity – the Internet is commandeering the experience of reading for the development of writing consciousness.

It takes a writer to know a writer

"*For you, writing is intellectual,*" a financial adviser said to me, the academic, at one point in our interview. "*You have your parameters. You define them. But it's a different obligation that I have. We're dealing with people's money, their future, their retirement, their children's education.*" These remarks came as the financial advisor was addressing my questions about government regulation and institutional surveillance that bear on writing in his industry, and he did so in part by drawing an implicit contrast with the tradition of academic freedom that he knows surrounds the writing of educators and scholars. In his remark he attributed to me, an academic writer, a certain kind of mental experience, which he called intellectual, and characterized both my writing conditions (*"You have your parameters"*) and writing process (*"You define them"*). The remark also came with an accompanying attitude, at least as I heard it: an implication that his writing is more consequential than mine. The financial advisor wanted me to know that regulation does not debilitate or demean his writing. It serves as proof of its social importance.

People who write think about other people who write. They often use that thinking to understand themselves or carry out their own writing responsibilities. This form of cognizance is strongly attached to writing postures: it develops from dwelling in the writing mindset every day and/or dealing with others who do so. These postures – contoured by power relations – can sometimes invite the construction of quite elaborate inner worlds of writing that contain keen observation, intimate knowledge and even bold speculation, sometimes gratuitous but often necessary and hard won, about other writing people. According to the traditions of rhetorical studies, writers should know about or at least speculate about their readers and use that knowledge to develop their writing. Audience awareness has been well observed and analyzed in writing studies.[5] Here, in contrast, the focus is on knowledge or thoughts about other writing people, who technically may be one's readers, but whose existence as writers stands in some relationship to one's own – as colleagues, collaborators, competitors, or controllers.

Orienting one's self

People I interviewed often invoked awareness of other writers as a way to orient or characterize themselves. Occasionally the move was sociological, as in the following remarks from a freelancer writer: *"The challenge I've always had, even with groups like the Society of Technical Communicators, is I have a very different set of experiences from other people in the group"*; and from a government analyst: *"The first thing I say is that I'm not an investigative journalist."*

Occasionally self-orienting was in relationship to received wisdom – what other people in general say or believe about writing. For example, a health industry publicist said: *"I've always been suspicious of people who say they love to write."* A government analyst said: *"A lot of people fear writing. I don't fear it."* A mortgage broker said: *"A lot of people believe you have to write as if you are talking to someone about something for the first time. Don't project that you're intelligent. Don't use larger words. I've never agreed with that."*

However, the majority of such self-orienting expressions had to do with making particular distinctions or affiliations, favorable or unfavorable, explicit or implicit, with the writing skills, habits, processes, or outlooks of other writing people: a young poet who admired the courage of a peer who wrote *"personal things"* and was *"so experienced in letting people in"*; a police officer who knew he intimidated rookies *"by how quickly I can do a really significant report"*; a policy analyst perturbed by *"the routine grammatical errors and lack of rereading that go on around here"*; a professional writer who observed how *"some people write a rough draft and come back to it but I edit as I go"*; or a college student who was *"the only person I knew on Facebook who was using the note function to post essays."* The scenic and strongly comparative nature of these expressions suggests how self-knowledge as a writer rests in seeing, knowing, or imagining something about other people who write.

Interdependencies

Thinking about other writers, then, is a way to cultivate self-knowledge, self-assessment, self-understanding. It is important to the subjective experience of writing. But in the workplace, knowing things about other writers can also be fundamental to getting the job done. Because information workers depend on the productivity, accuracy, and reliability of other writing people, they internalize knowledge about the writing processes and rhythms of those others and incorporate that knowledge into their own decisions and practices. Where others might see organizational charts, workaday writers see writing territories differentiated by known or imagined conditions and constraints.[6] It was common especially among the government bureaucrats that I interviewed to understand hierarchy in terms of who was in charge of what kind of writing (*"I don't have to show the flavor of the agency; that's written at the secretarial level"*) or to see similarities and differences with writers in other agencies in terms of the pressure they were under or the audiences they needed to placate (*"They do what we do but their process is much more because they deal with so many more people."*) Working in large organizations of any kind could lead to perceptions about different writing workloads (for instance, *"A lot of writing came out of Tammy's office"* or *"Those people in the publishing area write seven or eight hours a day."*) Some interviewees expressed sympathy for colleagues who wrote under less than ideal circumstances: *"You see bad writing* [from that area] *but it's because it has to be so technical and because of all the regulation"* or *"They can't respond because of the volume of cases they get. The public sees it as non-responsiveness but they just don't have the human resources to do it."*

Those who seemed most cognizant of other writers' conditions, processes, or attitudes were individuals whose own success as writers depended on those others. Consider the following case of a communications specialist who works for a state government agency and has the responsibility of making his agency's initiatives visible to the general public. To advance the messages of his agency, he needs print journalists to pick up the press releases that he writes and use them to make their own stories. As a result of trial and error, success and failure, he developed ideas about how local media people think and how their thinking relates to the conditions in which they write. In the following extended account we can see how deeply this writer projects himself into the minds and circumstances of other writers:

Some topics will be instantly newsworthy if they are tangible and involve taxpayer dollars. But reporters still need topics that work with journalistic conventions where they need two sides to a story. They will say, okay, we have this press release over here and we can get this over here and it falls together for them. But some important things, like Medicaid spending, for example, just don't break down very well for news articles. No clear winners and losers, no clear two sides. And [reporters] don't have the luxury of writing a magazine-article length piece. If you're the Associated Press, you're probably writing more than one article a day. If you're the Journal Sentinel, you could probably fill your allotted space before you even get around to answering the Medicaid issue. So I understand there are certain things that are difficult for them to cover.[7]

Indeed, it was instructive in the course of the interviews to see the extent to which information workers learn about each other's writing lives by generating and sustaining writing for each other. Many prepare proto-texts that will be taken up into other people's work. Collectively they create a vast informational infrastructure for mutual use: press releases, databases, summaries, compilations, spreadsheets, newsletters, meeting notes, agendas, etc., most posted and available through the web. Information workers use the web to give and take writing (that is why, as one of the interviewees observed, *"The web can make you so much more productive."*). In these circulatory systems, writing is fungible, and its value lies in how much more writing it can generate. Another state policy analyst, for instance, uses postings on the websites of the Office of Management and Budget, Congressional committees, and the Library of Congress among other sources to identify and analyze pending federal legislation or regulations with implications for interests in his state. He circulates his analyses to a range of government personnel who, in turn, take up his writing into theirs. Notice in the following account how the analyst characterizes his multiple audiences not in terms of what they have to learn from his texts but in terms of what they are likely to have to write, listing these responsibilities until he reaches the limits of his imagination:

They need [my analysis] because they might need to do some analysis in their own office on the impact of federal dollars. They might need it to start thinking ahead to plan their budget for next year. They might need it to communicate with other people in their field. It may help citizens in other states pool together their resources to get changes in the bill or something like that. For other people, it's more just information for them to have and it's not clear what they might do with it.

Power

Some of the most acute thinking about other writers occurs in relationships of power and control, especially between superiors and subordinates in the workplace, where writing is produced collaboratively within hierarchies and where investment in that writing is high. In these cases, knowing how other writers think can keep you out of trouble. For subordinates, calibrating to the writing rhythms or preferred linguistic styles of supervisors may avert negative responses (*"My supervisor was very upset with what I wrote. She was clearly frustrated. So you take it and lesson learned."*). Or it may relieve the extra work of revising to someone else's specifications (*"Then one day I sent* [a draft of a letter] *and they wrote back and said 'looks good' and after that they said you don't have to send them to us any more."*). Or it may be to emulate the style of more experienced professionals (*"I try to write like the people who supervise me. Their writing is just really beautiful."*). Or it may simply be what a supervisor expects (*"I've worked for him for almost two years so I've learned how to write like him."* Or: *"People on my staff understand my thinking and my style and my values, and they try to adapt to that in their writing."* Or *"You don't want to turn* [younger employees] *into carbon copies of your own style unless you happen to write for the same client, in which case you sort of are indoctrinating them into the voice."*).

For some, close observation of supervisors' compositional rhythms can be quite strategic:

There are times that I will present [drafted] *letters to* [my boss] *and times not. I know if she is getting ready to leave she won't spend a lot of time. If she is here for the duration, if she is going to sit down and have lunch at her desk, that's the worst time possible because she starts rethinking all the messages.*

Reviewing other people's workplace writing is a ubiquitous practice, whether as a formal job responsibility or as an informal favor extended to colleagues, supervisors, or even in some cases friends and family members. Descriptions of these experiences are rife with sensitivity to writing egos and the attachments writers develop toward their own writing. Editorial incursions are understood as power plays: *"My responses depend on the individual,"* said the head of a communications department about her editorial feedback. *"How closely are you working with them? Have you had a long relationship with them? There is always a little bit of whether they will be receptive or not."* A human resource staffer with a reputation for strong writing skills said: *"A few people* [at work] *will ask me to take a look at things. I always have to apologize when I give it back because I'm brutal.*" Here a professional writer discusses the help she sometimes provides to her husband: "*For him it is much more of a personal process than it is for me. With him it's been mostly a lot of encouragement and a lot of feedback on how he can improve things.*"

Interestingly, the red pen, culturally associated with the persnickety schoolteacher, continues to index expressions of power and control even in workplace situations. A development director for a medical facility said: "*My administrator and I always read each other's writing. And we tease each other because we have red pens.*" An FBI agent observed: "*If you have a decent supervisor they will say, well, I wouldn't have said it this way but it conveys the facts, it's clear, there is no need to put my two cents in here. But sometimes they will kick your work back. And, really, do those red marks change anything?*" The supervisor of a branch office of a securities institution, who used to teach high school, said: "*I have to be careful being a former teacher. You can get carried away. I don't use a red pen. I don't highlight. I suggest, something like, 'If I were writing this, I wouldn't send it out in this form.' There was a time in my life when I would have underlined it. I don't do that any more.*"

Writing among other people who also write has become a typical daily experience for millions of Americans, and a highly formative one. Proximity to other writing people invites, and often requires, close attention to their habits, working conditions, and potential attitudes. It is as if the writing posture gives individuals the prerogative (and the insight) to project themselves into other people's composing processes, including their experiences, feelings, resources, and reactions, and use these projections to explain, calibrate, situate, anticipate, maneuver, and especially to compare and orient oneself as a writing person. People get to know each other as writers well beyond the words they might actually write and share with each other. Such person-to-person knowledge facilitates the intensive teaching and learning about writing that goes on in workaday and digital environments.[8] It feeds an expanding consciousness that underlies the production of texts in a world where people address each other not merely and not mostly as audiences but explicitly or tacitly as mutual writers. Indeed, in many cases, the rhetorical aim of writing is to stimulate others to write. Writing among others who write develops sensitivities toward the diversity of compositional rhythms and styles, power flows that accompany text production, and the existence of distinctive writing territories whose varying material and regulatory conditions bear on morale, expression, and practice – all of which might carry implications or instructiveness for one's own writing. This knowledge is developed not mainly through reading and not mainly through abstract apprehension of collective discourses but in ongoing, concrete interactions with particular others whose influence may be deliberately or tacitly rendered and resisted.

Having routine written exchanges with others can lend to sometimes intimate or elaborate conceptions of their writing processes, problems, or working conditions. Some of this is simply scenic. But often such conceptions are inferred during interactions with friends, or relatives, or colleagues who write, among other reasons: from reviewing, editing, or providing feedback; from taking up other people's texts to use in one's own writing; or from having to account for the volume or quality of writing that one encounters. In both work and leisure there is more writer-to-writer, peer-to-peer engagement with writing than at any time before in history and in more genres than ever before. On any given day, people I interviewed are more likely to read something written by somebody with whom they interact through writing than by an author they will never know. These may be emails, of course, but also reports, analyses, protocols, summaries, questionnaires, fiction, poetry, blogs, and many other kinds of text.

Further, the intense care that must be taken with written products in many information-based and service-based organizations brings high-stakes scrutiny, talk, teaching, and learning about writing into the course of the routine workday. Supervisors often have formal responsibility for developing the writing skills of their staffs, even as reviewing, editing, and feedback go on informally as well. Writing texts collaboratively can throw people into direct engagement with other people's writing habits and language styles, heightening awareness of their own. Engaging with others through mutual or reciprocal acts of writing enriches conceptions and knowledge about the craft of writing and the diversity of individual style while encouraging identifications with, distinctions between, and judgments toward other writing people. In this way, writing becomes embedded in everyday sociological consciousness.

Stereotypes

Given the integration of writing into routine sociological consciousness, it should not be surprising that stereotypes enter. Earlier chapters have addressed how writers subjected to discrimination by race, gender, sexual orientation, and language heritage use their own writing to manage and contest that hostility. Here, however, the focus is on stereotypes that have a basis in writing and find their justifications there. These observations show how connections are made between styles of writing and kinds of people. Here are some examples:

You know, those Ph.Ds with that itty bitty prose that nobody's going to read.

A novelist, I don't know if they think that consciously.

There is something about people who write editorials. They are controversy people.

Everybody thinks they can write. The worst people are English majors, which is scary because they all wind up in the weirdest places in business.

I think academics are sort of like that. They provide all this stuff and then they come up with a solution to a problem that sounds kind of lame.

I've read about authors being jerks but I almost think that is a put-on because you need to distance yourself to be a writer.

Entrepreneurs definitely think and act differently from the corporate America mold, and it's going to come out in the writing.

I think like a poet. I act like a poet. But I don't identify with the poetry crowd.

The engineering department didn't want to have anything to do with me at first because they thought the news people were all morons.

When I show people my work they are very surprised because they don't expect that I write what I write.

The most prevalent stereotypes that arose in the interviews were generational. The presumption that the younger generation is less literate than the older generation is a powerful belief in society, and it turned up frequently.[9] This perception was expressed mainly but not exclusively by older people toward younger people, and it was mainly attributed to falling standards in education or degrading effects of new writing technologies. These observations rested on the presumptions that, when it comes to writing, the way things were in the past differs from the way they are now and often to the detriment of society. I include many examples below to underscore how ubiquitously the generational divide came up in the interviews, as well as the forms it took:

I don't think young people can write sentences any more. It's horrible. The newer people, they can't write anything or express themselves.

They actually type their ums. And I'm like, wow, I try to edit ums from my speech. Why would I write them?

It's just crazy to think that the younger generations will not know how to write cursive. How are they going to sign their checks? It's disturbing to think about, oh, I don't need to learn this skill because I can just click and get it on the computer. It's going to make people lazy.

You can't blame these kids for not being able to put a sentence together because nobody made them. But, boy, some of the writing is atrocious.

I guess I'm a traditionalist but I see all these grammatical errors and I'm thinking, where is our society going?

The older accountants think they can write better than the younger accountants, that people coming out of school now aren't as top notch as the previous generation. I personally don't believe that's the case.

From what I have seen my generation is the last one that still kind of reads books, still kind of wants to go for coffee and talk face to face. A shocking percentage of younger kids I see, my little cousins, it's all Facebook, it's all digital.

Part of me feels like a fuddy duddy but I do think people of a certain age were taught to write, taught basic writing structure, and I think that has been under siege for a long time.

I think that there are generational differences in how people write. And I think people are losing the ability to write. When people apply for jobs here they have to write a couple of pages about two or three different subjects and I was just appalled at the poor writing that I saw. I don't know why. I'm guessing these people are younger because they write as if they were texting someone.

Writing skills are not skills that everyone has. And that particularly becomes somewhat generational because many people either don't read as much or they don't invest as much in cultivating the skills of writing.

With the teenagers doing so much email amongst each other and coming up with their own abbreviations and hidden meanings and words and so forth, when they get into let's say a business writing situation, are they going to be able to differentiate what they did casually in the evening and what they are doing during the day?

It was also the case that some older and some younger people perceived younger people as more adept writers, especially when it came to using computers and handling emergent forms of writing. The youths' edge was attributed to more recent education, genetic propensity, or finer cultural attunement:

I'm not as good at online research as some of the younger lawyers. They just seem to be born knowing how to do it.

At this point anyone you hire knows more about computers than people who have been around for a while.

A lot of the staff are much younger and so they have gone through communications or journalism courses within a shorter time frame. I graduated a long time ago so I learn a lot from my peers. I learn from my interns too, how to put together a website, how to tweet.

I'm helping my mom make a website and she asked me how to do something and I said, really, mom, just look at the symbols. That's definitely a generational thing. I just feel that I have a vision of how websites should be, just being my age and at this time.

Most youth writers are probably better than adult writers. They are just so uninhibited.

Finally, at least one older person, a 58-year-old editor for a trade association, linked a decline in the influence of print culture with a decline in respect for members of a generation reared on print:

I think older people such as myself and our upbringing, our love of books and the writ-ten word, have more of a linear way of approaching information and communication whereas a lot of young people who are being hired nowadays are into quick communi-cation. The shiny, bright new technologies get a lot of attention. People who are thought of as being associated with print are older and out of touch. So I notice that a lot of times people I report to aren't even conscious that they are sneering at people who have been associated with print.

The fast-moving changes associated with digital technologies make generational thinking palpable (*"I grew up in the non-computer generation." "My generation more than any other generation is constantly tuned into everything." "Some of the older staff are reluctant to learn new technologies."*). Further, some people aligned identities and affiliations with rising or fading communication technologies or practices (*"We were the last class to use electric typewriters." "People in our generation live on email." "I got to campus in the declining age of blogging."*). As we saw with the scenic significance of writing, meanings attributed to a generational divide could vary in substance. These conceptions intermingled with broader, age-based stereotypes. The declining quality of schooling – or at least the declining power of the school to overcome broader cultural trends – was a widespread presumption, as was the belief that younger people have an innate knack for new technologies. Overall, using age or generational membership to make sense of writing literacy appeared to be a common practice among those I interviewed.

Mass writing, opportunity, and social structure

So far I have tried to collate and characterize individual expressions of some of the most common, taken-for-granted social facts associated with writing and living among others who also write, at least as those facts were expressed, largely on the fly, by participants in this study. I also have explored variations in the meanings individuals ascribe to these facts and some of the sources from which they are derived. The focus has been on how proximity to and interactions with other writing people condition writing practices, judgments, and sensibilities, including people's concepts of their own standing as writers.

Here the focus shifts to considering how mentalities of mass writing manifest as aspects of social structure and change, shaping the terrain over which individual writing careers move through time. The aim is to show how the production of mass writing – especially its role in processes of competition and cooperation – conditions opportunities for working, earning, and communicating. The section focuses in depth on the accounts of two adults, one an IT and web pioneer and the other an elder care provider, whose working careers over the last several decades overlapped with the emergence of digital technologies and the accompanying explosion in online writing. As the Internet became infrastructural to social life and economic productivity, the tangible effects of other people's writing registered in the worlds of these two individuals in profoundly contrasting ways, continually destabilizing the writing (and economic footing) of the IT entrepreneur and gradually stabilizing the writing (and improving the economic footing) of the elder care provider. As new forms of mass writing structure and condition the contexts in which people think, write, and work, they can become a powerful agent of disruption, reorganization, and change.

Marvin Clark is a self-proclaimed and largely self-taught geek, a European American born in the Midwest in 1963 into middle-class conditions. In the early 1980s he enrolled at his state public university with an interest in radio engineering and computer programming. As a work-study student, he found a job at a public radio station on campus, editing audiotapes with razor blades, and also helping to write the news. (*"My writing was terrible but they needed a writer,"* he explained.) Clark eventually dropped out of college and took a position as an installer, and then technical support manager, and then technical writer for a now defunct company that made weather graphics systems for TV. He then moved into full-time technical writing for a software company working on email integration programs in the early days of email, and eventually founded his own company as an early commercial pioneer on the World Wide Web. He did all of this over the course of twelve years, from the early 1980s to the mid-1990s, a period characterized by a rapid spread of digital technologies and aggressive efforts to exploit their commercial potential. Certainly Clark's ability to work both the underside of digital technologies – as a programmer and software writer – and the public side of digital technologies – as a writer of user manuals – gave him unusual flexibility and range in an economy with a need for both kinds of writer. Still, Clark's prescience, innovations, and job security were constantly overtaken as word processing, email, and web-based interaction became mass practices. In response to other people's writing, Clark repeatedly had to rearrange and reinvent his own writing literacy, not to mention his ways of making a living. As Clark told his own story, the story of shifting mentalities for mass writing became prominent.

At one level Clark was often a step ahead of communicative transformations that were beyond the vision of those around him. As a student employee in both the engineering and news departments of the radio station in the early 1980s, Clark recalled:

Those word processing terminals were starting to make their way around. The radio station traffic managers had one and were using it to type up station logs. I got my nose in on this thing and said, you know, this could save a lot of time in the news department. So when I took over doing final prep work for [the morning news show] *I started putting it on a computer. The computer was way over in the traffic department so I was stealthily going off there. But I couldn't save the stuff. You didn't have a computer record of it because storage was expensive. But at the time it was really revolutionary to have a pristine piece of paper with no corrections on it.* [The news host] *was impressed. God, I'm sounding old.*

Clark also innovated in his position as a technical support manager for the weather equipment company by writing a software program to track his department's activities and setting up a bulletin board for customers to post their questions. Here are his recollections from that period:

We had been logging all of our calls and all of our interactions with customers on paper. Then you would put the paper in a drawer and forget about it because [the information] was totally inaccessible. So I developed a logging system. Nowadays there are sophisticated help desk software systems. This was an amateur version of it. Nobody would write their own program now. My last year [at the company] I set up a bulletin board system, kind of like a predecessor to a website, where customers could dial in to post or download software fixes, which was pretty revolutionary at the time.

Similar patterns of innovation and obsolescence characterized his brief stint at a company dedicated to integrating email programs. As more and more writing migrated to the Internet, standardized technological supports for that writing became commercially viable, forcing some businesses under and requiring constant readjustment in entrepreneurial efforts. Here are Clark's recollections of what he called a *"quaint"* transitional period in which he wrote software and served as a volunteer cataloguer of websites. This account illuminates changing relationships among emergent technologies, mentalities, and writing practices:

At the time all different kinds of email systems were coming on board, lots of different vendors with their own propriety systems. So we were building integration software so that these systems could talk to each other. It's not really an issue any more but at the time it was huge. We were pretty heavily involved in the Internet by then so I set up a gopher server. Remember gopher? We were experimenting to see if this was a way to communicate with customers. So I was emailing with a friend of mine who worked at an academic library and he said, well, I'm proud of your gopher service but check out the World Wide Web. I said, huh? Then I said, oh, gopher's dead, and I started fooling around with websites. There was a guy in Sweden who was maintaining a list of all the websites in the world, which one person could do at the time. He had it segmented by country, province, state, so I volunteered to maintain a list of websites in [my state]. It was a one-page list. When a new one went up, the owner would email me and I would add it to the list. But it raised a lot of questions, like where is this website? Is its headquarters in the state? Is it on a computer in the state? So very rapidly it started not to make any sense any more and then Yahoo was starting to build a comprehensive list of all websites in the world organized in all the different possible ways you can think of organizing it, so we figured out doing this geographic thing was just, well, goofy. It seems preposterous now.

But it was the founding and the fortunes of Clark's own website design company that most dramatically demonstrates how mentalities associated with emerging writing practices can scramble economic and organizational structures and affect an individual's writing literacy. In the mid-1990s Clark and his friend began offering web design and maintenance services to local businesses at a time when *"if you said website to somebody they didn't know what you were talking about."* He explained:

> We started with a computer in my basement hooked up by modem to the Internet and at the time it was hard to buy an Internet connection. There was only one company that was doing this in town and it was really expensive, so just finding a way that we could have a computer connected to the Internet, let alone connected all the time, was an expensive proposition. We were writing code by hand. And setting up the server was very difficult and just getting all the technology to actually work. We bought a laptop because we realized that the only way we were going to sell this stuff was to go out and show people what it was 'cause nobody knew. They may have read an article about the Internet but nobody had seen it. So we had to use all these analogies from broadcasting. There was so much education required.

The company began by offering their product gratis to a local government tourism office as a way to generate more publicity. Marvin Clark recalled: *"We made them this offer and they patted us on the head and said, sure, whatever, go do whatever you want. It just wasn't on their radar."* Very soon, though, he said, things began to change: *"It wasn't very long before they started to care what was on the website and we started working more and more with their communications department to control what was on the site."*

Ten years later, the company no longer was composing many websites but instead was developing custom-made software systems so that clients could create and maintain their own websites. Clark was uncertain about what was next for the company:

> When we first started out, we were more of an ad agency kind of business and now we're really a software company. But there are a billion companies out there that write website software and, while we're really good at it, it's hard to compete with a billion.

Clark's account demonstrates how the massification of websites and web-based literacy practices rearranged an organization, albeit a small and scrappy one, redefining it from something like an ad agency to something like a software company and, as Clark mentioned later in the interview, something like a writing consulting firm. As the website moved from the hands of the few to the hands of many, it became more valued, more supported, more known, more used, more dispersed, more standardized. From Clark's perspective, this change created new competitive challenges that affected his writing roles within his company, as he moved from being chief geek writing code to chief account executive, writing proposals, communicating with clients, and doing the increasingly difficult work of finding new business. (He had recently started a blog to help in this effort.) Clark welcomed the volatility that marked his career: *"The pace of change hasn't bothered me,"* he said. *"It's what makes things interesting. If you're doing the same stuff over and over it's boring,*" adding that there is a constant in his career: "*balancing the technical with the understandable.*"

Still Clark's experiences do demonstrate how new writing mentalities can be a destabilizing force as they enter economic and social arenas and change how people write and communicate as well as how they perceive their needs for technical support. While these processes are often attributed to technologies per se, Clark's account allows us to appreciate how people and their writing habits are the precipitators of these changes.

If Marvin Clark, the IT entrepreneur, was writing in contexts that seemed to be perpetually coming apart, elder care manager Jan Mahoney was writing in a context that was coming together: as a program planner in a non-profit health and social service network for older Americans. Over the course of the 1980s and 1990s, amid spikes in the population of people over 60 years old, this network was actively professionalizing, stabilizing, and consolidating. As we will see, the process of consolidation was enhanced by some of the very same writing practices that destabilized Clark's writing efforts. In Mahoney's world, the rise of Internet-based, networked writing practices and their accompanying mentalities served to strengthen a pre-existing human network. In the process, Maloney's writing and reading literacy became more assured, intensive, and global in outlook.

Maloney, a European American, was born in 1952 in the Midwest into working-class conditions. After high school she worked as a waitress and a pet store clerk before entering technical college in her late 20s to earn a two-year paralegal degree. She then joined VISTA and was assigned to an agency providing social services to older Americans, one of hundreds of decentralized, non-profit organizations around the country that were part of what was called the aging network, a mostly federally funded effort launched in the early 1970s to keep older Americans in their communities and homes. Maloney took the position at a time when, she said, the aging network in her state was "*in a period of development, expansion, program building,*" adding that "*it has grown an incredible amount since then.*" Maloney stayed committed to her newly found profession, returned to college in her mid-40s ("*To move up I really needed a bachelor's degree,*" she observed), and in the late 1990s became one of three regional program planners for a large agency in south-central Wisconsin. This agency contracts with state government to disperse and monitor funds directed to various municipalities and other local aging agencies that provide transportation, meals, recreation, legal protection, and health and social services for thousands of senior citizens annually.

Maloney recalled knowing very little about the field when she was first hired and describes a kind of pre-professional era of which she was a part:

The director just said, read through the files, you'll pick it up. Another person suggested that I read through the Older American Act. Well, the Older American Act is voluminous!

There were chapter titles and every program was broken down into a different chapter. There was a lot to learn.

Maloney said most of the writing she did at the time passed through the mail, in the form of funding proposals with the government and information-seeking with local service providers. She explained the accountability it entailed:

The aging network revolves around a three-year planning cycle. Now everything is done by email but then you'd get documents by mail that would set out objectives for the next three years and we would have to tell [the legislators] *what steps we were going to take and how we were going to measure things to ensure we made a difference.*

With the large-scale adoption of email, government funding announcements and proposal submissions began to flow electronically. But more important, Maloney noticed, communication patterns shifted from a "*hierarchy*" into more of a "*wheel,*" as planning became more collaborative, deliberative, and iterative:

There is a lot more communication back and forth now. When we do an assessment, it's in a draft form and I will even email it back to an agency and ask, "Did I get this right? Is there anything else you want to say?" Before we get the final written version done we will send it to them and they will share it with their staff and committees. We recently received a copy of a letter that one of the aging unit directors had sent out to her advisory group. She was asking for their input about what they need to do over the next two years. Did they have any thoughts? She emailed a copy of that letter to us, so I was able to send it out [to other directors in the field of aging] *and say, "this is a best practice."*

Maloney said she is "*on email most of the day,*" continuing:

If I'm in my office, I'm in a communication mode, emailing or phone calling but typically emailing. We use email rather than phone because it's more convenient, for one thing, and, for [the grantees] *it's a cost reduction. They are not making that long-distance phone call every other day to our office. Also, I prefer to have something in email so I can mull it over a little while before I respond.*

Maloney recounted how another innovation, the initiation of digital data collection, affected the agencies with which she worked, especially as those agencies learned to think and work with the affordances of the new system:

Everything is going online. We've been working with aging units over the last few years to start using a particular software that the state has made available. They enter all the names of their participants and every time a participant accesses a program, that information is recorded. Comfort with this software can vary from county to county depending on how much they have been using computers and doing data entry. It's a learning curve. But as they get more comfortable, it will actually make their programs more efficient and bring better quality to their reports. It all used to be on paper but names were not attached. Now the individual agency has a better look at the person. They have a more holistic look. So when a director says we don't do case management the way that social workers do case management, I can say, yes, you do, you just don't call it that. Look: you are providing this person a ride, a meal, some respite. You are juggling a lot for that person.

Maloney's first contact with computers was in a basic programming course that she took in 1983, although she did not continue to program. Through her employer she took additional courses in Windows and in website development. A self-described computer enthusiast, she manages the website for her agency and continually is revising content and appearance:

When I give information to people I want them to have more than a name of an agency. I want them to have a clue about whether the agency will be able to help them or whether they need to keep looking for something else. So websites really fit into the information assistance programs that I had been working with all along. That is why you will find a links page. [Designing the website] was easy to do. The format was already set up. When I couldn't figure something out, I went to the help documents or just looked around online. I can be somewhat of a sleuth. So I just pretty much learned how to do it myself.

Maloney also discussed how she used the Internet to upgrade her own knowledge about the field, relying especially on the contributions of peers working in other states and even other countries. Here we see how members of the aging network use digital writing (and reading) practices to upgrade their professionalism:

All of the counties [in my region] have contracts with us for elder abuse investigations, and I spend a fair amount of time working with them on appropriate uses of the funding. I subscribe to a national elder abuse list serve that is facilitated by someone at the American Bar Association. I use it to keep up on what's going on. People weigh in from all over the country and from other countries too. I'm signed up for other Yahoo groups as well. Every morning there will be a digest email that will have full articles from all over the country on elder abuse. You can see what's happening in our state, in California, even in Ireland. Financial abuse is in the news quite a bit. Caregiver issues, caregiver abuse, caregiver needs. I use the Internet in general to access services, get assistance with information, find resources for colleagues. If I have to put together a PowerPoint for training I find out who might have something out there so I don't have to reinvent the wheel. I look to see how services are being provided in other areas. There are some states that have exceptional aging programs similar to ours. Oregon does. How is it working for them? Elder abuse. San Diego County has the best elder abuse system in the country only because they have a district attorney who is really tuned in to that. I found that out through the list serve. His name kept coming up. So one of our counties is actually having him come to do a conference.

When the aging network was established by federal legislation in the 1970s, *network* was meant to denote a loose and decentralized affiliation of service providers receiving allocations of federal funds to carry out mandated services under state oversight – a deliberate "patchwork" alternative to the creation of a centralized government bureaucracy and one that would ideally stay responsive to local needs and conditions (Gelfand 2006; Niles-Yokum and Wagner 2011).

But Maloney's account, from inside a network that was growing in size and professionalizing in the process, shows how its temporal overlap with the emergence of mass, Internet-based writing practices could turn it into a more connected, global, and consolidated network in the new, digital sense – how professional consciousness could be developed regionally, nationally, and internationally through the uses of email, digitized databases, and websites, among other means. Whereas in Marvin Clark's experiences the mass uptake of these practices destabilized his writing environments, as he was forced to move to the next new thing, in Maloney's experience these same mass practices strengthened her writing environment by deepening, extending, and improving systems that were already in nascent existence. This was especially obvious in how the website became an improved tool for providing information to older Americans by putting more and better information at their disposal and allowing them to customize their own processes of information gathering. Underlying software that standardized and streamlined web development was key to this process. Whereas this software put negative economic pressure on Clark's small business, it enabled Maloney to become an independent website designer. Further, the mass turn to websites assisted Maloney in her own sleuth-like forms of professionalizing, as she viewed the websites of other agencies (i.e., other people's writing) as locations of professional conduct from which she could learn.

Clark saw his entrepreneurial plans scrambled by processes of standardization and massification, but for Maloney these same processes made planning easier, cheaper, and of higher quality. "Email integration" took on a different connotation in Maloney's context, as the integration of email into planning processes and working relationships meant she could more fully realize her long-standing values of inclusion in decision-making, as electronic communication closed geographic distances and allowed rounds of consultation that were previously infeasible. The rise of Yahoo turned Clark's social contributions obsolete and "goofy," but helped Maloney's social contributions to become more current and informed. She traveled a long distance from a VISTA volunteer reading the Older American Act as her primary resource for action to consulting a global array of sources and cycling that knowledge and perspective back into her own writing consciousness and sharing it with others.

As the accounts of Marvin Clark and Jan Maloney illustrate, the force of other people's writing not only enters the thoughts, perceptions, and actions of individuals in the everyday but also helps to constitute (and at times dissolve) the material structures in which an individual works and acts. As new communication practices and genres are adopted on a mass scale they affect the configurations of economic and social possibilities in which people find themselves. These configurations are not deterministic; rather their meanings and impacts vary by context.

Conclusion

In this chapter I have tried to capture patterns of social cognizance associated with the entrenchment of a mass writing literacy, particularly the awareness that one writes among other people who also write. As we have seen, this awareness not only attunes people to the coordinated production contexts in which they must work and communicate but also serves as a basis of self-understanding and orientation within a diverse world of writing and writers. Among the participants in this study, routine comparisons with other writing people appear to be widespread and commonsensical, even as they often serve to form distinctions between self and others, whether in terms of generational mindsets, skills, values, styles, resources, attitudes, responsibilities, or other criteria. We have also seen how this cognizance draws from the scenic nature of writing and the daily proximity to other writing people, other acts of writing, and other people's writing. Active and passive observation of other people writing is an obvious yet powerful dynamic in the building of a writing society, and no doubt plays an important role in the development of individual writing skill. Yet it is a dimension of literacy that is rarely noticed, defined, studied, or assessed as part of literacy and one that is not often figured into analysis of inequality of access. Other people's writing also shapes forms of competition, cooperation, and survival that characterize social and organizational structures in these times. Especially, as writing has become a dominant form of labor, it has become a force that increasingly conditions the contexts in which we work, learn, and live. That the practices of mass writing have been undergoing such change, innovation, and turbulence over the last several decades only makes that force more formidable.

This chapter has offered one, most limited and exploratory foray into mass writing mentalities expressed by a small set of people who write electively or for pay. The historical rise of these mentalities, the means by which they circulate, and their change or stability over time unfortunately elude the scope and methods of this study and must await further research. Still, they suggest that people who write every day carry with them sophisticated understandings of a wider world of writing, including insights into other people's composing processes and writing conditions, their diversity of skills and styles, the relationship of writing to power, and the contexts of production and publication from which writing emerges. People who write develop intersubjective awareness of others who write, because of the need to coordinate with them, or the desire to learn from them, or the responsibility for teaching them, or the need to stimulate their writing, or to survive oppression along with them, or just from sheer daily proximity. This awareness can be rife with judgment, attitude, bias, and injurious feeling, even as it lends people insight into their own standing as a writer.

People who write every day possess a working awareness of their own writing development over time, and, when asked, can express ad hoc theories of the factors that have contributed to that development, factors that are at least as likely to come from what one participant called "hard experience" as from the formal designs of school curriculum and instruction. Writing develops as part of surviving and striving, self-defending, seeking to belong, and responding to surprise or change, but especially by noticing one's standing as a writing person among other writing people. How mentalities associated with writing societies contribute to individual writing development across the lifespan is an urgent research question.

In closing, my thoughts return to where this chapter began, with Edward Stevens' account of how the spread of reading in late nineteenth-century America infiltrated a society's conception of what is just and fair and normal, creating dangers and insecurities for non-readers trying to get by in a reading world. It is easy to see in the testimonies compiled in this chapter how membership in a society of writers becomes second nature to those who labor each day in contexts of intense text production, where encounters with other writing literates are routine, formative, and consequential, where those processes are fortified by powerful writing technologies and economic incentives, and where writing-based forms of getting things done can be casually carried into other spheres of life. Further, members of the writing society – often more highly educated and often more highly employed than average – take positions in government and private enterprise that carry with them decision-making and gatekeeping responsibilities: child custody decisions, statute-writing, mortgage granting, criminal investigating, program design, financial advising, news reporting, and drug development, to name only some. Through words and actions undertaken on a daily basis, members of the "writing class" lay down the conditions with which others must cope.

Certainly people I interviewed expressed sensitivity toward people who lacked access to writing literacy in some form or other: "I've learned," a lawyer told me "that you can't make assumptions whatsoever about the literacy level of a client." A retired small business man noticed that some employment ads in newspapers "give only an email address, not a street address, not a telephone number, so they assume every respondent is computer literate and has access to a computer and I'm not sure that is the case." "In the early 1980s," a university-based translator of Hmong recounted, "a lot of the elders had relatives in the refugee camps [in southeast Asia] and when they needed to write a letter back to their relatives they came to me." In discussing constituents who contact his office, a legislative aide said, "When folks contact us because they are in trouble for failing to fill out paper work, responding with a detailed letter is not going to help them." Yet law, business, higher education, and government, among other fields, are organized around a writing intensity embedded in organizational rationales and communication habits, large and small, that are not easily consciously controlled or mitigated. It would not be an exaggeration to say, in the experiences and estimations of many, that how people write is largely how the world works. The two are concomitant. The testimonies in this chapter certainly open one's eyes to how proximity to other writing people – ample, ongoing, routine proximity – plays myriad, formative roles in the development and calibration of writing, writing skill, and writing consciousness. Such taken-for-granted, casual access is layered into the mental and material structures of a dominant writing society even though it is far from available to everyone. The assumptions of a writing society increasingly define the facts of life as all people find them.

Conclusion: deep writing

In his well received book *The Shallows: what the Internet is doing to our brains*, Nicholas Carr (2011) argues that our capacity for "deep reading" – sustained immersion in extended, linear text – is going out the window. Fidgety, fragmented, associational, and overloaded, our susceptible brains are being reshaped by how the Internet invites us to read: surf, sample, browse, scan. Like the minds of other generations of humans before us, he says, our minds are adapting to the character of a new and profound technology and leaving behind the old. As traditional print fades from use, the cognition of literacy – including its intellectual effects – will be compromised. As we attend to more, we will want to understand less, and there will be no going back.

To his credit, Carr briefly addresses the irony of presenting his argument in long-book form, an effort that obviously required sustained immersion in his own extended text. But otherwise the cognition of writing gets short shrift in his treatment – even though writing has to be counted among the prominent activities that digital systems solicit and support. For the first time in history, masses of humans have keyboards under their hands that connect them to people at a distance and screens that shine back at them the public look of their own written utterances. Yet these profound social and cognitive changes in the direction of mass literacy go unremarked. That is because Carr, like others, assumes that our literacy can only develop through how we read, and that how we read will condition how we write. If the cognition of text comprehension becomes fragmented and shallow, he assumes, so will the cognition of text production. But might his argument itself be a holdover from the social arrangements of a disintegrating print culture, from a time when readers were presumed to be many and writers were presumed to be few? Is it possible to contemplate a mass literacy based on new relationships between writing and reading such that how and why we write will condition how and why we read? Is it possible – indeed necessary–to contemplate new approaches to literacy based primarily in writing?

This book has argued for both the possibility and the necessity for changing perspectives on the future of mass literacy. Before we decide what the Internet is doing to literacy, we need to attend to writing much more centrally than we have in the past. Whatever the fate of *deep reading*, we are just now entering an era of *deep writing*, in which more and more people write for prolonged periods of time from inside deeply interactive networks and in immersive cognitive states, driven not merely by the orchestration of memory, muscle, language, and task but by the effects that writing can have on others and the self.

Consider the experiences of 27-year-old Eileen O'Grady, who works as a financial coordinator for a pediatric dental clinic that sees about 150 patients a day. It is her job to figure out how much a patient's health insurance company will pay for a particular dental procedure and how much the patient's family will have to co-pay. She has had to familiarize herself with the details of approximately 300 different policies. She estimates that she spends 20 percent of her workday writing letters to insurance companies setting out the case for payment in situations where *"you could genuinely make an argument either way."* She explained:

I write for both the policyholder and the doctor. So it's a juggling act for what I can say that is medically necessary, truthful, and within the bounds of our position. You have to be very clear with what you are writing, very careful about how you are saying it. You learn a lot of legal language. I use language from the policies themselves, quoting them directly. But at the same time you have to twist their words on them.

Eileen O'Grady attaches to the letters pertinent dental records, x-rays, and other materials that she sequences as part of making the case.

In the event that an insurance company declines payment or if a procedure falls into the category of "special circumstances," O'Grady will draft an appeal letter. Sometimes appeals require soliciting second opinions from experts. Appeals and solicitations that she composes will be reviewed and sent out under the name of one of the dental surgeons. O'Grady finds these ghostwritten letters the most difficult to write:

I have to sound like somebody who has a Ph.D. It's difficult to have a five-minute discussion with a doctor about a procedure like a skin graft and then write a two-page letter about why it is important and write that letter to a plastic surgeon who is a bigwig in the field. It's complicated. [The doctors] have a particular language and a particular way of saying things. Because of confidentiality laws, you are very limited as to what you can say. There is a lot of pressure in those situations, not necessarily pressure other people are putting on me but pressure I am putting on myself.

From the posture of the clerical worker, Eileen O'Grady wrestles with the power and consequence of writing in her society. She enters converging systems of law, medicine, and insurance, choosing language to mediate multiple interests, audiences, regulations, and knowledge, ventriloquizing and twisting these systems as she can, with implications for others and herself. These are the hallmarks of deep writing: consequential, complicated, dramatic. And, as we have seen, these conditions are coming to typify the ways that workaday people routinely engage their literacy.

In one of Eileen O'Grady's computer files, she organizes the letters she writes not by patient name but by the type of argument she has made, so that when a similar case arises she can recoup and repurpose her strategies. She also surfs the Internet with the eyes of a writer: "*A lot of times I will go out online and look at how other people have worded things, picking and choosing language that I think is effective, that could get my point across,*" she said. O'Grady looks to her supervisor for additional guidance, explaining: "*She is a good role model. She has a way of using language with people to get them to do things they don't want to do, and she makes them feel it was their idea and what a great idea. That is how I have to communicate too.*" As with many of the people encountered in this book, O'Grady reads through the lens of writing and calibrates with others who write in her proximity.

Yet Eileen O'Grady does not consider herself a writer by disposition or training: "*I don't particularly like writing. It is not something that's been easy for me. It is not something I would choose to do with my personal time. But it is something I have had to try to learn.*" The writing course she took as part of a two-year accounting program at a local community college did not serve so well. She said: "*I had a written communication course but it did not prepare me for the things I try to accomplish. The course was just about different kinds of letters and their formatting. Spelling. Grammar. That is what we were scored on. But that is not the most important part of a letter, and it is not the most important part of your writing.*" Rather, O'Grady learned to write through experience in place, explaining: "*It is something I have gained through the experience of saying the wrong thing and having it backfire. Or putting something a certain way and having it not go over well. It is something I have had to acquire and work on.*" O'Grady has experienced the gap between reading-based writing instruction, organized around texts and their formal features, and a worldly, craft-based style of learning, based in response to rhetorical hard-knocks. This latter kind of learning travels into other domains of life: "*I'm more conscious now of what I am saying as a result of this job,*" she observed about the wider effects of her workplace writing. "*When I am trying to communicate something effectively, I find myself taking more time to think about how I'm going to say it instead of just blurting out whatever is on my mind.*"

This book has argued that we are making a turn in the history of mass literacy in which relationships between writing and reading are undergoing profound change. Writing is overtaking reading as the skill of critical consequence. The rise of writing has been accompanied and stimulated by changes in communications technology, but the two should not be conflated. The emergence of mass writing developed gradually across the twentieth century with the emergence of the so-called information economy, as literacy was pulled more deeply into the modes and means of economic production and profit. Until only recently, writing was a minor strain in the history of mass literacy, including schooling. But it is surging into prominence, bringing with it a cultural history and developmental arc that stand in contrast to reading.

Writing is crowding out reading and subordinating reading to its needs. This shift is driven largely by the role that writing plays in the nation's economic life. In the information economy, reading proceeds functionally, as input leading to output, as both workaday and elective writers convey, synthesize, or formulate new information, monitor the writing of subordinates, peers, or competitors, or use reading to hone or develop their writing. Production demands change reading habits, favoring skimming, surfing, and sampling, practices that too often are attributed to the influence of technology. "Reading to write" in school has usually meant using reading to stimulate ideas for writing or else incorporating written sources into writing for academic purposes (Asencion Delaney 2008; Flower *et al.* 1990). But in the wider world, reading to write actually stands for a broader, more diverse, more diffused, more sustained, and more comprehensive set of practices.

We write among other people who also write. This is a simple and obvious state of affairs yet its implications are historic and profound. Learning to write with other people who write (rather than from authors who address us abstractly) is a new condition for mass literacy development. People learn from peers who undertake similar kinds of tasks or produce similar sorts of text, and often serve as audiences or editors for each other.[1] Audiences are made up not merely (or mostly) of receptive readers but also responsive writers; increasingly people write to catalyze or anticipate other people's writing (Lunsford and Ede 2011). Even more profound, writing in the proximity of other writers builds up awareness of other people's composing processes, language styles, and the conditions in which they write, favoring comparison and calibration and adding social texture to literate understandings.

Writing is a site of intellectual, moral, and civic development. Because writing unleashes language into the world, it engages people's sense of power and responsibility, even when they are writing anonymously or under someone else's name. In the throes of composition, writers see their words take public shape, and the effects of these words do not stop with the reader. The residual impact of writing on the writer surpasses the ostensible purposes of a text. It is an excess that can register as development, satisfaction, despair. A staff member of a small business organization told me he figured out how to write meeting agendas so as to engender deeper discussions on issues he believed deserved deeper thought. *"You make sure the agenda asks open-ended questions,"* he explained. *"You might put something in there that you know the answer to but phrase it in a certain way to get them to think about it."* A former clerical employee I interviewed had to compose and duplicate a meeting agenda for a trade group planning an intervention that troubled her conscience. *"Later, I went into the meeting room to clear away the papers and saw what was written on the white board,"* she said. *"I quit that job."* A social worker told me: *"People are going to interpret your words in a certain way. It's part of your responsibility to understand that and work through it. It helps to develop you as a person."* Literacy has long been essentialized as an internal and internalizing process, but only because reading has been privileged. Writing externalizes, yet one's own writing ricochets, returning from the outer world with implications that can pierce the mind and soul. What is internalized, what shines into writers during writing, are the potential consequences of their own words at work in the worlds of others. The effects of writing on readers have been considered from every imaginable angle. Meanwhile, the effects of writing on the writer – positive or deleterious – go largely unexplored. Yet increasingly these effects will give human definition to mass literacy.

As mass writing reshapes the future of literacy, it brings along a past that troubles the traditional values and meanings associated with a reading-based literacy. As we have seen, mass writing was not included in the initial campaigns to universalize literacy. Reading was the technology of choice for churches and schools seeking to socialize and integrate mass populations. The regulation of reading became bound up in the relationships of citizens to their government, its protections enshrined in the Bill of Rights. Writing was left for work, production, practicality. Its regulation became bound up in relationships of private contract, ownership, copyright, and libel, leaving it weakly protected in the civic sphere. Most ordinary writing that is done every day in this society is hired speech, corporate speech, not free speech; the government is more apt to regulate or surveil the writing done by everyday citizens than to protect its autonomy. Further, the association of writing with the inkier, vocational, material side of life made it an uneasy fit with the reading-based school. Writing is a low-prestige enterprise within the cerebral liberal arts, where canonical texts are adulated and writing instruction, where it occurs, is forced to fit into reading's regime. Mass writing has been shunted to the periphery of nation-building and culture-building. So as it ascends as the dominant half of people's literacy, its potential for taking on these hallowed projects rests on precarious foundations.

Among the most precarious foundations is the location of mass writing in the employment sphere, where traditional associations among literacy, democracy, and freedom of speech are inoperative and where people's civil rights and literacy skills must bend to the rules of labor and contract. When people write for pay, they write at the will and under the control of the employer, and their skills and experience as writers belong among the assets of their organizations. That so much writing literacy is trained on these endeavors gives mass writing a weak civic tradition. Many of the people I interviewed are highly educated and highly articulate professionals who have spent decades accumulating knowledge about topics of urgent public concern – health care, the environment, monetary matters, social welfare, and civil rights, among other pressing issues. Yet many expressed reticence about writing in public in their capacities as citizens, sure that such public displays would not be looked upon favorably by their employers or would not be taken as sincere by a wider population. Now, as we have seen, individuals do try to use their workplace writing to bring about desirable outcomes where they can, within the limits of their positions. And, of course, as one government employee told me: "*I may not have the right to speak out but I still have a right to go to the ballot box and that says it better.*" But when it comes to writing, people's expressive voices seem inevitably entangled with interests and liabilities of the organizations that employ them – and often cannot be comfortably extricated even off the job. While democratized technologically, writing and publishing can be dangerous enticements if they put at risk an employer's interests or reputation. A weak civic tradition for mass writing means that courts these days find it easier to uphold the free speech rights of corporations than the free speech rights of individuals who work for them. Courts have demonstrated little curiosity or concern about the effects of paid expression on citizens' overall capacity for independent thought or action. Meanwhile, the spheres in which many of us may safely express ourselves in public grow narrow.

At the same time that writing-reliant workplaces can compromise the citizen voice, they have become formidable engines of literacy production. Businesses invest considerable time and resources in the development of writing literacy among those whose scribal skills they depend upon, sometimes through sponsoring formal classes and professional seminars but more often through informal teaching and learning. For many people, literacy learning at work happens as part of routine processes of planning, production, and oversight. As people work in rhetorically consequential conditions with powerful technologies at hand and with regular invitations to reflect, revise, and talk about writing, they also find their literacy amplified by the economic, political, and cultural power of the individuals or organizations they represent through writing. In the workplace, literacy development is not a civic duty but a by-product of production and a matter of productivity. Who gets what support for their literacy depends on their position in the production process, and that means there is less support at the bottom of an organizational hierarchy than at the top, where more original writing is produced and where the consequences of the writing are sharpest. Few employers will sponsor or subsidize basic literacy or English language instruction for employees who may need it, leaving that responsibility to oversubscribed public programs. Yet almost every writing-intensive employee I interviewed benefited from some sort of help with writing at work. Indeed, an attorney I interviewed who was a partner at a prosperous law firm had a small army of assistants who researched, edited, and corrected his writing and covered up his admittedly low level of computer skills. In the workplace, support for writing literacy is specific to the needs of production. Unlike the school, the workplace has no universalizing mandate when it comes to literacy.

When writing is a form of labor, access to instruction, opportunity, and reward are stratified as a matter of economic principle. Many of the workaday writers I interviewed found their literacy learning or opportunities to write halted by downsizing or buyouts, or by moving from well-endowed work sites to barebones ones, or by shifts in corporate priorities. Just as workplaces are formidable sites of literacy production, they are formidable sites for the production of literacy inequalities. While we are used to hearing business leaders chide the public school to lift the literacy achievement of more students, little attention is given to how businesses as de facto schools for literacy stoke inequality. Nor are these enterprises asked to be more conscientious with the literacy resources that circulate under their roofs and to engage those resources more productively for the benefit of more people. I write this from the grounds of a public university, where the ongoing literacy development of enrolled students and employed faculty is generously supported through the provision of space, material, equipment, workshops, consultations, and technical assistance of every kind and at nearly every hour of any day. But by policy and practice, service workers on campus are excluded from such supports for their literacy, with ramifications for them and their children. Today the growing gaps in wealth and well-being stem in part from the stratified patterns of access, investment, and reward that accompany the role of writing in society.

Given all that, the rise of writing presents its greatest challenge to the educational enterprise, which is growing increasingly out of step with the wider world. From its start, the school has defined literacy as reading and has treated writing skill as a branch of reading skill. Although recent educational initiatives have begun to emphasize more writing in the curriculum, writing remains untaught or undertaught in the nation's schools, and most public school teachers have had inadequate preparation in the teaching of writing (Applebee and Langer 2006). Only in specialized professional training like creative writing or journalism are teachers likely to be practicing writers themselves. In school, good writing is thought to proceed from the good reading of good texts. But recent cognitive research, although still rudimentary, illustrates how writing is not a mirror process of reading. Reading and writing fire up distinctly different parts of the brain, even as they both implicate a shared language region. As Alice Flaherty (2004) has observed: "What we do in our heads when we are daydreaming or reading, however many of our thoughts we are bringing in, has key neurological differences from writing" (p. 175). From the point of view of our brains, we are undertaking a different kind of literacy when we write and even a different kind of reading when we read our own emerging texts during composition.[2] These findings ask us to ponder the cultural and social differences between writing and reading that relate to such differentiation in brain function. At the very least, these findings beg for more attention to the writing brain, which has attracted considerably less interest than the reading brain among researchers and the general public. The instinct to communicate and connect with others surges during writing. This is a drive that is now in overdrive, stimulated and exploited by the purveyors of interactive media. Yet we lack understanding – or even good prediction – about how literacy develops from a base primarily in writing.

Even more challenging to the school going forward is the historical affiliation of writing with art, artisanship, craft, vocation, performance, publicity, and earning – parts of the human world that have been suppressed in the abstract, symbol-based routines of the school. Writing instruction has been wrestled under the wing of reading and at all levels remains too reading- and text-focused, as if what writers need most to learn can be gleaned from communion with written language (typically, in school, confined to literature or academic discourse). But, as those in this study attest, being in the company of other writing people seems critical to the development of writing know-how, sparking aspiration, emulation, craft consciousness, and better awareness of the roles of writing and writers in the world. Unlike reading, writing is a process of externalizing one's thoughts, and even more than reading it is a making. It bends toward the creation of value. These active processes remain too rare for students in the quiet, sedentary classroom, except, that is, when it comes time to be tested on what one has read or heard. When writing is treated pedagogically in all of its fullness, it engages ethics and a sense of risk and responsibility. It becomes consequential, dramatic, dangerous, demanding, rewarding, and capable of changing self and others.

If the public schools were to become committed to a full-fledged, writing-based literacy, they would give the society its best hope of recuperating mass writing for civic purposes and not just commercial and corporate ones. Schools are a place that could revive the revolutionary concept of writing and publishing as natural rights of individuals that deserve to be pursued "with decency and freedom" and with the same vital protections as reading. At the very least, schools could help citizen-students think through the implications of one day putting their literacy out for hire. Although unimaginable at the founding of this country, we have indeed become a nation of writers. What kinds of writers we are capable of being will matter to the kind of nation we can have.

In the meantime the writing imperative only deepens. In the course of interviewing for this book, I visited a research farm that on first appearance looked like any other dairy farm in my neck of the woods. There were cornfields, outbuildings, implements, pickup trucks, and a lot of mud. The facility was

staffed by farm hands whose main job was to feed, milk, and clean the livestock. But the livestock were participants in research projects, and everything
that was done on the farm had to be documented and documented correctly to
protect the integrity of the scientific projects. One of the feeders told me she that
she was so intent on accuracy that she would write instructions and protocols
on her bare arms with a ballpoint pen so as to be able to check her actions
as she physically worked with the animals. In the barn, computer screens and
keyboards sat on small desks next to hay piles. As the farm supervisor explained
to me: "*Everybody here has recording responsibilities. Down to our entry level
people.*" In fact, these recording responsibilities went deeper than that. With
digital devices implanted in their ears, the livestock sent information to computers as they ate and moved around the barn. In this setting, even the cows
were required to write.

Appendices

Appendix 1
Profile of sixty workaday adult writers

	Adminis-tration	Business	Communi-cations	Finance	Human services	IT	Law and law enforcement	Science	TOTAL
Female	6		7	2	6	1	3	2	27
Male	6	5	7	3	1	2	6	3	33
African Am.	2	1			1		1		5
Asian/Asian Am.			2		2				4
European Am.	7	4	12	5	4	3	7	5	47
Latino/Latino Am.	3						1		4
Born 1930–1940s	2	3	3	2			2		12
Born 1950–1960s	8	1	8	1	6	2	4	1	31
Born 1970–1980s	2	1	3	2	1	1	3	4	17
TOTAL	12	5	14	5	7	3	9	5	60

Appendix 2
Interview topics for workaday writers

Background:

> Year and place of birth
> Schooling and brief work history
> Current position; length of time in position
> Writing for which you are responsible
> Learning how to carry out this writing
> Interests for which your writing is responsible
> Stances, voices, representations taken in the writing
> People to whom writing is addressed
> People who read or review the writing
> Regulations on writing
> Time spent on job-related writing
> Where work writing takes place

Instruments/technologies used
Reading, reviewing, or editing other people's writing
Formal and informal learning about writing on job
Formal and informal teaching about writing on job
Awareness of changes to writing over time
Concrete consequences of work writing
Writing and reading outside of work
Sharing of workplace literacy resources with family members or others
Effects of workplace writing on you
Difficulties of writing
Satisfactions of writing

Appendix 3
Profile of thirty writing-intensive youth

	Fiction/poetry	Journalism	Non-fiction	TOTAL
Female	10	2	3	15
Male	6	2	7	15
In college	8	2	9	19
In high school	6	1		7
Working	2	1	1	4
Middle-class upbringing	10	3	7	20
Poverty upbringing	2			2
Working-class upbringing	4	1	3	8
African Am.	6		2	8
Asian/Asian Am.	1	1	1	3
European Am.	8	2	7	17
Latino/Latino Am.	1	1		2
TOTAL	16	4	10	30

Appendix 4
Interview topics for writing-intensive young adults

Place and date of birth
Schooling and occupation of parents
Own educational/employment background
Earliest memory of writing
Earliest memory of reading
First awareness that texts are written by people
Learning/knowing how to write what you write
Being taught and teaching
Significant achievements around writing
Motivations for writing

Relationships between writing and reading
Preference for writing or reading
Typical writing process
Materials and tools and their sources
Times and locations for writing
Sharing writing
Collaborating
Reading, reviewing, editing other people's writing
Awareness of own writing or writing identity developing over time
Preserving writing
Internet use
Publishing and/or performing
Effects of writing on you
Future goals
Difficulties of writing
Satisfactions of writing

Notes

INTRODUCTION

1. See Veit *et al.* (1991); also Cogan (1997). Legislative debate on what became the free speech clause of the First Amendment focused mainly on the parameters of the press and the issue of libel. For helpful context see Starr (2004: 62–82).
2. This lopsided attention to reading over writing is a condition endemic to historical studies, as observed recently in other contexts by Martyn Lyons (2010) and Ursula Howard (2012). Lyons (2012) continues to contribute valuable information about the history of writing practices.
3. For useful treatments of the range of narrative inquiry in the social sciences and their relative strengths and weaknesses, see Holstein and Gubrium (2012); also Riessman, (2007). Also see the editors' introduction in Chamberlayne *et al.* (2000) for an informative overview of biographical methods and their critics.
4. I do not claim that participants in this study are representative of their occupations or social groups in a predictive sense. Rather, each life reveals something about how the social system operates on and through a life and can illuminate structures and processes that are broadly explanatory.
5. Because language as a structuring agent was not the focus of my interest, my transcriptions omitted false starts and the like as well as words that could have disclosed a participant's real identity, as pseudonyms are used in all cases. For ease of reading, quoted passages appear in standard written English with punctuation provided by me. In some cases quotes include noncontiguous talk when, as was sometimes the case, we would return to a topic after brief divergences or if a participant elaborated on a statement later in an interview. In no cases did I use editing intentionally to misrepresent a participant or change substantive meaning.
6. Thanks to Carol Mattingly of the University of Louisville for urging me to include elective writers in this study.

CHAPTER 1

1. I am not even counting here the additional hours people spend writing as part of their leisure activities. Clive Thompson (2013a) reported that, worldwide, people produce 3.6 trillion words on the web every day.
2. Some critics claim that reading is being undermined by digital technologies that are turning us into skimmers, surfers, and shallow readers (see Carr 2011). It is worth noticing that none of the interviewees' comments about changes in their reading has to do with the effects of the web on reading. Rather, they relate to the pressures

on people who produce or monitor writing in contexts of work and production or otherwise take on the mantle of the writer.

3. For a good discussion of the issues, see Patricia Sanchez Avril *et al.* (2012). See Chapter 2 for more about regulatory pressures on workaday writers.

4. This discussion of legal regimes around workplace writing is based on a number of sources. For excellent overviews of work-for-hire doctrine see Angel and Tannenbaum (1976); also Tussey (2007). For a history of common law that shaped the 1909 US Copyright Law and its subsequent amendments, see Clark (1997). For another especially fascinating critical history, see Fisk (2009). My understanding of First Amendment law and its relevance to workplace writing comes from Baker (1989). Also see Neuborne (1989); Schauer (2004); and Norton (2009). The unique case of government workers is explored in more depth in Chapter 2. For discussions of the intersections between copyright and First Amendment, see Nimmer (1970). The "work made for hire" provision is just one small and exceptional part of copyright law. For the most part, copyright law does define the author as the person who does the work of writing, and this is the figure we associate most readily with copyright protection (at least, we have done until now). In a landmark 1976 copyright case, *Community for Creative Non-Violence v. Reid*, Supreme Court Justice Thurgood Marshall observed that, "As a general rule, the author is the party who actually creates the work that is, the person who translates an idea into a fixed, tangible expression" (quoted in VerSteeg 1996, p. 1326). When disputes have broken out under the general provisions of copyright law, courts have appealed to a much more writer-centered set of criteria to determine authorship, looking for evidence of originality, expression, and communication – criteria, in other words, that adhere closely to the act of writing itself. Here we have a different yet equally longstanding legal protection in play: protection of the rights of individuals to control and benefit from the fruits of their own intellectual labor. My interest remains in how workaday writers navigate these conflicting concepts of authorship when they compose.

5. For a discussion of the assumptions of corporate endeavor behind work-for-hire legislation, see Clark (1997). For an examination of distinctions between moral rights and economic claims and their historical imbalance in US copyright law, see Fielkow (1997). Fielkow argues that: "Despite the employer's economic rights in copyright, most employers cannot claim moral rights in a work if they did not physically create it. Moral rights can only apply to one whose personality was embodied in the art during its creation. In this case, moral rights should vest in the employee who physically created and often originated and designed the work" (p. 233); but for complicating arguments, see Saunders and Hunter (1991). For a fascinating defense of writers – rather than financiers – see Wu (2008), who argues that control by creators is necessary to be sure that the world of writing itself – including the development of new forms of text – is being invigorated and replenished.

6. For more positive outlooks on the current arrangements, see Orbach (2009), who dismisses the "genius construct" that surrounds authorship, brings attention to the moral rights of managers and directors (but not financiers) in work-based creations, and concludes that the "properties of creative activities" do not justify unique allocations or protections. For an explication of the defense of the employer's claim to ownership, see Hardy (1987), who explains it this way: "Copyright ownership

should go to the party in the better position to exploit the value of the disputed work by bringing it to the public's attention. In practice, this meant that copyright ownership went to the party with the greater resources or better market position – the one who could, in short, more cheaply distribute the work to the public" (p. 181). However, for a fascinating account of the public-good ideology of print, including inevitable state interest in the dissemination of writing, see McGill (1997); and for an interesting account of how protection of "the work" can lead to the alienation of the author, see Jaszi (1991). For an argument that author interests and social good interests must be balanced, see Yen (1990). What is so interesting to me is how all of these conflicts over ownership occur to workaday writers in the course of carrying out their tasks and/or condition their contexts of composition.

7. Orren (1991) provides a compelling legal and historical account of the reemergence of the master–servant legacy in late nineteenth century and twentieth century hierarchical workplaces.

8. Government agencies, including the courts, eventually were required to render all of their decisions in their own writing and to place their writing in the public domain, off limits to copyright by anybody. See Fisk (2009).

9. The fruits of reading can have productive and transactional value but first must be converted into externalized, transactional form (i.e., writing, in many cases).

10. For insightful discussions of legal backgrounds of this controversial case, see Norton (2008, 2009). To see how all this matters to workaday government employees, see my Chapter Two.

11. The one exception was a member of a family-owned mortgage brokerage who wrote for other family members.

12. For a thoughtful study of surrogate writers, see Kalman (1999).

13. For fascinating historical perspectives on illiteracy and the courts, see Stevens (1998).

14. This controversy shows no signs of abating. Even as journals, universities, and professional organizations enact ghostwriting policies, this less than transparent practice continues. For discussions of the ethics see, for instance, Bosch *et al.* (2013); Fugh-Berman (2005); Gorski and Letkiewicz (2010); McHenry (2010); Tierney and Gerrity (2005).

15. Empirical evidence suggests that industry-sponsored writing has less credibility with readers (one of the reasons that transparency is having a hard go of it). See Lacasse *et al.* (2012).

16. Both Slager and the legislator are European American and from the middle class.

17. One of the few pieces of scholarship I have been able to find that treats work and its effects on personhood is Schultz (2000). She writes here about work but I would say this is especially true of work *writing*:

Work is a site of deep self-formation that offers rich opportunities for human flourishing (or devastation). To a large extent it is through our work – how it is defined, distributed, characterized, and controlled – that we develop into the "men" and "women" we see ourselves and others as being. Because law's domain includes work and its connection to other spheres of existence, the prospect of who we become as a society, and as individuals, is shaped profoundly by the laws that create and control the institutions that govern our experiences as workers. (pp. 1883–1884)

CHAPTER 2

1. See Wilson (1999) for an account of Jefferson's steadfast belief that reading cultivated the perspective-taking and critical habits of mind needed to sustain a democratic government. Brown (1997) provides an historical account of the growing ideological association among reading, a free press, and a free citizenry in the context of Revolutionary America. Brown recognizes that this association did not allay struggles around who counts as a citizen, but this history helps to explain how literacy came to be used both as a standard to exclude people from citizenship and a basis for laying claim to citizenship. As Brown establishes, definitions of all the pertinent terms – citizen, reading, and the informed – continued to change across time. Also see Warner (1992) for an important demonstration of how the public was trained to read as a strategy in the struggle for independence. For an updated and more skeptical view, see Lidsky (2010). For a contemporary empirical argument about how "reading is illustrative of a lifestyle that aids citizenship," see Bennett *et al.* (2000). (I could find no equivalent studies about what mass writing illustrates in terms of the citizen lifestyle.)

2. Alexander Meiklejohn (1948) is generally credited with establishing the public's right to know as the credible basis of First Amendment protections. He writes:

> The point of ultimate interest is not the words of the speakers, but the minds of the hearers . . . The First Amendment, then, is not the guardian of unregulated talkativeness. It does not require that, on every occasion, every citizen shall take part in public debate. Nor can it even give assurance that everyone shall have the opportunity to do so . . . What is essential is not that everyone shall speak, but that everything worth saying shall be said. (p. 25)

For another interpretation, see Emerson (1976). While Emerson accords more importance to individual free speech than Meiklejohn, he nevertheless argues that expressive speech rights will be most firmly secured by the rights of the public to know. In other words, a speaker's best protection against an intrusive government is a citizenry broadly entitled to information. Tussman (1977) examines the foundations of the right to inner, mental privacy. He writes: "Government, we are told – and by the Supreme Court – may not invade the sphere of intellect and spirit" (p. 3). And, "Public authority is unlicensed in the private world" (p. 5). The thoughts of readers lie in this inner domain and enjoy this ring of privacy. (Tussman goes on in his study, however, to look at how the government indeed influences minds, most directly, through mandatory public education.) In case law, the right to privacy in reading choices is conceptualized as part of a broader right to privacy, generally thought to lodge in the First, Fourth, Fifth, Ninth, and Fourteenth Amendments. Case law has upheld citizens' rights to receive extremist mail and read obscenity in the privacy of their homes. Most of all, the American Librarian Association has developed professional principles guarding the records of library patrons. These principles have come into conflict with the Patriot Act. For a brief history, see Bowers (2006). Private writing can have a harder time of it. Visible and permanent, writing is more easily discoverable, searchable, and susceptible to subpoena.

3. Frankel looks at how central governments in the nineteenth century sponsored major studies and inquests as a way to represent their power to the citizenry. The US government was a heavy publisher by the early 1850s; some government-commissioned ethnographic and geological studies of this period in fact became best sellers. Frankel is a rare scholar, who pays attention to the writers of these reports – many of them independent scholars – and how they carried out their work. Also see Scott (1998). Government writers today number in the tens of millions. According to recent Bureau of Labor Statistics figures (www.bls.gov/oes/current/999001.htm) government employs over 1 million people in management; 1.8 million in business and financial services; nearly 400,000 in computer and math; more than 300,000 in architecture and engineering; more than 448,000 in science; nearly 760,000 in social services; nearly 256,000 in law; 6.5 million in teaching and library services; 34,000 in public relations; more than 5,700 in editing and writing; 19,000 in translating and interpreting; 1.1 million in health care; around 2 million in protective services; and 3.4 million in office support.
4. For a basic explanation of the government's need to advance its own viewpoints, see Bezanson and Buss (2001). For measured cautions about the powers of government to speak in public forums, see Bezanson (2010); Norton (2003–2004); and Yudof (2009).
5. Scott E. Casper (2007) observes: "From the founding of the United States, governments at all levels have been among the nation's most prolific publishers" (p. 178). Seavey and Sloat (2009) track the prodigious government print production in the late nineteenth century, concluding that, "The US government had become (and is) the largest publisher in the world" (p. 260). For follow up, see Nord and Richardson (2009).
6. Migdal's theory challenges structuralist and so-called statist conceptions of government authority, legitimacy, and control, including those influenced by Talcott Parsons, who stresses shared goals and predictable stages of collective development, and Max Weber, who treated the State as an homogeneous institution that uses military and political might to impose its policies. Influenced by Bourdieu and interested in comparative politics, Migdal embraced a more decentralized and practice-centered framework, one that I found attractive for helping to explain the accounts of participants in my study.
7. I located participants by using government websites that posted the names and email addresses of individual agency employees. Not all agencies made this information available. I looked for websites at the local, state, and federal level and in the executive, legislative, and judicial branches. I then randomly contacted employees using the email lists, continuing to seek individuals who were willing to talk with me. In some cases those individuals referred me to supervisors, who then assisted me in locating participants.
8. I chose these four focal individuals out of the thirty government employees I interviewed in order to represent different branches of government and different occupations within government, and to represent the gender and race diversity of the participants. While these four individuals addressed issues of representation in their writing in interesting and thought-provoking ways, they were certainly not unique for this. In many ways the selection of these four was arbitrary.

9. In *Public Opinion* (1922), Walter Lippmann wrote: "I argue that representative government, either in what is ordinarily called politics or industry, cannot be worked successfully, no matter what the basis of election, unless there is an independent, expert organization for making the unseen facts intelligible to those who have to make decisions" (pp. 31–32). Lippmann found it unrealistic that every citizen would be able to develop informed opinions about every matter before a government. In *The Public and Its Problems* (1927), John Dewey argued that citizens "inspired by democracy" could rise to the obligations of overseeing even a complex government and be thoughtful contributors to the deliberations. Only the public, he maintained, will understand the public interest.

10. I am helped in this discussion by Foerstal (1999). For a critical treatment of government obstruction in providing information, see McDermott (2007).

11. Simmons' views were not necessarily shared by other government employees I contacted. Many did not respond to my request to interview them or else declined my request.

12. The entire Wisconsin open-record law can be found at: http://nxt.legis.state.wi.us/ nxt/gateway.dll?f=templates&fn=default.htm&d=stats&jd=19.31

13. This ruling has met with considerable criticism by legal scholars. See, particularly, a symposium on the *Garcetti* decision that appeared in the Fall 2008 issue of *First Amendment Law Review.*

14. For scholarly treatments of this fluid area of the law, see Fabian (2010); Kirkland (2006); Shooman (2005–2006).

15. Interestingly, when I asked Rollins if he wrote outside of work he said he did not because he lacked an audience.

16. One of the legislative aides I interviewed was heavily involved in political activity as a private citizen. To obey state statutes that regulated political activity of government employees during work hours, it was important that he segregate that activity, so he stayed up late at night writing on behalf of this volunteer community action group. By law, he was strictly prohibited from conducting any partisan activity while he was physically working in his state capitol. At the same time, he talked about how his experiences at work helped him to craft rhetorically effective messages for the volunteer political organization for which he worked. Under the same set of regulations, Diana Garcia, the legislative aide introduced earlier in this chapter, said that when she campaigned for her boss, she took vacation time.

CHAPTER 3

1. For a dated but still informative overview of claims for the role of reading in writing development, see Stotsky (1983). On how writing reinforces reading, see Graham and Hebert (2010). Learning to write by imitating texts is a tenet of classical rhetorical education; see Edward P.J. Corbett (1971). For a thoughtful, expansive update see Fleming (2003). For a more cognitive treatment, see Bereiter and Scardamlia (1984). In general, the fields of education and writing studies have moved toward a view that reading and writing share underlying pragmatic functions and discourse processes, not that one necessarily leads to the other (see Note 2). Still, the belief that writing skill requires reading experience remains strong. Given changes to writing and reading wrought by digital technologies, the need for updated research on this premise is obvious.

2. The consensus now is that reading and writing are both constructive, meaning-driven discourse processes that engage overlapping resources of language, pragmatics, and world knowledge, such that experiences with one can, under certain conditions, feed the other. For excellent overviews, see Fitzgerald and Shanahan (2000); also Langer and Flihan (2002).

3. This discussion is largely informed by the work of Cornelius (1992); Gallegos (1992); Gross (2007); Monaghan (2005); and Soltow and Stevens (1981). Also see Nelson and Calfee (1998).

4. Evan is a European American who was born in 1985 and raised in the middle class.

5. It is an important detail that when Evan Davies was offered a book contract, the publishing house that made the offer had recently been bought out by one of the largest corporate providers of pet supplies, a national company that was also buying up smaller pet supply companies as a way to consolidate its market share. Before that, the publishing house had been small and independent. The company corralled Evan's knowledge, which he had been giving away for free, to make it profitable, a classic move in what Burton-Jones (2001) calls knowledge capitalism.

6. I assigned socioeconomic status on the basis of what participants told me about the educational attainment and occupations of their parents or guardians, confirmed through other details that emerged during the interviews.

7. A most expansive account of all dimensions of authorship in the US is offered in the magisterial *A History of the Book in America, Volumes 1-V* (Hall 2007–2010). Also see Woodmansee and Jaszi (1994). For treatments of the rise of working writers see Weber (1997); and for important histories of professional writing instruction in colleges and universities see Adams (1993) and Myers (2006).

8. For an important treatment of changing conditions for authorship, see Laquintano (2010).

9. You will notice that I use the terms *writer* and *author* interchangeably in this discussion, largely because most of my participants did. Some wanted to differentiate between a *writer* (someone who writes) and an *author* (someone who publishes). For a more nuanced treatment of *author* than the one offered here see Haswell and Haswell (2010), who define authoring in terms of a psychological experience during writing. Also see Eubanks (2010) and Tomlinson (2005).

10. 19-year-old middle-class African American male

11. 16-year-old middle-class European American female

12. 22-year-old middle-class European American male

13. 20-year-old middle-class European American male

14. 24-year-old middle-class Latina

15. 20-year-old working-class European American female

16. 21-year-old working-class European American female

17. 18-year-old upper-class European American male

18. 19-year-old low-income African American female

19. 16-year-old middle-class European American female

20. 20-year-old middle-class European American male

21. 22-year-old middle-class African American female

22. 16-year-old low-income African American male

23. 22-year-old working-class European American male

24. 22-year-old middle-class European American male

25. 20-year-old middle-class Asian American male
26. 24-year-old middle-class African American female
27. 16-year-old middle-class European American female
28. 20-year-old middle-class European American male
29. 24-year-old working-class European American female
30. 17-year-old middle-class Asian American female
31. 17-year-old working-class Latina
32. 22-year-old low-income European American female
33. 23-year-old middle-class European American male
34. 18-year-old upper middle-class European American male
35. A fourth participant published a novel some months after our interview.
36. For a discussion of vocational–liberal currents in early writing instruction in England that is relevant to this discussion, see Christen (1999).
37. This is a pseudonym.
38. Akira and her team did not win the competition.
39. For an interesting treatment of the hand and changing conceptions of authorship, see Goldberg (1990).
40. For an argument on how this identification can happen by way of texts and reading, see Brooke (1988). This style of reading is a key move in what I call writing-based literacy.
41. Beginning at least from the 1970s in the work of such writing pedagogues as Donald Murray and Donald Graves, continuing with Peter Elbow and Nancie Atwell, and instantiated most broadly in the National Writing Project, efforts have been made to make authoring and authors a centerpiece of liberal-arts writing instruction, both in terms of attending to how real writers work and in terms of arranging learning environments in such a way that student authors gain access to readers and publishing. In this tradition, teachers also write and model the writer's life for students. While two of the participants in this study did experience writing instruction in this "workshop" tradition throughout their schooling, and a couple more had sporadic experience with it, most of the participants in this study were largely untouched by this tradition. See Atwell (1998); Elbow (1998); Graves (2003); Gray (2000); Murray and Newkirk (2009). In the writing curriculums at the post-secondary level, the working writer of interest is mostly the discipline-based scholarly writer. These writers rarely model work in person; rather their texts are studied and analyzed (see, for instance, Herrington and Moran 2005).
42. I have been helped in my thinking on this point by the ethnographic work of Anne Dyson (1997, 2003), who shows how even very young writers can fully inhabit powerful popular genres and advance them for their own social and intellectual purposes. I have also been helped by the wonderful progress being made in genre theory over the last couple of decades, especially in writing studies. Genres are now understood not as text types or static forms but as traveling sets of social resources that mediate interpersonal and intrapersonal relations. For particularly nimble and incisive uses of these recent understandings of genre, see Bawarshi (2003).
43. For a good and thorough treatment of the rising social significance of blogs, see Rosenberg (2010).
44. A surprising number of young people I interviewed preferred to do their writing in longhand, in notebooks, instead of on a computer. Speculatively, I link this preference to their formative years, when they used notebooks to carry their writing

with them to school, where they worked on it under the guise of taking notes or doing seatwork. A few said they kept notebooks in order to preserve drafts over time, a record that helped them gauge their own growth as writers.

45. For an interesting study of the use of writing in reading assessment, including evidence that reading assessments that use writing can underestimate reading comprehension, see Jenkins *et al.* (2004).

46. The experiences of at least three of the study participants departed in some ways from this privileging of reading. Valeria Rojas, who was born and schooled in Colombia, said writing was much more stressed than reading in the society around her and in the curriculum of her schools there. When she arrived in the United States as a teenager, she encountered the heavy focus on reading as different from her home society. Carla King started inventing stories at the age of 2, and her father, a graphic designer, illustrated them and produced them as what she called *"little books."* Alexis Harrison said her parents *"put a journal in my hands when I was 4 years old"* and she began writing from that time.

47. I suspect that is why it has been difficult to establish consistent findings about reading–writing relationships and why some proficient readers have been found to write poorly and vice versa. For a good overview, see Fitzgerald and Shanahan (2000).

48. There was one exception. Throughout my interview with political blogger Maury Lowell, he consistently minimized his writing and rejected the label of writer, even though he did write avidly and thought about a career in political journalism. He characterized his reading and writing quite differently from other participants, more in line with what I would call a reading-based literacy. Speaking here about his childhood literacy, he said: *"I don't think I ever focused on the author. It was always about the story. I got so absorbed in some of those books. I would read straight and want to read the next one right away and want to live in the fantasy world. That's why I wrote. When I wrote I pictured myself as the main character."*

49. In *Songs Of Ourselves: the uses of poetry in America*, Rubin (2007) observes, "There is a key difference between the audience spurring the recent boom [in poetry] and their late nineteenth-century and early twentieth-century predecessors: present day poetry devotees are more likely to be writers as well as – and, in some cases, instead of – readers" (p. 384).

50. For general histories, see Kaestle (1983); Kaestle *et al.* (1991); Soltow and Stevens (1981). I use the word *belief* throughout the discussion to distance myself from the many claims made for the power of literacy, yet to show how these beliefs have their own organizing power when it comes to literacy. I also use the term *experience* to capture both the larger social situations that accompany reading and writing and to inquire into how people interpret those experiences. Graff (1979, 2010) has been especially critical of unsubstantiated claims that literacy in and of itself improves people's lives. For a subtle treatment of how beliefs about literacy can be recruited for social and political advancement, see Bibbs (2011).

51. The literature on the effects of reading is vast and diffuse. For historical perspective see Brown (1997); also Waples *et al.* (1940). For cultural and critical perspectives see, for instance, McHenry (2002); Sicherman (2010); Warner (1992). For more empirical approaches, see Cunningham and Stanovitch (2001); Nell (1988); Oatley (2011). And for a treatment of reading and civic participation, see Bennett *et al.* (2000); also Milner (2002).

52. For writing and self-disciplining, see Miller (1998). For a rare sustained treatment of lay writing see Burton (2008). On writing and learning, see Emig (1977); Langer and Applebee (1987); Applebee (1984); National Writing Project and Carl Nagin (2006). On writing for therapeutic ends, see, for instance, Daniell (2003) and the fascinating work of James W. Pennebaker (1997); Pennebaker and Chung, 2006).

53. I have noticed that some popular writing guidebooks do take up issues of courage, including in terms of managing relationships between art and life. See Keys (2003). Learning to write involves learning to overcome fear, even though writing instruction too often serves to cultivate fear.

CHAPTER 4

1. Of course other harsh disqualifications were in place in this period, including exclusions by race and gender.

2. See St. Clair (2004, Chapter 1) for a discussion of some of the methodological difficulties and potentials associated with this kind of scholarship.

3. In fact, candidates for jury duty are sometimes eliminated if, upon questioning, they appear too well informed about a case prior to trial. Admitting to avid consumption of news media can be a liability for citizens during a voir dire process.

4. This chapter does not focus mainly on digital transformations, as much has been written on the subject. For instance, see Shirky (2009); Carr (2011); Thompson (2013b). For a more grounded ethnographic treatment, see Selfe and Hawisher (2004).

5. Scholarship on writers and their audiences is vast, interdisciplinary, and disputatious. For recent syntheses of this literature from diverse perspectives see Miller and Charney (2007) and Rijlaarsdam et al. (2009).

6. For an interesting treatment of relationships between writing practices and workplace organization, see Karlsson (2009).

7. Several people I interviewed had regular interactions with news media, and it was striking to me how much they thought about, tried to work with and even manipulate the composing rhythms and habits of journalists. An information officer for a police department remarked: *"I do keep a journalist's mentality of what they want, what they need."* Another communications specialist observed about press releases: *"Everybody sends them. Everybody writes them. The news organizations get more of them than they know what to do with."* A legislative aide explains: *"We had all these graphics we wanted the press to know about and see but when we put them on a poster, nobody took a picture of them. So we burned CDs to hand out, with all of our talking points, our arguments, the graphics, everything on the CD. So some of them took the graph and put it right in the newspaper. We made it so easy, we controlled that."*

8. For some provocative empirical research on the beneficial effects of proximity to other writing people, see Braaksma et al. (2002, 2004).

9. For an entertaining historical treatment of wayward youth and the language crisis (which he dates back to ancient Sumeria), see Daniels (1983). Thanks to Chris Anson for this reference.

CONCLUSION

1. Interestingly these conditions pertain both in the workplace and in adolescent online writing communities. See Alvermann (2004); Black (2008). They also pertain in the blogosphere, where readers of blogs are often other bloggers (Lenart and Fox 2006).
2. In addition to Flaherty (2004), see Berninger *et al.* (2002) and Berninger and Winn (2006). Also Dehaene (2009); Wolf (2007).

Bibliography

Adams, Katherine H. 1993. *A History of Professional Writing Instruction in American Colleges: years of acceptance, growth and doubt*. Dallas, TX: Southern Methodist University Press.

Alvermann, Donna E. 2004. *Adolescents and Literacies in a Digital World*. New York: Peter Lang.

Angel, Dennis and Samuel W. Tannenbaum 1976. Works made for hire under S.22. *New York Law School Law Review* 22, 2: 209–239.

Anson, Chris M. and L. Lee Forsberg 1990. Moving beyond the academic community: transitional stages in professional writing. *Written Communication* 7, 2: 200–231.

Applebee, Arthur 1984. Writing and reasoning. *Review of Educational Research* 54, 4: 577–596.

Applebee, Arthur N. and Judith Langer 2006. *The State of Writing Instruction in American's Schools: what existing data tell us*. Albany: Center on English Learning and Achievement at Albany State University of New York.

Asencion Delaney, Yuly 2008. Investigating the reading-to-write construct. *Journal of English for Academic Purposes* 7, 3: 140–150.

Atwell, Nancie 1998. *In the Middle: new understandings about writing, reading and learning* 2nd ed. Portsmouth, NH: Heinemann.

Auer, John J. 1984. Ghostwriting and the cult of leadership response. *Communication Education* 33: 306–307.

Avril, Patricia Sanchez, Avner Levin, and Alissa Del Riego 2012. Blurred boundaries: social media privacy and the twenty-first century employee. *American Business Law Journal* 49, 1: 63–124.

Baker, C. Edwin 1989. *Human Liberty and Freedom of Speech*. New York: Oxford University Press.

Barlow, Aaron J. 2007. *The Rise of the Blogosphere*. New York: Praeger.

Bazerman, Charles 2007. *Handbook of Research on Writing: history, society, school, individual and text*. New York: Routledge.

Bawarshi, Anis 2003. *Genre and the Invention of the Writer: reconsidering the place of invention in composition*. Logan: Utah State University Press.

Beaufort, Anne 1999. *Writing in the Real World: making the transition from school to work*. New York: Teachers College Press.

Bennett, Stephen R., Staci Rhine, and Richard Flickinger 2000. Reading's impact on democratic citizenship in America. *Political Behavior* 22, 3: 167–195.

Bereiter, Carl and Marlene Scardamalia 1984. Learning about writing from reading. *Written Communication* 1, 2: 163–188.

Berninger, Virginia W., Robert D. Abbott, Sylvia P. Abbott, Steve Graham, and Todd Richards 2002. Writing and reading: connections between language by hand and language by eye. *Journal of Learning Disabilities* 35, 1: 39–56.

Berninger, Virginia W. and William D. Winn 2006. Implications of advancements in brain research and technology for writing development. In Charles A. MacArthur, Steve Graham, and Jill Fitzgerald (eds.). *Handbook of Writing Research*. New York. Guildford Press, pp. 96–114.

Bertaux, Daniel 1981. *Biography and Society: the life history approach in the social sciences*. Thousand Oaks, CA: Sage.

2003. The usefulness of life stories for a realist and meaningful sociology. In Robin Humphrey, Robert Miller, and Elena Zaravomyslova (eds.). *Biographical Research in Eastern Europe: altered lives and broken biographies*. Hampshire, England: Ashgate, pp. 39–52.

Bertaux, Daniel and Catherine Delcroix 2000. Case histories of families and social processes. In Prue Chamberlayne, Joanna Bornat, and Tom Wengraf (eds.). *The Turn to Biographical Methods in Social Science*. New York: Routledge, pp. 71–89.

Bezanson, Randall P. 2010. The manner of government speech. *Denver University Law Review* 87, 4: 809–818.

Bezanson, Randall P. and William G. Buss 2001. The many faces of government speech. *Iowa Law Review* 86: 1377–1511.

Bibbs, Maria 2011. "The African American Literacy Myth: literacy's ethical objective during the Progressive Era, 1890–1919," Ph.D. dissertation, University of Wisconsin-Madison, ProQuest 3488549.

Black, Rebecca 2008. *Adolescents and Online Fan Fiction*. New York: Peter Lang.

Boesky, Amy 2013. The ghost writes back. *Kenyon Review Online*. Winter: DOI 656342.

Bolter, Jay 2001. *Writing Space: computers, hypertext, and the myth of transparency*. New York: Routledge.

Bormann, Ernest G. 1960. Ghostwriting and the rhetorical critic. *Quarterly Journal of Speech* 66: 284–288.

1961. Ethics of ghostwritten speeches. *Quarterly Journal of Speech* 67: 262–267.

Bosch, Xavier, Christina Hernandez, Juan M. Pericas, and Pamela Doti 2013. Ghostwriting policies in high-impact biomedical journals: a cross-sectional study. *JAMA Internal Medicine* 173, 10: 920–921.

Bowers, Stacey L. Bowers 2006. Privacy and library records. *Journal of Academic Librarianship* 32, 4: 377–383.

Braaksma, Martine. A.H., Gert Rijlaarsdam, and Huub van den Bergh 2002. Observational learning and the effects of model–observer similarity. *Journal of Educational Psychology* 94, 2: 405–415.

Braaksma, Martine A.H., Gert Rijlaarsdam, Huub van den Bergh, and Bernardette H.A.M. Van Hout-Wolters 2004. Observational learning and its effects on the orchestration of writing processes. *Cognition and Instruction* 22, 1: 1–36.

Brandt, Deborah 2001. *Literacy in American Lives*. New York: Cambridge University Press.

2004. Drafting US literacy. *College English* 66, 5: 485–502.

2005. Writing for a living: literacy and the knowledge economy. *Written Communication* 22, 2: 166–197.

2009. *Literacy and Learning: reflections on writing, reading, and society*. San Francisco: Jossey-Bass.

Brodhead, Richard 1993. *Cultures of Letters: scenes of reading and writing in nineteenth-century America*. Chicago: University of Chicago Press.

Brooke, Robert 1988. Modeling a writer's identity: reading and imitation in the writing classroom. *College Composition and Communication* 39, 1: 23–41.

Brown, Richard D. 1997. *Strength of a People: the idea of an informed citizenry in America 1650–1870*. Chapel Hill: University of North Carolina Press.

Burguiere, Andre 2009. *The Annales School: an intellectual history*. Trans. Jane Marie Todd. Ithaca, NY: Cornell University Press.

Burk, Dan L. 2004. Intellectual property and the firm. *University of Chicago Law Review* 71, 1: 3–21.

Burke, Peter 2005. *History and Social Theory, 2nd ed*. Ithaca NY: Cornell University Press, p. 2.

Burton, Vicki Tolar 2008. *Spiritual Literacy in John Wesley's Methodism: reading, writing, and speaking to believe*. Waco, TX: Baylor University Press.

Burton-Jones, Alan 2001. *Knowledge Capitalism*. New York: Oxford University Press.

Buss, Kristine 2011. Ghosting authenticity. *Journal of Business and Technical Communication* 24, 2: 159–183.

Carr, Nicholas 2011. *The Shallows: what the Internet is doing to our brain*. New York: Norton.

Casper, Scott E. 2007. The census, the Post Office, and government publishing. In Scott E. Casper, Jeffrey D. Groves, Stephen W. Nissenbaum, and Michael Winship (eds.). *A History of the Book in America, Volume III: the industrial book, 1840–1880*. Chapel Hill: University of North Carolina Press, pp. 178–193.

Chamberlayne, Prue, Joanna Bornat, and Tom Wengraf 2000. *The Turn to Biographical Methods in Social Science*. New York: Routledge.

Chandler, Alfred 1977. *The Visible Hand*. Cambridge, Ma.: Harvard University Press.

Charmaz, Kathy 2006. *Constructing Grounded Theory*. Thousand Oaks, CA: Sage.

Chartier, Roger 1995. *Forms and Meanings: text, performances, and audiences from codex to computer*. Philadelphia: University of Pennsylvania Press.

Choi, Stephen J. Choi and G. Mitu Gulati 2000. Empirical measures of judicial performance: which judges write their own opinions and should we care? *Florida State University Law Review* 32 (Summer): 107–122.

Christen, Richard S. 1999. Boundaries between liberal and technical learning: images of seventeenth-century English writing masters. *History of Education Quarterly* 39, 1 (Spring): 31–50.

Clark, Jon 1997. Copyright law and work for hire: a critical history. *Copyright Law Symposium* 40: 129–164.

Cogan, Neil H. 1997. *The Complete Bill of Rights: the drafts, debates, sources and origins*. New York: Oxford University Press.

Cohen, Daniel A. 1993. *Pillars of Salt/Monuments of Grace: New England crime literature and the origins of American popular culture, 1674–1860*. New York: Oxford University Press.

Cornelius, Janet Duitsman 1992. *When I Can Read My Title Clear: literacy, slavery, and religion in the Antebellum South*. Columbia: University of South Carolina Press.

Corbett, Edward P.J. 1971. The theory and practice of imitation in classical rhetoric. *College Composition and Communication* 22, 3: 243–250.

Cunningham, Anne E. and Keith E. Stanovich 2001. What reading does for the mind. *Journal of Direct Instruction* 1, 2: 137–149.

Daniell, Beth A. 2003. *Communion of Friendship: literacy, spiritual practice, and women in recovery.* Carbondale, IL: Southern Illinois University Press.

Daniels, Harvey A. 1983. *Famous Last Words: the American language crisis reconsidered.* Carbondale: Southern Illinois University Press.

Darnton, Robert 1978. History of mentalities. In Richard Harvey Brown and Stanford M. Lyman (eds.). *Structure, Consciousness, and History.* New York: Cambridge University Press, 1978, pp.106–136.

Dehaene, Stanislas. 2009. *Reading in the Brain.* New York: Viking.

Dewey, John 1927. *The Public and Its Problems.* New York: Holt.

Doheny-Farina, Stephen 1986. Writing in an emerging organization. *Written Communication* 3, 2: 158–185.

Drucker, Peter F. 2003. The knowledge society. In *A Functioning Society: sixty-five years of writing on community, society, and polity.* New Brunswick, NJ: Transaction Press, pp. 147–194.

Durkheim, Emile 1982. *The Rules of Sociological Method* (1st Am. Ed.). Trans W.D. Halls. New York: Free Press.

Dyson, Anne Haas 1997. *Writing Superheroes: contemporary childhood, popular culture, and classroom literacy.* New York: Teachers College Press.

  2003. *The Brothers and the Sisters Learn to Write: popular literacies in childhood and school culture.* New York: Teachers College Press.

Ede, Lisa and Andrea Lunsford 1990. *Singular Texts/Plural Authors: perspectives on collaborative writing.* Carbondale: Southern Illinois University Press.

Einhorn, Lois J. 1988. The ghosts talk: personal interviews with three former speechwriters. *Communications Quarterly* 36, 2: 94–108.

Eisenstein, Elizabeth 1982. *The Printing Press as an Agent of Change.* New York: Cambridge University Press.

Elbow, Peter 1998. *Writing Without Teachers, Twenty-Fifth Anniversary Edition.* New York: Oxford University Press.

Emerson, Thomas L. 1976. Legal foundations of the right to know. *Washington University Law Quarterly* 1: 1–24.

Emig, Janet 1977. Writing as mode of learning. *College Composition and Communication* 28, 2: 122–128.

Erdal, Jennie 2004. *Ghosting: a double life.* New York: Doubleday.

Eubanks, Phillip 2010. *Metaphor and Writing.* New York: Cambridge University Press.

Fabian, Sarah L. 2010. *Garcetti v. Ceballos:* whether an employee speaks as a citizen or a public employee: who decides? *UC Davis Law Review* 43: 1675–1708.

Fielkow, Colleen Creamer 1997. Clashing rights under United States copyright law: harmonizing an employer's economic right with the artist-employee's moral rights in a work made for hire. *DePaul-LCA Journal of Art and Entertainment Law* 7: 218–263.

Fischer, Frank 2009. *Democracy and Expertise: reorienting public policy inquiry.* New York: Oxford University Press.

Fisher, Maisha T. 2007. *Writing in Rhythm: spoken word poetry in urban classrooms.* New York: Teachers College Press.

  2009. *Black Literate Lives: historical and contemporary perspectives.* New York: Routledge.

Fisk, Catherine 2000. Working knowledge: trade secrets, restrictive covenants in employment, and the rise of corporate intellectual property, 1800–1920. *Hastings Law Journal* 52, 2: 441–536.

2003. Authors at work: the origins of the work-for-hire doctrine. *Yale Journal of Law* 15, 1: 1–70.

2009. *Working Knowledge: employee innovation and the rise of corporate intellectual property, 1800–1939.* Chapel Hill: University of North Carolina Press.

Fitzgerald, Jill and Timothy Shanahan 2000. Reading and writing relations and their development. *Educational Psychologist* 35, 1: 39–50.

Flaherty, Alice W. 2004. *The Midnight Disease: the drive to write, writer's block and the creative brain.* New York: Houghton Mifflin, 2004.

Fleming, David 2003. The very idea of a progymnasmata. *Rhetoric Review* 22, 2: 105–120.

Fletcher, Robert J. 2005. Ghostwriting initiated by commercial companies. *Journal of General Internal Medicine* 20, 6: 549.

Flower, Linda, Victoria Stein, John Ackerman, Margaret J. Krantz, Kathleen McCormick, and Wayne C. Peck 1990. *Reading-to-Write: exploring a cognitive and social process.* New York: Oxford University Press.

Foerstal, Herbert N. 1999. *Freedom of Information and the Right to Know: the origins and applications of the Freedom of Information Act.* Westport, CT: Greenwood Press.

Fosko, T.J. 2012. Buying a lie: the harms and deceptions of ghostwriting. *University of Arkansas at Little Rock Law Review*, 35: 165.

Foucault, Michel 1988. *Technologies of the Self.* Amherst: University of Massachusetts Press.

Frankel, Oz 2006. *States of Inquiry: social investigations and print culture in nineteenth-century Britain and the United States.* Baltimore, MD: Johns Hopkins University Press.

Fugh-Berman, Adriane 2005. The corporate co-author. *Journal of General Internal Medicine* 20, 6: 546–548.

Furet, Francois and Jaques Ozouf 1982. *Reading and Writing: Literacy in France from Calvin to Jules Ferry.* Cambridge UK: Cambridge University Press.

Gallegos, Bernardo 1992. *Literacy, Education and Society in New Mexico 1693–1821.* Albuquerque: University of New Mexico Press.

Gelfand, Donald E. 2006. *The Aging Network: programs and services.* New York: Springer.

Gillespie, Thomas C. 2002. Let's stop ghostwriting reviewing officer remarks. *Marine Corps Gazette* October: 29–30.

Gilmore, William J. 1992. *Reading Becomes a Necessity of Life: material cultural life in rural New England, 1780–1835.* Knoxville: University of Tennessee Press.

Ginsberg, Jane 1990. Creation and commercial value: copyright protection of works of information. *Columbia Law Review* 90, 7: 1865–1938.

Goldberg, Jonathan 1990. *Writing Matter: from the hands of the English Renaissance.* Stanford, CA: Stanford University Press.

Goldschmidt, Jona 2002. In defense of ghostwriting. *Fordham Urban Law Journal* 29: 1145–1187.

Gorski, Andrzej and Slawomir Letkiewicz 2010. "Medical writing" and ghostwriting as ethical challenges in medical communication. *Transplantation Proceedings* 42, 8: 3335–3337.

Graff, Harvey J. 1979. *The Literacy Myth: cultural integration and social structure in the nineteenth century*. New York: Academic Press.

    1987. *The Legacies of Literacy: continuities and contradictions in Western culture and society*. Bloomington: Indiana University Press.

    2010. The literacy myth at 30. *Journal of Social History* 43, 3: 635–661.

Graham, Steve and Michael Hebert 2010. *Writing to Read: evidence for how writing can improve reading*. New York: Carnegie Corporation.

Graves, Donald 2003. *Writing: teachers and children at work, 20th anniversary edition*. Portsmouth, NH: Heinemann, 2003.

Gray, James 2000. *Teachers at the Center: a memoir of the early years of the National Writing Project*. Berkeley, CA: National Writing Project.

Gross, Robert A. 2007. Reading for an extensive republic. In Robert A. Gross and Mary Kelley (eds.). *A History of the Book in America Volume II: print, culture, and society in the new nation, 1790–1840*. Chapel Hill: University of North Carolina Press, pp. 516–544.

Grow, Brian 2010. As jurors go online US trials go off track. *Reuters Legal* (December 8). Web.

Hall, David D. 2007. The Chesapeake in the seventeenth century. In Hugh Amory and David D. Hall, (eds.). *History of the Book in America Volume I*. Chapel Hill: University of North Carolina Press, pp. 55–82.

    2007–2010. *A History of the Book in America, Volumes 1–V*. Chapel Hill: University of North Carolina Press.

Hardy, I.T. 1987. An economic understanding of copyright law's work-made-for-hire doctrine. *Columbia Journal of Law and the Arts* 12, 2: 181–228.

Haswell, Janis and Richard Haswell 2010. *Authoring: an essay for the English profession on potentiality and singularity*. Logan: Utah State University Press.

Henry, Jim 2000. *Writing Workplace Culture: an archaeology of professional writing*. Albany, NY: State University of New York Press.

Herrington, Anne and Charles Moran 2005. *Genre Across the Curriculum*. Logan: Utah State University Press.

Hitt, Jack 1997. The writer is dead. *New York Times Magazine*, 25 May: 38–41.

Holstein, James A. and Jaber F. Gubrium 2012. *Varieties of Narrative Analysis*. Los Angeles: Sage.

Howard, Ursula 2012. *Literacy and the Practice of Writing in the 19th Century: a strange blossoming of spirit*. Leicester, England: National Institute of Adult Continuing Education.

Hutton, Patrick H. 1981. The history of mentalities: the new map of cultural history. *History and Theory* 20, 3: 237–259.

Jaszi, Peter 1991. Toward a theory of copyright: the metamorphoses of "authorship." *Duke Law Journal* 2: 455–502.

    1994. On the author effect: contemporary copyright and collective creativity. In Martha Woodmansee and Peter Jaszi (eds.). *The Construction of Authorship: textual appropriation in law and literature*. Durham, N.C.: Duke University Press, pp. 29–56.

Jenkins, Joseph R., Evelyn Johnson, and Jennifer Hileman 2004. When is reading also writing? Sources of individual differences on the new reading performance assessments. *Scientific Studies of Reading* 8, 2: 125–151.

Johns, Adrian 2010. *The Nature of the Book: print and knowledge in the making.* Chicago: University of Chicago Press.

Kaestle, Carl 1983. *Pillars of the Republic: the common school and American society 1780–1860.* New York: Hill and Wang.

Kaestle, Carl, Helen Damon-Moore, Lawrence C. Stedman, and Katherine Tinsley 1991. *Literacy in the United States: Readers and Reading Since 1880.* New Haven: Yale University Press.

Kalman, Judy 1999. *Writing on the Plaza: mediated literacy practices among scribes and clients in Mexico City.* Cresskill, NJ: Hampton Press.

Karlsson, Anna-Malin 2009. Positioned by reading and writing: literacy practices, roles, and genres in common occupations. *Written Communication* 26, 1: 53–76.

Katz, Susan M. 1998. *The Dynamics of Writing Review: opportunities for growth and change in the workplace.* Stamford, CT: Ablex.

Keen, Andrew 2007. *The Cult of the Amateur: how today's Internet is killing our culture.* New York: Crown Business.

Keys, Ralph 2003. *The Courage to Write: how writers transcend fear.* New York: Holt.

Kirkland, Aaron 2006. You got fired on your day off: challenging termination of employees for personal blogging practices. *University of Missouri – Kansas City Law Review* 75, 2: 545–568.

Kwall, Roberta Rosenthal 2001. Author-stories: narrative's implications for moral rights and copyright's joint authorship doctrine. *Southern California Law Journal* 75, 1: 1–64.

Lacasse, Jeffrey R., Jonathan Leo, Andrea N. Cimino, Kristen F. Bean, and Melissa DelColle 2012. Knowledge of undisclosed corporate authorship ("ghostwriting") reduces the perceived credibility of antidepressant research: a randomized vignette study with experienced nurses. *BioMed Center Research Notes* 5. doi: 10.1186/1756–0500–5–490, 5 012, 5:490.

Langer, Judith A. and Arthur Applebee 1987. *How Writing Shapes Thinking.* Urbana, IL: National Council of Teachers of English.

Langer, Judith A. and Sheila Flihan 2002. Writing and reading relationships: constructive tasks. In Roselmina Indrisano and James R. Squires (eds.). *Perspectives on Writing: research, theory and practice.* New York: Routledge, pp. 120–146.

Laquintano, Tim 2010. Sustained Authorship: digital writing, self-publishing, and the e-book. *Written Communication* 27, 4: 469–493.

Lenart, Amanda and Susanna Fox 2006. *Bloggers: a portrait of the Internet's new storytellers.* Washington D.C.: Pew Internet and American Life Project.

Lerman, Lisa G. 2001. Misattribution in legal scholarship: plagiarism, ghostwriting, and authorship. *South Texas Law Review* 42 (Spring): 467–492.

Lessig, Lawrence 2005. *Free Culture: the nature and future of creativity.* New York: Penguin.

Lidsky, Lyrissa 2010. Nobody's fool: the rational audience as the First Amendment ideal. *University of Illinois Law Review* 2010: 799–850.

Lidsky, Lyrissa and Robert G. Wright 2004. *Freedom of the Press: a reference guide to the United States Constitution.* New York: Praeger.

Lippmann, Walter 1922. *Public Opinion.* New York: Macmillan.

Lunsford, Andrea and Lisa Ede 2011. *Writing Together: collaboration in theory and practice.* New York: Bedford/St. Martin's.

Lyons, Martyn 2010. *A History of Reading and Writing in the Western World.* New York: Palgrave MacMillan.

2012. *Writing Culture of Ordinary People in Europe c. 1860–1920.* New York: Cambridge University Press.

Machlup, Fritz 1972. *The Production and Distribution of Knowledge in the United States.* Princeton NJ: Princeton University Press.

McCarthy, Lucille 1991. A psychiatrist using DSM-III: the influence of a charter document in psychiatry. In Charles Bazerman and James Paradis (eds.). *Textual Dynamics of the Professions.* Madison: University of Wisconsin Press, pp. 358–378.

McDermott, Patrice 2007. *Who Needs to Know? The state of public access to federal government information.* Lanham, MD: Bernan Press.

McGill, Meredith L. 1997. The matter of the text: commerce, print culture, and the authority of the State in American copyright law. *American Literary History* 9, 1: 21–59.

McHenry, Elizabeth 2002. *Forgotten Readers: recovering the lost history of African American literary societies.* Durham, NC: Duke University Press.

McHenry, Leemon 2010. Of sophists and spin-doctors: industry-sponsored ghostwriting and the crisis of academic medicine. *Mens Sana Monographs* 8, 1: 129–145.

Meadows, Susannah 2004. Between the lines. *Newsweek* 12 January: 12.

Medhurst, Martin J. 1987. Ghostwritten speeches: ethics isn't the only lesson. *Communications Education* 36, 3: 241–249.

Meiklejohn, Alexander 1948. *Free Speech and Its Relationship to Self Government.* New York: Harper.

Migdal, Joel 2001. *State in Society: studying how states and societies transform and constitute one another.* New York: Cambridge University Press.

Miller, Carolyn R. and Davida Charney 2007. Persuasion, audience, and argument. In Charles Bazerman (ed.). *Handbook of Research on Writing: history, society, school, individual and text.* New York: Routledge pp. 583–598.

Miller, Susan 1998. *Assuming the Positions: cultural pedagogy and the politics of commonplace writing.* Pittsburgh, PA: University of Pittsburgh Press.

Milner, Henry 2002. *Civic Literacy: how informed citizens make democracy work.* Medford, MA: Tufts University Press.

Monaghan, E. Jennifer 2005. *Learning to Read and Write in Colonial America.* Amherst: University of Massachusetts Press.

Murray, Donald and Thomas Newkirk 2009. *The Essential Don Murray: lessons from America's greatest writing teacher.* Portsmouth, NH: Heinemann.

Myers, D.G. 2006. *The Elephants Teach: creative writing since 1880.* Chicago: University of Chicago Press.

Nash, Ray 1959. *American Writing Masters and Copybooks.* Boston: Colonial Society of Massachusetts.

National Writing Project and Carl Nagin 2006. *Why Writing Matters.* Berkeley, CA: National Writing Project.

Nell, Victor 1988. *Lost in a Book: the psychology of reading for pleasure.* New Haven: Yale University Press.

Nelson, Nancy and Robert C. Calfee 1998. The reading–writing connection viewed historically. In Nancy Nelson and Robert C. Calfee (eds.). *The Reading–Writing Connection: ninety-seventh yearbook of the National Society for the Study of Education Part II.* Chicago: University of Chicago Press, pp. 1–52.

Neuborne, Burt 1989. First Amendment and government regulation of capital markets. *Brooklyn Law Review* 55, 1: 5–64.

Nichols, Marie Hocmuth 1963. Ghostwriting: implications for public address. In *Rhetoric and Criticism.* Baton Rouge: Louisiana State University Press, pp. 35–48.

Niles-Yokum, Kelly and Donna L. Wagner 2011. *The Aging Networks: a guide to programs and services.* New York: Springer.

Nimmer, Melville B. 1970. Does copyright abridge the First Amendment guarantees of free speech and press? *UCLA Law Journal* 17, 6 : 1180–1204.

Nord, David Paul and John V. Richardson Jr. 2009. US government publishing in the postwar era. In David Paul Nord, Joan Shelley Rubin, and Michael Schudson (eds.). *A History of the Book in America, Volume V: the enduring book: print culture in postwar America.* Chapel Hill: University of North Carolina Press, pp. 167–180.

Norton, Helen 2003–2004. Not for attribution: government's interest in protecting the integrity of its own expression. *University of California – Davis Law Review* 37: 1317–1350.

    2008. Government workers and government speech. *First Amendment Law Review* 7, 1: 75–91

    2009. Constraining public employee speech: government's control of its workers' speech to protect its own expression. *Duke Law Journal* 59, 1: 1–68.

Oatley, Keith 2011. *Such Stuff as Dreams: the psychology of fiction.* New York: Wiley.

Orbach, Barak Y. 2009. "The Law and Economics of Creativity at the Workplace." Discussion Paper 356. Center for Law, Economics, and Business. Harvard Law School. Web.

Orren, Karen 1991. *Belated Feudalism: labor, the law, and liberal development in the United States.* New York: Cambridge University Press.

Pare, Anthony 1993. Discourse regulations and the production of knowledge. In Rachel Spilka (ed.). *Writing in the Workplace: new research perspectives.* Carbondale: Southern Illinois University Press, pp. 111–123.

    2002. Genre and identity: individuals, institutions, and ideology. In Richard M. Coe, Lorelei Lingard, and Tatiana Teslenko (eds.). *The Rhetoric and Ideology of Genre.* Creskill, NJ: Hampton Press, pp. 57–72.

Pennebaker, James W. 1997. Writing about emotional experiences as a therapeutic process. *Psychological Science* 8, 3: 162–166.

Pennebaker, James W. and Cindy K. Chung 2006. Expressive writing, emotional upheaval and health. In Howard S. Friedman and Roxanne Cohen Silver (eds.). *Foundations of Health Psychology.* New York: Oxford University Press, pp. 263–284.

Pitkin, Hanna Fenichel 1967. *The Concept of Representation.* Berkeley: University of California Press.

Porat, Marc Uri 1977. *The Information Economy.* Washington, D.C.: U.S. Department of Commerce.

Prose, Francine 2007. *Reading Like a Writer: a guide for people who love books and for those who want to write them.* New York: Harper Perennial.

Riessman, Catherine Kohler 2007. *Narrative Methods for the Human Sciences*. Thousand Oaks, CA: Sage.

Rijlaarsdam, Gert, Martine Braaksma, Michel Couzijn, Tanja Janssen, Marleen Kieft, Mariet Raedts, Elke van Steendam, Anne Toorenaar, and Huub van den Berg 2009. The role of readers in writing development: writing students bringing their texts to the test. In Roger Beard, Debra Myhill, Jeni Riley, and Martin Nystrand (eds.). *Sage Handbook of Writing Development*. Los Angeles: Sage, pp. 436–452.

Riley, Linda and Stuart C. Brown 1996. Crafting a public image: an empirical study of the ethics of ghostwriting. *Journal of Business Ethics* 15, 7: 711–721.

Robbins, Ira P. 2010. Ghostwriting: filling in the gaps of pro se prisoners' access to the courts. *Georgetown Journal of Legal Ethics* 23, 2: 271–321.

Rose, Mark 1995. *Authors and Owners: the invention of copyright*. Cambridge, MA: Harvard University Press.

Rosenberg, Scott 2010. *Say Everything: how blogging began, what it is becoming, and why it matters*. New York: Crown Publishing.

Rothermich, John C. 1999. Ethical and procedural implications of ghostwriting for pro se litigants: toward increased access to civil justice. *Fordham Law Review* 67: 2687–2729.

Rubin, Joan Shelley 2007. *Songs Of Ourselves: the uses of poetry in America*. Harvard University Press.

Saunders, David and Ian Hunter 1991. Lessons from the literatory: how to historicize authorship. *Critical Inquiry* 17, 2: 479–509.

Schauer, Frederick. 2004. The boundaries of the First Amendment: a preliminary exploration of constitutional salience. *Harvard Law Review* 117, 6: 1765–1809.

Schemo, Diana Jean 2006. Schoolbooks are given Fs in originality. *New York Times* 13 July: A1, A21.

Schryer, Catherine F. 1994. The lab vs. the clinic: sites of competing genres. In Aviva Freedman and Peter Medway (eds.). *Genre in the New Rhetoric*. London: Taylor and Francis, pp. 105–124.

Schultz, Vicki 2000. Life's work. *Columbia Law Review* 100, 7: 1881–1964.

Scott, James C. 1998. *Seeing Like a State*. New Haven: Yale University Press.

Seavey, Charles A. and Caroline F. Sloat 2009. The government as publisher. In Carl Kaestle and Janice A. Radway (eds.). *A History of the Book in America, Volume IV: print in motion: the expansion of publishing and reading in the United States, 1880–1940*. Chapel Hill: University of North Carolina Press, pp. 260–275.

Selfe, Cynthia L. and Gail Hawisher 2004. *Literate Lives in the Information Age: narratives of literacy from the United States*. Mahwah NJ: Lawrence Erlbaum.

Shirky, Clay 2009. *Here Comes Everybody: the power of organizing without organizations*. New York: Penguin.

Shooman, Jeffrey 2005–2006. The speech of public employees outside the workplace: towards a new framework. *Seton Hall Law Review* 16: 1341–1371.

Sicherman, Barbara 2010. *Well Read Lives: how books inspired a generation of American Women*. Chapel Hill: University of North Carolina Press.

Slack, Jennifer D., David J. Miller, and Jeffrey Doak 2006. The technical communicator as author: meaning, power, authority. In J. Blake Scott, Bernadette Longo, and Katherine V. Willis (eds.). *Critical Power Tools*. Albany, NY: State University of Albany Press, pp. 25–46.

Smith, Donald K. 1961. Ghostwritten speeches. *Quarterly Journal of Speech* 67: 417–420.

Soltow, Lee and Edward Stevens 1981. *The Rise of Literacy and the Common School in the United States: a socioeconomic analysis to 1876.* Chicago: University of Chicago Press.

Somers-Willett, Susan 2009. *The Cultural Politics of Slam Poetry: race, identity, and the performance of popular verse in America.* Ann Arbor: University of Michigan Press.

Spinuzzi, Clay 2003. *Tracing Genres Through Organizations: a sociocultural approach to information design.* Cambridge, MA: MIT Press.

Starr, Paul 2004. *The Creation of the Media.* New York: Basic Books.

St. Clair, William 2004. *The Reading Nation in the Romantic Period.* New York: Cambridge University Press.

Stevens, Edward W. 1988. *Literacy, Law and Social Order.* DeKalb: Northern Illinois University Press.

Stewart, Thomas A. 1998. *Intellectual Capital: the new wealth of organizations.* New York: Doubleday.

Stotsky, Sandra 1983. Research on reading/writing relationships: a synthesis and suggested directions. *Language Arts* 60, 5: 627–642.

Surrency, Edwin C. 1981. Law reports in the United States. *American Journal of Legal History* 25, 1: 48–66.

Swank, Drew A. 2005. In defense of rules and roles: the need to curb extreme forms of pro se assistance and accommodation in litigation. *American Law Review* 54, 5: 1537–1591.

Tendler, Joseph 2013. *Opponents of the Annales School.* London: Palgrave McMillan.

Thompson, Clive 2013a. How successful networks nurture good ideas. *Wired Magazine* 21, 10. Web.

2013b. *Smarter Than You Think: how technology is changing our minds for the better.* New York: Penguin.

Tierney, Robert and Timothy Shanahan 1991. Research on the reading–writing relationship: interactions, transactions, and outcomes. In Rebecca Barr, Michael L. Kamil, Peter Mosenthal, and P. David Pearson (eds.). *Handbook of Reading Research Volume II.* New York: Routledge, pp. 246–280.

Tierney, William M. and Martha S. Gerrity 2005. Scientific discourse, corporate ghostwriting: journal policy and public trust. *Journal of General Internal Medicine* 20, 6: 550–51.

Tomlins, Christopher L. 1993. *Law, Labor, and Ideology in the Early American Republic.* New York: Cambridge University Press.

Tomlinson, Barbara 2005. *Authors on Writing.* New York: Palgrave Macmillan.

Torrance, Nancy and David Olson 2009. *Cambridge Handbook of Literacy.* New York: Cambridge University Press.

Tussey, Deborah 2007. Employers as authors: copyrights in works made for hire. In Peter K. Yu (ed.). *Intellectual Property and Information Wealth: issues and practices in the digital age, Volume I.* Westport, CT: Praeger, pp. 71–92.

Tussman, Joseph 1977. *Government and the Mind.* New York: Oxford.

Veit, Helen E., Kenneth R. Bowling, and Charlene Bangs Bickford 1991. *Creating the Bill of Rights: the documentary record from the First Federal Congress.* Baltimore, Md.: Johns Hopkins University Press.

VerSteeg, Russ 1996. Defining "Author" for purposes of copyright. *American University Law Review* 45: 1323–1366.

Waples, Douglas, Bernard Berelson, and Franklyn R. Bradshaw 1940. *What Reading Does to People.* Chicago: University of Chicago Press.

Walter, David L. 2003. Ghostwriters In the Sky. *American Journal of Family Law* 17, 2: 61–63.

Warner, Michael 1992. *The Letters of the Republic: publication and the public sphere in eighteenth-century America.* Cambridge, MA: Harvard University Press.

Weber, Ronald 1997. *Hired Pens: professional writers in America's golden age of print.* Athens: Ohio University Press.

Weeman, Lauren A. 2006. Bending the (ethical) rules in Arizona: ethics opinion 05–06's approval of undisclosed ghostwriting may be a sign of things to come. *Georgia Journal of Legal Ethics* 19: 1041–65.

Wenger, Etienne 1998. *Communities of Practice: learning, meaning and identity.* New York: Cambridge University Press.

Wilson, Douglas L. 1999. Jefferson and literacy. In James Gilreath (ed.). *Thomas Jefferson and the Education of a Citizen.* Washington, DC: Library of Congress, pp. 79–90.

Winsor, Dorothy 1993. Owning corporate texts. *Journal of Business and Technical Communication* 7, 2: 179–195.

Witham, Larry 2000. Ghostwriting haunts Christian publishing. *Insight on the News* 16, 30: 26–27.

Wolf, Maryanne 2007. *Proust and the Squid: the story and science of the reading brain.* New York: Harper.

Woodmansee, Martha and Peter Jaszi 1994. *The Construction of Authorship: textual appropriation in law and literature.* Durham, NC: Duke University Press.

Wu, Tim 2008. On copyright's authorship policy. *University of Chicago Legal Forum* 2008: 335–354.

Wyatt, Ian D. and Daniel E. Hecker 2006. Occupational changes during the twentieth century. *Monthly Labor Review* (March): 35–57.

Yates, Joanne 1993. *Control Through Communication: the rise of system in American management.* Johns Hopkins University Press.

Yen, Alfred C. 1990. Restoring the natural law: copyright as labor and possession. *Ohio State Law Journal* 51: 517–559.

Yudof, Mark G. 2009. *When Government Speaks: politics, law and government expression in America.* University of California Press.

Index